Democratic Beginnings

Democratic Beginnings

Founding the Western States

Amy Bridges

 University Press of Kansas

© 2015 by the University Press of Kansas
All rights reserved

Published by the University Press of Kansas (Lawrence, Kansas 66045), which was organized by the Kansas Board of Regents and is operated and funded by Emporia State University, Fort Hays State University, Kansas State University, Pittsburg State University, the University of Kansas, and Wichita State University

Library of Congress Cataloging-in-Publication Data

Names: Bridges, Amy, author.
Title: Democratic beginnings : founding the Western States / Amy Bridges.
Description: Lawrence, Kansas : University Press of Kansas, [2015] | Includes index.
Identifiers: LCCN 2015026180 | ISBN 9780700621729 (cloth : alk. paper) | ISBN 9780700625215 (paper : alk. paper) | ISBN 9780700621491 (ebook)
Subjects: LCSH: Constitutional conventions—West (U.S.)—History. | Constitutional history—West (U.S.) | West (U.S.)—Politics and government. | State governments—West (U.S.) | Democracy—West (U.S.)
Classification: LCC KF4530 .B75 2015 | DDC 342.7802/92—dc23
LC record available at http://lccn.loc.gov/2015026180

British Library Cataloguing-in-Publication Data is available.

Printed in the United States of America

10 9 8 7 6 5 4 3 2 1

The paper used in this publication is recycled and contains 30 percent postconsumer waste. It is acid free and meets the minimum requirements of the American National Standard for Permanence of Paper for Printed Library Materials Z39.48-1992.

Contents

Preface and Acknowledgments *vii*

1. Upon the Shores of an Unknown Sea *1*

2. Frontier Foundings *27*

3. Managing the Periphery *59*

4. Progressive Settlements *103*

5. Creating the Western States *137*

Notes *157*

Index *191*

Preface and Acknowledgments

Years ago I began work on a book, *The Progressive West,* meant to provide an account of politics in the western states in the early twentieth century. Chapter 2 was to be about the constitutions of the eleven western states. I thought that since California wrote the first in 1849, and New Mexico and Arizona wrote the last in 1910, a review of the constitutions would be an efficient way to bring myself and my readers from the middle of the nineteenth century to the midpoint of the Progressive Era. I began by reading the minutes of the Colorado constitutional convention (1875–1876). A great read. Articulate delegates, interesting debates about many, many things. So well transcribed, the minutes are a veritable "You Are There" of that convention as, later, were the minutes of most of the other constitutional conventions. I presented a talk, "Making a Place for Themselves," about the Colorado convention at the University of Wisconsin–Madison. My audience—mostly historians—thought I should forsake *The Progressive West* and instead write a book about the initial constitutional conventions of the western states. *Democratic Beginnings* is that book.

    It is a pleasure to acknowledge the people who have helped me. I am deeply grateful to the National Endowment for the Humanities and the American Council of Learned Societies, which funded a year for me to devote to research. I owe much, too, to Fred Woodward, longtime director of the University Press of Kansas. Fred was my faithful academic suitor for years; I enjoyed our conversations at many academic conferences and have been sustained by his confidence. It is my good fortune that Charles Myers is the current director of the University Press of Kansas; he has not only the post but also the patience and tact of his predecessor. Paul Emerson Herron and Paul Frymer have been generous colleagues and critics; I regret that I have not (yet) taken all of their advice. I am grateful to Robin Einhorn for suggesting the title *Democratic Beginnings,* exactly right. The editors of *Studies in American Development* published "Managing the Periphery," portions of which appear in chapters 1 and 3, and provided helpful commentary as I wrote and revised it. Julie Novkov, Bruce Cain, Melanie DuPuis, Charles Anthony Smith, John Dinan, Howard Schweber, and Alan Tarr provided careful and instructive readings, as did readers of the manuscript of *Democratic Beginnings* for the University Press of Kansas.

Richard Kronick, among many other gifts, read and commented on many chapter drafts and has maintained the effective balance between insistence that I finish this book and patience that partners of academics strive for. Along with Rick, Emma and Zach, and Dorothy and Etan bring joy to my life and remind me of what is important.

Amy Bridges
Bethesda, MD

ADDRESS TO THE PEOPLE

Your Representatives, in convention assembled... for the purpose of framing a Constitution for the State of Colorado, have completed their work, and herewith submit the result of their labors for your adoption or rejection.... The Convention labored assiduously to frame a fundamental law, wise and wholesome in itself, and which would be adapted to the general wants of the people....

... we believe it contains not only all of the primitive rights guaranteed in our National Constitution, but most of those reformatory measures which the experience of the past century has proven to be wise and judicious....

The maintenance of free public schools, and the gratuitous instruction therein for all children between the ages of six and twenty-one is forever guaranteed....

Probably no subject has come before the Convention causing more anxiety and concern than the troublesome and vexed question pertaining to corporations. The Legislatures of other States have, in most cases, been found unequal to the task of preventing abuses and protecting the people from the grasping and monopolizing tendencies of railroads and other corporations. Experience has shown that positive restrictions on the powers of the Legislature in relation to these matters are necessary.

To this end we have provided for the wiping out of all dormant and sham corporations claiming special and exclusive privileges. We have denied the General Assembly the power to create corporations.... We have declared that railroad corporations shall be liable as common carriers... [and] must subject themselves to all the provisions and requirements of this constitution.... We have carefully guarded the right of eminent domain ... while some of our sister States have not gone far enough in placing restrictions on the legislative power, others have gone too far, and have had to recede. We have endeavored to take a middle ground, believing it to be more safe....

Let us now look at the political and substantial advantages of Statehood as contrasted with our present condition of Territorial vassalage....

... Let us cherish, then, this occasion with more than ordinary zeal, actuated by the memories of the past, and inspired by the rewards for us in the future; let us arouse ourselves to the responsibilities of the hour and, as citizens of a free republic, become, in fact, as well as in name, citizens of the American Union of Sovereign States.

William M. Clark, Chairman,
and nine other Delegates
March 14, 1876

Proceedings of the Constitutional Convention Held in Denver, December 20, 1875, to Frame a Constitution for the State of Colorado, Together with the Enabling Act Passed by the Congress of the United States and Approved March 3, 1875 (Denver, CO: Smith-Brooks Press, 1907), 723–734.

1. Upon the Shores of an Unknown Sea

In *Democratic Beginnings* I offer accounts of the constitutional conventions that founded the western states—Arizona, California, Colorado, Idaho, Montana, Nevada, New Mexico, Oregon, Utah, Washington, and Wyoming—and the constitutions they wrote.[1] California was the first of these; its constitution was written in 1849. Arizona and New Mexico were the last, holding their conventions in 1910. State constitutions are fundamental law, blueprints for government institutions, statements of principles, values, and goals, and declarations of collective identity, written with fostering settlement and prosperity in mind. In this extended essay, I describe the puzzles and dilemmas delegates faced, their arguments about remedies and responses, and the compromises they reached. Delegates had a long list of achievements to their credit. Delegates extended the reach and enhanced the authority of state governments. They wrote law where little existed, in water and protections for working men, women, and children. Delegates created new institutions (mine inspectors, departments of agriculture and labor, corporation commissions) and familiar ones (elementary and normal schools, universities, prisons, grand juries). They reformed court systems and added duties to lower courts and county officials. They expanded bills of rights, elaborating those in the federal Constitution, adding positive rights, and including sweeping injunctions for state governments to fulfill new obligations to their residents. They chipped away at the law of master and servant.

Two themes are prominent across the western conventions. First, their distinctive mission, and second, delegates' frequent encounters with new and puzzling situations, for which they were without precedent in law or policy. At the conventions reviewed here, it is striking how very different delegates' understanding of their task was from what the federal Founders set out to accomplish. In 1787 the Founders above all desired the permanent and successful existence of the democratic republic they were founding. They created a government of three branches, each of which had a critical virtue, and—since politicians always sought to expand their power—also posed a distinctive threat. The executive, which promised unity and threatened tyranny; the legislature, which promised to tie the several interests of both the many and the few to government but which, unrestrained, might grow to self-serving oligarchy; and the people, whose rights were ascendant in a republic, but whose unrestrained control of government would bring disorder and destruction. In this they faced an eighteenth-century social choice problem: How to allocate the authority and prerogatives of the three branches to enable their strengths and stymie their threats? How to arrange the powers of each branch to create a government that was permanent, peaceful, and secure? The Founders' success was, as Michael Kammen felicitously phrased it, that they created "a machine that would go of itself,"[2] a democratic republic that is still our frame of government.

By contrast, authors of state constitutions, as John Dinan explained, prized the accumulated wisdom and "the institutional knowledge and experience that was unavailable to the eighteenth-century founders."[3] Delegates to state constitutional conventions were at work in the democratic republic the Founders created, a young nation they understood to be learning as it practiced republican democracy. Continuous learning required that state governments and their constitutions be revised and updated. This was exemplified in the conventions considered here by praise of the Indiana Bill of Rights at the Oregon convention in 1857. There, Delazon Smith proposed that the constitution include an article to be a Bill of Rights.[4] One of his colleagues was dismissive, remarking that bills of rights were frivolous, mere Fourth of July orations. Smith defended his proposal, praising Indiana's Bill of Rights. Not confined to the ten sections of the federal constitution, the Bill of Rights in Indiana's 1851 constitution included others discovered in "seventy years of progress."[5] Similarly, in 1876, Colorado delegates, in their Address to the People, explained that the constitution they proposed had "not only the primitive rights guaranteed in our National Constitution, but most of those reformatory measures which the experience of the last century has proven to be wise and judicious."[6]

In addition, as the country grew, changing conditions meant some provisions became outdated. This was best explained by J. F. King, a delegate to Oklahoma's founding convention, held 1906–1907. "Time," he said,

> impairs constitutions as it does all things and if they be not amended and repaired to meet changed conditions, new questions, and the ever-altering situations of an enterprising and progressive people, there is an end to good government.... And as fast as great questions of government policy emerge settled from the political arena, the field and the forum they should be embodied in the Constitution that they may become a permanent guide to the official and an inspiration and a protection to the people.... This and every other generation of a free people has its own peculiar problems to face in Constitution making.... We would be unworthy sons of worthy sires if we fail to meet and courageously solve the problems now pressing upon our people for solution.[7]

Even Matthew Deady, who, of all the delegates at the conventions reviewed here was most committed to maintaining his territory just as it was, declared, "Let every day and generation do for itself as it needs it."[8]

Changing conditions and rethinking citizenship in a democratic republic enjoined delegates to design state constitutions with provisions that had demonstrated greatest utility and prescribed practices that followed the guidelines of contemporary understandings of equity and justice. The commitment to learning from the past, and adding "improvements" or progress to the constitutions they wrote, was a constant across conventions. Delegates might, from a federal Founder's point of view, look a bit feckless, as when one said, "We are a new people, free as air to select what is good from all republican forms of government."[9] And another, that he did "not believe in sacrificing to any time-honored evil, simply because it has the sanction of time."[10] Authors of state constitutions were neither feckless nor cavalier. The obligation to be attentive to progress and accumulated wisdom informed delegates' deliberations at every convention. Nor did delegates believe their work marked an end to new wisdom; the commitment of delegates to the idea that constitutions should incorporate accumulated wisdom is revealed not only in their general deliberations but also in provisions for amendment and revision in the future. Dinan argued that provisions for amendment and greater ease of amendment than the federal constitution were motivated by delegates' adherence to the principle that constitutional revision was necessary in the democratic republic of the United States.

The second theme is the appearance of new challenges. Over the course of eleven founding conventions, delegates again and again were faced with new questions, developments new to them and to their generation. This happened at the Washington convention. In the foreword to the proceedings, Charles Gates wrote:

> There was a disposition on the part of a number of delegates to view such conventions as laboratories where the states might correct existing political weaknesses by introducing corrective measures. For some of these matters history offered no precedents; the problems called for new solutions even though they might be untried and experimental. Thus members of the convention put up propositions and counter propositions for consideration on a wide variety of points.... The opening weeks of the convention featured especially this kind of originality and inventiveness.[11]

Water was the occasion for several of these dilemmas. On January 14, 1879, Wiley Tinnin presented the report of the Committee on Water and Water Rights to California's second constitutional convention. Tinnin explained that "the use of water for ... irrigation and mining was, until the last twenty-five or thirty years, practically unknown to the American people." Other societies had managed irrigation for decades. Yet their "experience ... cannot be fully applied to this free Government, for the reasons that governments that have brought forward and completed great irrigation schemes were arbitrary governments ... whose citizens had no privilege, no right to use water." By contrast, in the United States "the rights of the citizens are paramount in a great sense, in many respects, to the government." For the United States, or state governments, to attempt to "place [water] under legislative control, we are embarking on a new era. We stand upon the shores of an unknown and unexplored sea."[12] The absence of appropriate precedents was often a challenge at the founding conventions of the western states. In 1876, when William Clark introduced the section on mines and mining to the Colorado convention, he explained that the committee "had much difficulty ... because of the absence of all precedent."[13] And one delegate to California's 1849 convention, as banks were discussed, compared the territory to New York State, explaining "how very different are [our] circumstances, representing as we do a young and virgin territory, without banks, and whose great natural wealth is unparalleled." For these reasons, they were starting afresh; "this is an original question with us."[14] Each generation faced its own, new challenges. California, Oregon, and Nevada puzzled over the limited liability corporation and weighed the claims of race on suffrage. Colorado, Idaho, Montana, Washington, Wyoming, and Utah grappled with the prospects of distant investors assisting their growth or failing to, worried about industrial conflict in the mines, and settled on a few protections for labor. Deliberations in Arizona and New Mexico were much taken up with direct democracy; Arizona abrogated, and New Mexico declined to consider, the fellow servant doctrine.

Democratic Beginnings is, first, a study of state constitutions. The chapters that follow include every founding constitutional convention in the West, enabling the reader to trace the evolution of issues and writing constitutions in the West across the sixty years from 1849 to 1910. I compare western constitutions to constitutions in other states to demonstrate ways constitutional law and, by inference, politics in the West differed from the constitutions and politics in other regions. My presentation of the proceedings includes much more of the argument and debate that took place in their meetings than will be found in other accounts. The proceedings, arguments, and debates are the evidence for my claims about the intentions, differences, and eventual agreements of the delegates.[15] Delegates' conversations show what they saw to be at stake in their debates and the process of reaching majority consensus. One of the pleasures of reading the proceedings of the conventions is that the verbatim accounts recorded by stenographers and journalists offer an immediacy to convention debates not available elsewhere. Sharing delegates' words and arguments with the reader seemed to me far superior to any paraphrase I might offer. Among other things, the sophistication of many of the arguments, how deeply delegates felt their positions on some issues, and how articulate and well versed in history, myth, and the Bible speakers were are especially impressive in light of the absence of any—or the existence only of rudimentary—systems of public education in the states. Until well into the twentieth century many American children, and like them many of these delegates, were educated by their mothers. The debates and conversations reproduced here also show the tenor and content of delegates' deliberations. Their conversations display, too, the roles of time and place in their deliberations.

Democratic Beginnings is also a study of American political development, adding an account of the West to state constitutions, and a report of western development to US politics and history. Political scientists have paid scant attention to the West. Although there is a long tradition of western studies among historians, for a generation historians turned away from politics and political economy. Scholars of American political development have also neglected the West. Like other scholars of politics and history, our understanding of the United States rests heavily on the history of the Northeast, secondarily on the South, and on the West hardly at all. Writing about the Colorado Constitution in 1903, Elbert Meyer observed, "The pioneers of the West labored, like their fathers in the East, through years to establish free institutions; but, while the children of Colorado know well the history of the great struggle of the Puritans and the founders of Virginia, they know relatively nothing of the pathfinders of the mountains and the plains." The same observation is true of students in Kansas, Oregon, and New Mexico. If we were to follow carefully the trajectories of constitutional development in the nation's regions, our studies would, as Meyer suggested, "result . . . in a broader view of American institutions and in a realization that the work of the founders was to transplant the old institutions and to transform them, in a measure, to fit new conditions" of varying sorts from place to place.[16] *Democratic Beginnings* follows the transplants and transformations of old institutions, and the development of new ones, in the western states.

Richard Bensel has been attentive to region in a different way. Beginning with *Sectionalism and American Political Development,* Bensel has written a history of, and explained, the development of the federal government.[17] In his work the central tensions underlying US political economy are those between the politically and economically dominant Northeast (the "core") and the quasi-colonial South (the "periphery"). *Democratic Beginnings* is about the *other* periphery in the United States, the West. The vast West had its own distinctive geography and political economy, centered not on farming but on mining and ranching. There were areas devoted to farming, especially in Washington and Oregon, and also in Colorado, Idaho, California, and Montana, but the West did not have the densely populated agricultural areas of the South or the plains. The West also had a distinctive population, counting tens of thousands of Native Americans, few African Americans, populous Mexican regions incorporated by the US conquest of Mexico, Anglos from the East, and—working alongside them in the mines, towns, and forests and on ranches and the railroads—European immigrants, Mexicans, and Chinese.

The West has not had the substantial presence in national politics that the South has enjoyed. For much of the nineteenth century, most of the West was territorial, with only nonvoting representation in Congress. The West joined the Union slowly and was thinly settled. In 1880, only four of what became the eleven western states had voting representation in Congress. In 1890, when there were eight western states, the population of the West was so slight that the region sent only sixteen representatives to the House, while the South sent eighty-seven. In 1912, when all eleven western states were represented in Congress, twenty-four representatives spoke for them, while ninety-eight representatives were sent to the House from the eleven states of the South. Population was not the only political resource of the South; each region sent twenty-two senators to Washington, so in the Senate southern strength might have been matched by the West. It was not. In the Senate the presence of the South was bolstered by its staunch one-partyism, shared political economies, and policy unanimity, while the western states were divided by party, as well as by their quite different terrains, societies, and economic foundations.

Democratic Beginnings includes sustained attention to territorial government and political economy. In the nineteenth century, when the federal government was a state of courts and parties, it was also a state of states. State governments performed the long list of tasks assigned to them, sometimes by default, in the federal constitution—family policy and law (marriage, adoption, divorce, custody of children, assignment of property); education; law enforcement and prisons; roads, water, sewerage, and other infrastructure; fire protection and building codes; and poor relief. States also managed, as best they could, the local consequences of federal economic policies (the tariff or the gold standard, for example) and the deprivations of a depression ("panic") in every generation: 1833, 1853, 1873, and 1893. In thinly settled areas, territorial and state governments worked as best they could to encourage settlement and growth. Well before the federal government addressed these issues, politicians in state governments, as well as ordinary citizens, argued about what was fair and appropriate in a democratic republic (that, for example, imprisonment for debt was wrong), enacted protective legislation for children and adults at work, and implemented "reformatory measures which... experience... has proven to be wise and judicious."[18] For many issues to which the general population and its leaders were attentive, Washington was distant and oblivious. The result was that, even as they pleaded with Washington for assistance, states developed policies to address their problems; not a few of their solutions provided precedents for federal courts and policies. We can make better sense of the history and politics of the United States in the nineteenth and early twentieth centuries by paying attention to territories and states.

In this chapter I introduce the arguments of *Democratic Beginnings*, present a general understanding of state constitutional conventions and constitutions, offer a way to study state constitutions, and preview the chapters to follow. In chapters 2, 3, and 4, I show that the constitutional convention was an institution with distinctive characteristics, making it more sensitive and responsive to public opinion than territorial or state legislatures. I argue that delegates to state constitutional conventions had a mission quite different than the task the federal founding fathers undertook. I observe that in convention deliberations there were two narratives, one national and the other territorial. I present dilemmas and challenges that were new to each generation, and so without precedent in public policy. Although delegates routinely denounced placing "legislation" in constitutions, they did so nevertheless; I present their reasons and argue that their choices were sensible.

Conventions and Constitutions

Scholars long disparaged state constitutions—for their meandering length, their adoption of provisions of other constitutions, the apparent haste of their composition, and the seeming absence of legal or political theory. By contrast, contemporary scholars offer more positive accounts, recognizing delegates' seriousness of purpose, system in borrowing, commitment to revision and ease of amendment, and inclusion of positive rights and the role of the states in the practice and creation of American constitutionalism. *Democratic Beginnings* builds on this more recent reading of state constitutions.[19]

The constitutional convention was quite different than territorial and state legislatures, and its distinctive characteristics resulted in conversations and decisions more representative of and responsive to public opinion than state and territorial legislatures were. Delegates' elections, their representation of territorial occupations, and their attention to the sentiments of their constituents were the special institutional characteristics of the constitutional convention. Together they created a setting that provided opportunities for popular voices to make an imprint on the law. Constitutional conventions were the setting for the founding of the western states, and it was the institutional characteristics of the conventions that made the foundings *democratic* beginnings. First, in almost every case delegates to state constitutional conventions were elected by popular vote. Election gave delegates democratic legitimacy and also enabled delegates to speak authoritatively about what their constituents wanted to see in the constitutions and what they were likely to oppose. Moreover, delegates had every reason to believe the public was attentive to their deliberations. A steady stream of memorials and petitions was delivered to the conventions; occasional guest speakers argued strongly for one provision or another. The territorial press was very attentive to the conventions, much more attentive than they were to territorial, and later state, legislatures. Newspapers introduced the delegates, followed the debates, explained partisan differences, and offered analysis and evaluation both in their reports and in their editorials. Since the constitutions required endorsement by popular vote, information and threats about how constituents were likely to vote were always important, and sometimes dispositive, for what appeared in the document.

Second, state constitutional conventions were not elite assemblies in the style of the Federal Convention of 1787. Delegates reflected the societies and the partisan tendencies of the communities that elected them. In western conventions there were delegates who had long lived in the territory, as well as migrants from other territories or states, some of whom had participated in a constitutional convention elsewhere. There were aspiring politicians and men with long political careers, many lawyers, small businessmen, farmers, and representatives of larger interests; in smaller numbers, there were populist partisans, farmers' advocates, workers from the mines, and Mexican Americans (there were no women, Native Americans, Asians, or African Americans). In most conventions there was representation of a territory's major occupations, if well short of representation in proportion to their presence in the population. This was important. In these small meetings, an articulate and effective spokesman might well turn the outcome of a debate. That said, that representation of occupations was not proportional to their presence in the population was central to many outcomes. The leading example is that in every convention, farmers' preferences for riparian rights to water were defeated by mine owners' insistence on the doctrine of first in claim, first in right, and not without some bullying of farmer delegates by their better-heeled colleagues.[20]

Third, delegates were attentive to constituent sentiment not only because they took that attention to be part of their job but also because proposed constitutions had to be ratified by popular vote. The specter of defeat of the constitution at the polls, Henry Bromwell reported the Colorado convention "tended to modify the action of the some of the [Republican] majority of the convention, in deciding upon the questions affecting corporations, railroads, water rights, and fees and salaries . . . which gave especial effect to the opposition from without to the measures proposed and urged by a minority in dealing with those subjects."[21] Not only was the public very attentive to convention debates, but resistance to statehood was common and could threaten ratification. In Oregon, Colorado, and Wyoming, majorities expressed a preference for territorial status in several elections, often to avoid increased taxes and, in Colorado in the early 1860s, for fear of the draft.[22] As a result, delegates had every reason not to alienate the public.

Delegates saw themselves as superior in talent and intent to state or territorial legislators, and the territorial press agreed. "The territory has never been represented as it is represented here today," the *Idaho Weekly Statesman* reported, concluding, "It is a grand Convention. They are making a superb Constitution. They are a superb company of men. . . . The State of Idaho will for years rejoice in their work.[23] John Hicks argued that delegates to constitutional conventions were men of better character than state legislators. Writing the history of the constitutions of the northwest states, Hicks observed, "Many citizens of national reputation, rarely or never available for service in a state legislature, willingly assumed the burden of leadership in the constitutional convention. Third rate politicians were seldom candidates. They cared little for the hard work of convention delegates, which was not necessarily rewarded by future prominence, and might leave an embarrassing record on the questions of the day."[24] Lord Bryce made similar observations, seeing the constitutions as "the work of abler, or at any rate honester, men, acting under a commission which imposes special responsibilities."[25]

Writing constitutions was difficult, intense, and time-consuming (see table 1.1). Delegates met a minimum of five days a week, and often six days, and into the evenings. Wyoming and Montana wrote their constitutions in about a month; the second California convention in 1878 was the outlier, with delegates spending five months at argument and compromise. Delegates regularly complained of long days in meetings and many days away from work and family. Possibly for this reason, conventions brought forward more serious and honest delegates than served in territorial legislatures. If the *Idaho Weekly Statesman* exaggerated the eminence and wisdom of delegates to Idaho's founding convention, it was surely the case that among the delegates to constitutional conventions were men of more political experience and higher public regard than most territorial or state legislators. Former territorial governors, once denounced as carpetbagging and incompetent patronage appointees, were highly valued members of founding conventions, both because of their time served as chief territorial executives and because of their experience negotiating with the federal government. Once the constitutions were ratified, convention veterans accounted for several elected state governors, among them Joseph Toole in Montana and George W. P. Hunt in Arizona.

Delegates and deliberations at the conventions shared other values and practices. Alongside their mission of learning from the history of the Republic, delegates were required to innovate. In their effort to resolve "great issues of government policy . . . settled"—and sometimes newly posed, or fiercely debated—in "the political arena, the field, and the forum," delegates were creative and constructive, increasing the authority and reach of state governments, creating new institutions, new rights,

Table 1.1 Constitutional Conventions

State	Dates	Duration	Delegates Total	Republican	Democrat	Other
CA	9/1/1849–10/13/1849	48 days	48	—	22	15 Whig, 11 unknown
OR	8/17/1857–9/22/1857	36 days	60	—	43	17 anti-Democrat
NV	7/4/1864–7/27/1864	23 days	45	—	—	45 Union
CO	12/20/1875–3/14/1876	50 days	39	24	15	—
CA	9/28/1878–3/13/1879	167 days	152	11	10	77 Nonpartisan, 51 Workingmen, 3 Independent
ID	7/4/1889–8/3/1889	30 days	72	38	33	1 Labor
WA	7/4/1889–8/3/1889	30 days	75	43	29	3 Independent
MT	7/4/1889–8/17/1889	38 days	75	36	39	—
WY	9/2/1889–9/30/1889	28 days	49	32	17	—
UT	3/4/1895–5/7/1895	64 days	107	59	48	—
NM	10/3/1910–11/21/1910	49 days	100	71	29	—
AZ	10/10/1910–12/9/1910	60 days	52	11	41	—

Sources: California 1849: Dates, J. Ross Browne, *Report of the Debates in the Convention of California, on the Formation of the State Constitution, in September and October, 1849* (Washington, DC: John T. Towers, 1850; repr., Ann Arbor: University of Michigan,), 7, 477; delegates, David Alan Johnson, *Founding the Far West: California, Oregon, and Nevada 1840–1890* (Berkeley: University of California Press, 1992), appendix 1A, 354–357.

Oregon: Dates, Charles H. Carey, ed., *The Oregon Constitution and Proceedings and Debates of the Constitutional Convention of 1857* (Salem, OR: State Printing Department, 1926), 57, 399; delegates, Johnson, *Founding*, 358–361.

Nevada: Dates, Andrew J. Marsh, *Official Report of the Debates and Proceedings in the Constitutional Convention of the State of Nevada: Assembled at Carson City, July 4, 1864, to Form a Constitution and State Government* (San Francisco: Eastman, 1866), 1, 779; delegates, Johnson, *Founding*, 362–365.

Colorado: Donald Wayne Hensel, "A History of the Colorado Constitution in the Nineteenth Century" (PhD diss., University of Colorado, 1957), 98, 217 (dates); 98 (delegates).

California 1878: Carl Brent Swisher, *Motivation and Technique in the California Constitutional Convention 1878–1879* (Pomona, CA: Claremont College, 1930), 32 (dates); 24 (delegates).

Idaho: Dates, Federal Writers Project, *The Idaho Encyclopedia* (Caldwell, ID: Caxton Printers, 1938), 91. Delegates, 233–234. Dennis C. Colson, *Idaho's Constitution: The Tie That Binds* (Moscow: University of Idaho Press, 1991).

Washington: Beverly Paulik Rosenow, ed., *Journal of the Washington State Constitutional Convention, 1889* (Buffalo, NY: William S. Hein, 1999), I, 464 (dates); iv, v (delegates).

Montana: Dates, *Proceedings and Debates of the Constitutional Convention Held in the City of Helena, Montana, July 4, 1889 to August 17, 1889* (Helena, MT: State Publishing Company, 1921); delegates, Michael P. Malone, Richard B. Roeder, and William L. Lang, *Montana: A History of Two Centuries* (Seattle: University of Washington Press, 1991), 197. Peter Breen is identified in some sources as a Labor delegate; I assume he is counted among Democrats in the count from Malone et al.

Wyoming: Dates, *Journal and Debates of the Constitutional Convention of the State of Wyoming: Begun at the City of Cheyenne on September 2, 1889, and Concluded September 30, 1889* (Cheyenne, WY: Daily Sun, Book and Job Printing, 1893); delegates, T. A. Larson, *History of Wyoming* (Lincoln: University of Nebraska Press, 1978), 238.

Utah: Jean Bickmore White, *Charter for Statehood: The Store of Utah's Constitution* (Salt Lake City: University of Utah Press, 1966), 45, 88 (dates); 49 (delegates).

New Mexico: Dates, Robert W. Larson, *New Mexico's Quest for Statehood, 1846–1912* (Albuquerque: University of New Mexico Press, 1968), 276, 282; delegates, *Santa Fe New Mexican*, September 8, 1910, 1.

Arizona: Dates, *Minutes of the Constitutional Convention of the Territory of Arizona* (Phoenix: Phoenix Printing, 1910), 5, 429; delegates, *Albuquerque Morning Journal*, September 13, 1913, 1.

and broad imperatives for state responsibility. These efforts meant that deliberations at the conventions were both national and specific to each territory. From the first to the last, the territories show themselves as anything but island communities. At the early conventions, in California (1849), Oregon (1857), and Nevada (1864), antagonism between North and South was a looming presence. The central narratives of the Gilded Age—the appearance of large corporations, clashes between labor and capital, the mobilization of farmers, the rise of populist sentiment, and the settlement of the West—were all elaborated at western conventions held between 1876 and 1895: Colorado, Washington, Wyoming, Montana, Utah, Idaho, and California's second (1878). The issues that consumed the political energy of leaders across the country were also central concerns of western leaders. The taxation of corporations, which raised all sorts of puzzles, is an example. Even as the delegates to the constitutional conventions of Idaho, Wyoming, Montana, and Washington were debating how to tax corporations, E. R. A. Seligman was charting the progress of the states in that project in *Political Science Quarterly*.[26] As they were debated across the country, issues of the Progressive Era—direct democracy, protections for labor, and the regulation of corporations—were central at conventions that authored constitutions for New Mexico and Arizona in 1910.

In every decade the Congress and President were critical audiences for the delegates; they decided whether admission was granted. That authority made delegates attentive to increasingly detailed enabling acts. Compromises were tailored with congressional, and later presidential approval in mind, and sometimes in defiance of anticipated disapproval. Across the West, political leaders resented the always distant and sometimes indifferent, sometimes hostile, sometimes patronizing, sometimes racist attitudes of members of Congress, revealed as they wrote enabling acts for the territories. Both when delegates were discussing national questions and as they worked to create governments for their new states, delegates engaged the central issues and challenges of American life in their generation.

Conversation and debate at the conventions were specific to each territory and in that way demonstrate the importance of place. Each territory had its own political history, demographics, natural setting, prominent leaders, and economy; these, too, shaped the constitutions delegates wrote. The economies of Arizona, Nevada, Colorado, Idaho, and Utah were dominated by mining.[27] Stock growers held sway in Wyoming and New Mexico. In Montana, mining and ranching were twin contenders. Farmers were very important in Washington and Oregon and, along with the timber industry, were primarily responsible for settlement and growth. In Colorado, Idaho, and Utah, farmers and miners wandered in and out of alliance and competition. California, Colorado, Montana, and New Mexico had sizable Mexican and Mexican American populations who, since they voted, required political attention. Native Americans and Chinese worked in and suffered violence in almost every state; populations of the Native Americans declined precipitously. In California, where the Chinese population was larger than in other states (both in absolute numbers and as a proportion of the population), politics was seared by the mobilization of anti-Chinese sentiment.

At every convention, region mattered; region was another important meaning of place for residents, as it should be for scholars. The West is not an academic construct placed unnaturally over these territories and states. Delegates spoke often of themselves and their territories as western. Many politicians and delegates to conventions had careers that spanned several western states. For example, Peter Breen was a mine worker who chaired the labor committee at the Montana convention after years as a labor activist there and in Idaho.[28] Henry Bromwell led the Granger faction in the Colorado convention. Long a prominent Republican, Bromwell cast his Electoral College vote in Illinois for Fremont in 1856 and for Lincoln in 1860 and was a delegate to the convention revising the Illinois Constitution in 1869.[29] Regional identity was also important when borrowing constitutional provisions. Although delegates looked to older states to see how issues they were facing had been managed by those with more experience of industrial relations, or railroads, or school systems, more often than not, delegates relied for precedent on other western states.

Delegates frequently borrowed sections and even articles from other state constitutions, a practice once dismissed as hasty cutting and pasting. Marsha Baum and Christian Fritz showed that borrowing was not thoughtless; it was a deliberative process. Delegates were equipped with digests of the provisions of state constitutions in order to consult systematically decisions of their predecessors across the country. The digests informed "extended debates over . . . different constitutional practices of other states."³⁰ At the conventions reviewed here, delegates sought to borrow from a state that was arguably like their own. The subsequent prosperity, or peace, or consensus in the lending state demonstrated the provision's utility.³¹ In this book, chapters 2, 3, and 4 also show borrowing to have been careful. Delegates at the conventions reviewed here were especially attentive to other western states. In 1876 Colorado delegates borrowed from Illinois, as other states borrowed from Missouri, because in the 1870s and even later, delegates thought of Illinois and Missouri as western states. Delegates to later western conventions borrowed from Colorado, a regional cousin, and a state where prosperity in the years after admission to the Union spoke well of its constitution and laws. And when western states considered direct democracy, they most often spoke not of South Dakota, the first state to adopt the initiative, but of Oregon, the first *western* state to adopt initiative, referendum, and recall. The frequency of reading and borrowing suggests that constitutional conventions, whenever they were held, sustained a far-flung and constructive conversation among the states.

State constitutions are long and detailed. It was not uncommon at the conventions for a delegate to object to putting "legislation" in the constitution. Indeed, the long and detailed provisions do resemble ordinary legislation more than organic law. Delegates argued for these provisions on several grounds. One claim was that state legislatures were not responsive to demands for some laws. Despite repeated pleas in California, for example, the state legislature had failed to regulate private companies in control of water. Too, legislatures were corrupt. A delegate favoring a provision was likely to say, "Don't leave it to the legislature." Placing legislation in constitutions was defensive. So-called legislation in the constitution was more secure than ordinary legislation. Constitutional provisions were safe from territorial courts. This was a particular concern for labor because territorial supreme courts were likely to declare laws protective of workers unconstitutional, as they declared laws enfranchising women unconstitutional.³² Finally, since the western states, unlike states in other regions, had competitive party politics, laws passed by one partisan majority in the legislature might well be repealed when the other party (or a third party) held sway. Each of these arguments in support of detailed provisions in constitutions appears in chapters 3 and 4. In all three circumstances, placing so-called legislation in state constitutions was defensive, securing laws more than ordinary legislation would have, and so, rational.

State constitutions contain provisions limiting the reach of the governments they created. One reason follows from constitutional theory. The federal constitution created a government of enumerated, delegated powers. All powers not granted the federal government—"plenary legislative powers"[33]—reside in the states. It followed that if the states were not to become little Leviathans, their constitutions had to limit the reach of state authority; many restrictions were put in place. By the middle of the nineteenth century there were additional reasons to limit legislative discretion. Large state debts, often incurred to assist railroads, cautioned delegates to place severe limits on government debt and to forbid future subsidies. The corruption of territorial assemblies and state legislatures by large interests was common enough that constitution writers felt compelled to put explicit and specific limits on legislative discretion, thereby "hamstringing" state legislatures. The "shall not" sections of articles creating state legislatures are lengthy and detailed. The California Constitution of 1879, for example, listed thirty-three cases "in which the Legislature shall not pass local or special laws." The Pennsylvania Constitution of 1893 has an even longer list.[34] The wording "local or special" is central here. The language is a legacy of principled Jacksonian evenhandedness, and it appears in every state constitution. Prohibitions of local or special legislation, and, similarly, objections to "class" legislation, were efforts to forestall legislative favors to specific individuals or groups. Later in the century the same language was used to object to laws for the protection of labor. Kermit Hall best described the result. In his essay "Mostly Anchor and Little Sail," Hall argued that state constitutions were "diffuse, overly long, negative documents that generally prevented the positive exercise of public authority."[35] In Hall's telling, state constitutions thereby crippled, by design, the very governments they were creating.

There is another reading of state constitutions, emphasizing their generative capacity. John Hicks observed in 1924 that rather than crippling state government, in the Gilded Age "people were confronted . . . by the need of an immediate expansion of state activities to meet new and unprecedented conditions."[36] Similarly, describing California's 1878 constitutional convention in 1930, Carl Swisher wrote, "Undoubtedly, the sentiment of the country favored more government, not less," and more elected officials, not fewer.[37] In chapter 3 the reader will see that "more government" meant bureaus of labor, mine inspectors, and assertions of state government's authority on a list of issues. Kermit Hall's conclusions might well have been different, had he paid more attention to western state constitutions. There were as well sweeping constitutional directives to newly formed state governments. The Wyoming Bill of Rights provided that "the rights of labor shall have just protection through laws calculated to secure to the laborer proper rewards for his service and to promote the industrial welfare of the State." Utah's constitution included a nearly identical provision, as well as this directive: "The Legislature shall prohibit . . . the political and commercial control of employees."[38] In "State Constitutions and the Evolution of Positive Rights," Burt Neuborne argued that the capacity for the design and implementation of positive rights was ever part of state constitutionalism. Neuborne lamented that "a generation of intense effort to mine positive rights for poor people from the federal Constitution ended in failure." No one should have been surprised. The federal document, Neuborne argued, had no textual basis for positive rights, lacked a positive rights tradition, was inflexible, and was "laissez-faire" rather than populist. State constitutions differed on all four measures and so were likely to be more productive ground for such an effort.[39] More broadly, Neuborne claimed that

> most state constitutions are enabling documents designed to authorize, not restrain, the government. Most state constitutions are acutely aware that it is the responsibility of the states to deal with education and . . . breakdowns in the availability of food, shelter, and health care. Indeed, if the federal Constitution can be confidently described as a laissez faire document, many . . . state constitutions can fairly be described as communitarian; even populist.[40]

Not only the legislature but also the courts had this capacity. Neuborne wrote that "state courts are imbued with the power and creative ethos of the common law tradition."[41] Judith Kaye wrote that the common law tradition provided an opportunity: "Nourished by our bedrock constitutional values and updated by our evolving sense of justice, the common law can embolden state courts . . . and encourage the sort of experimentation that has long been a strength of the American justice system," including "the development of an expanded sense of rights."[42] While Neuborne and Kaye were speculative and prospective, Emily Zackin's work is historical and empirical. Zackin argues that the United States has a history of long-recognized government obligations, positive rights that are products of "vigorous campaigns Americans have waged" in the states.[43] In chapter 3, I call attention both to the positive rights included in Gilded Age constitutions and to the broad imperatives for state governments to be found in the texts of western state constitutions. More broadly, the creativity of delegates and their design of new institutions support these authors' understanding of state constitutions' generative character. The same positive rights and injunctions to state governments were among the responses delegates devised to the unprecedented dilemmas they faced.

How to Study State Constitutions

Every serious study of state constitutions begins with the records of the constitutional conventions. These records are lengthy and detailed. A good stenographer captured both the speeches and something of the audience response (usually in a parenthetic expression, for example, applause, cheers, laughter). As extensive as the minutes are, they are not comprehensive. For example, there are few if any notes or journals from committee meetings, where one imagines there were many tough arguments, allowing provisions to be drafted before being discussed at the convention. And the minutes are an insufficient source for explanation. Secondary sources and other primary sources give greater depth both to constitutional debates and to their resolutions. Newspaper coverage, which was all explicitly partisan, is a source for party positions on various issues, not always clear in convention debate. Newspapers closely followed and reported convention debates. Newspaper coverage also discussed which interests lobbied for, or were likely to benefit or suffer from, possible constitutional provisions. For *Democratic Beginnings*, I read convention coverage in pursuit of this information. Contemporary newspaper coverage explains territorial politics, sometimes providing accounts of bargaining not found in the minutes; for some conventions, the press offered brief sketches of delegates' lives and political activities. I also read some of the delegates' and politicians' papers. Newspaper coverage suggests that the press was reluctant to criticize convention proceedings, possibly for the same boosterish and political reasons that led the press to present idealized descriptions of the delegates. Delegates' post hoc discussions of the conventions can provide more frank appraisals of the proceedings (although sometimes self-congratulation inhibits full disclosure), as well as discussions of pressures from lobbyists and constituents not provided by the proceedings.

Understanding the decisions delegates made requires attention both to the institutional characteristics of constitutional conventions and to time and place—the historian's most basic tools. Time and place matter both in the large and in the small. Chronology matters; the familiar nomenclature of political and economic change—the antebellum generations, the Gilded Age, the Progressive Era, the New Deal, and the Cold War—each signify social structure, demography, dominant issues, and political patterns. The central narratives of these eras were the concerns of delegates to western constitutional conventions. For that reason I have grouped my discussion of the conventions into three generations: antebellum (California, Oregon, Nevada), Gilded Age (Colorado, Idaho, Montana, Utah, Washington, Wyoming, and California's second), and Progressive (Arizona and New Mexico). Accepting that delegates were serious in purpose and rational in pursuit of goals for their communities, attention to time and place provides insight into their decisions. Each generation of delegates to state constitutional conventions had their own concerns, from the infant states of the 1780s to the states revising constitutions late in the twentieth century, and these have not been independent of national and international developments. We read delegates' considerations of events beyond their territorial communities in every report of convention proceedings; it is in those contexts that their deliberations and decisions make the most sense.[44] The same markers designate assumptions and beliefs common to their time.

Time also matters in the shorter intervals of sequence. Every commentator on state constitutions has been attentive to "borrowing." There is much in any state constitution that is not original; often the published minutes and journals of state constitutional conventions dutifully list the sources of their provisions. It was borrowing that led many students of state constitutions to infer that they were hastily produced, with little creative effort. Later commentators have viewed borrowing more generously. In my reading of constitutional conventions, I see delegates conscientiously seeking states that might model the future of their own. These considerations were clearly stated by the delegates, whose conversations reveal the importance of sequence: every convention and constitution added choices for the consideration of delegates at later conventions. Presidential comments on public policies and the federal government's innovations, too, affected convention debates and policies in the states. Changes in federal law, and rulings on state law by federal courts, changed the substance of convention deliberations. State conversations about regulating corporations were different after *Munn v. Illinois* (which confirmed the authority of states to regulate common carriers) than before, after the creation of the Interstate Commerce Commission than before, and after the passage of federal legislation on mining than before.

Place matters in history, politics, and economy and so also in state constitutions. Region made its mark on state constitutions. Regions have distinctive political, social, and economic histories; we have every reason to expect their trajectories of constitutional development to differ. In *Understanding State Constitutions,* in addition to showing elements shared by nearly all state constitutions, Alan Tarr showed that regions exhibit different patterns of constitutional development. Tarr provided overviews of constitutional development in New England and the South. His account of southern state constitutions began with antebellum constitutions much like those in the North, with the addition of protections for slavery. Seven of the eleven Confederate states wrote new constitutions as the Civil War began. In the wake of the Civil War, Reconstruction constitutions appeared in every state below the Mason-Dixon Line. These reflected the Radical Republican agenda imposed on the South, as they "guaranteed the rights of African-Americans, encouraged government support for economic enterprise, ... expanded the scope of government responsibility with provision for ... public education, poor relief, [and other government tasks, as well as] reconstructing local government to dislodge local oligarchies."⁴⁵ The demise of Reconstruction brought new constitutions renouncing the activist states of the years following the Civil War. At the turn of the twentieth century, new constitutions in southern states consolidated white supremacist regimes. The short life of southern state constitutions followed from the many sharp changes in political direction taken by those states.⁴⁶ So too the West had its own constitutional path, moving through the Gilded Age and arriving at the Progressive Era with its own distinctive politics.

Regions also have strategic relations with one another. Immanuel Wallerstein recognized these relations on an international scale in *The Modern World-System*.⁴⁷ Wallerstein argued that trading partners around the globe resided in areas with different roles in the world economy. "Core" countries controlled a preponderance of capital; this enabled the most advanced economies to draw resources from other, "peripheral" economies. Countries in the periphery lacked sufficient capital to fund their own development and provided raw materials or primary products to core countries. Richard Bensel has applied a parallel framework to the United States, arguing that the northeastern core succeeded at establishing federal policies that enhanced its ability to draw resources from the South. In the Gilded Age the most important of these policies was the gold standard. The West and the South displayed the characteristics Wallerstein described for areas peripheral to the world economy—both regions exported primary products, lacked resources necessary for their own development, and were dependent on distant investors and the equally distant federal government for their future prosperity. Delegates to state constitutional conventions hoped the state governments they created would protect their communities from the worst potential outcomes of these relations and foster the best ones.

Place mattered as well in the characteristics of the territories. Not least, territories had histories of government and law that were the prologue to convention deliberations and served as a resource for delegates. Delegates did not start from nothing. Strategies, tactics, and precedents were created in practice, in courts, and in territorial legislatures. The initial forays of the territories form the subtext, and sometimes provide the actual text, of convention deliberations. The text of the constitutions was merely the tip of an iceberg of common law, legislative compromise, judicial decision, and extragovernmental practice. And for all the efforts of convention delegates to bring order and clarity to their nascent states, legislative compromise, judicial decision, extragovernmental practice, and the incremental change of common law continued once the constitutions were in place. It could hardly have been otherwise. Constitutions did not stop debate, disagreement, or conflict, much less history. Rather, they created institutional and legal settings for resolving disagreement and finding consensus.

In the chapters that follow, I discuss each of the three generations of western state constitutions. I report the issues, debates, and compromises of each generation's conventions.

"Frontier Foundings" is devoted to the conventions and constitutions of California, Oregon, and Nevada. Broadly speaking, the three constitutions were not very different from contemporary constitutions in other states, no doubt in part because, as David Johnson wrote, they shared the antebellum values that were nearly universal in their time. The three western states, like states across the country, denied the vote to people of color, were unsettled by the appearance of limited liability corporations, and insisted that corporations be granted charters only by general laws rather than by legislation specific to a particular company. At the California and Oregon conventions, delegates confronted the dilemmas caused by corporations and banks. These institutions were an affront to central antebellum values of citizen character and evenhanded government. Nevada, already a society of large corporations, debated the value of assistance to railroads and struggled with choices for taxing corporations more than thirty years before taxing corporations became a question for states across the nation.

Although they shared these values, the three territories were home to quite different societies. California territory was home to gold rush society in the north and conquered Californio society in the south. At the 1849 convention, the state's future as regional hegemony was not visible to the delegates. Oregon was a territory of family farmers, dependent on imports to meet many of their needs. Nevada was an industrial society, advanced beyond its years by the end of placer mining and the beginnings of large-scale industrial mining. Distance from the existing states, and recent settlement of the three territories encouraged delegates to resist the examples of older states and declare themselves free to construct governments appropriate to their own communities.

In "Managing the Periphery," I present the proceedings, and offer analyses, of the Gilded Age conventions. The central narratives of the Gilded Age—the appearance of large corporations, clashes between labor and capital, the mobilization of populist sentiment, the appearance of the Farmers' Alliance and the People's Party, and the settlement of the West—are prominent themes in the deliberations and the constitutions of these states. This generation of delegates completed three tasks. First, as in every constitutional convention, delegates in these territories fashioned government institutions. Second, they expanded bills of rights. Third, they made an effort to manage the periphery. Just as "the West" is not an artificial construct imposed on the region, so the region's quasi-colonial relation to the eastern states and Europe is not very different from delegates' own understandings (although they did not speak of themselves as the "periphery"). Both eager for investment and its benefits, and anxious about its possible ill effects, western delegates spent considerable effort trying to maximize the former and minimize the latter, the goals of managing the periphery. Managing the periphery also required law and institutions for managing competing social forces within the territory, claims on water, and relations between workers and employers. To these ends they created both law (for example, for property in water) and new government institutions (for example, mine inspectors). I examine debates about rights to water, railroads and other corporations, and the protection of labor on which delegates spent considerable time and energy; the resolutions of their debates appear in the constitutions.

The character and tenor of each convention also appear in this chapter. Colorado was the last cheerful and optimistic moment in the deliberations of western delegates; Idaho delegates were concerned, systematic, and resolute; Wyoming debates reveal open bullying about water law, mutual respect in consideration of the protection of labor, unity in hostility to railroads, and support of woman suffrage; Montana was a territory of cattle ranching and mining, with the latter contributing a significant worker contingent to the Populist Party; California's convention was plagued by heated rhetoric and ad hominem denunciation, its delegates most perceptive, thoughtful, and vexed by the dilemmas of writing law for property and corporations. Chapter 3 is the heart of this book, not least because there were more conventions. More substantively, the Gilded Age—the strength of the Populists and their agenda, the conflicts between labor and capital, and the role of state governments in those crises—birthed the agendas of the Progressive Era in these states as well as in the nation.

"Progressive Settlements" is devoted to the founding constitutional conventions of Arizona and New Mexico, which met in 1910. The constitutions they adopted were in their time extreme, Arizona to the left of Wilson and New Mexico to the right of Taft. Extremism was a product of the territories' lopsided party systems. In Arizona Democrats usually drew a majority of votes; in New Mexico Republicans had the advantage. However, in neither territory was party ascendance secure. Republicans regularly won elections in Arizona as Democrats did in New Mexico. At each convention the agenda of the partisan majority was to increase and secure their standing among their central supporters. For Arizona Democrats, the central supporters, and the majority of their supporters, were organized laborers. For workers, Democrats supported direct democracy, protections for labor, and abrogation of the fellow servant doctrine. For New Mexico Republicans, Mexican American laborers, mine workers, and farmers provided a majority of votes. For their Mexican American constituents, Republicans delivered provisions forbidding segregation in schools, requiring bilingual teachers, and guaranteeing that speaking or writing English was not to be a requirement for voting or holding office. These policies bound workers to the Democrats, and Spanish-speaking New Mexicans to the Republican Party, for many years.

Three issues were central to their convention debates, and distinguished left from right in the nation: direct democracy, the law of master and servant, and the attempt to regulate corporations. In national politics differences on these issues distinguished Democrats, Progressive Republicans, and stand-pat Republicans from one another. Direct democracy had been on the agenda in several states since the late 1890s. In Arizona there was little doubt that there would be constitutional provisions for direct democracy. Similarly, in New Mexico the failures of initiative and recall were forecast as soon as delegates were elected; the inclusion of the referendum was a compromise. President Taft rejected both constitutions. Taft judged the New Mexico Constitution as proposed too difficult to amend and insisted on revisions to make amendment easier. Taft objected to the recall of judges in Arizona's constitution. The law of master and servant posed contentious issues for decades and received attention in Gilded Age conventions. Arizona's conversation began where those left off; delegates furthered discussions of fairness and prudence in the protection of labor and were decisive in their rejection, the first among the states, of the fellow servant doctrine in all employments. The regulation of corporations by the states was uncertain territory everywhere. Both conventions created the broad outlines of sturdy political settlements that endured for decades to come.

"Creating the Western States" reviews the achievements of the conventions and discusses what the proceedings reveal about the conventions as deliberative bodies. I show how the conventions trace the development of the West and briefly look ahead to the western states on the eve of World War I. I argue that at the middle of the second decade of the twentieth century, the western states were distinguished by their greater commitment than states elsewhere to the protection of labor and to democratizing reform. The Gilded Age constitutions of the West provide earlier evidence of greater commitment to labor; studies of law subsequently show the same commitment. There is a great deal of evidence about the adoption of democratizing reform in the West, some of it appearing in state constitutions, and much of this too brought about by ordinary legislation. I argue that if, in the first instance, protections for labor and democratizing reform were created at constitutional conventions, in their wake those commitments were sustained by broad popular support. Among those supporters, the presence of many organized workers was the motive force of progressive reform.

In *Democratic Beginnings,* I present the constitutional conventions of the western states held between 1849 and 1910, and the constitutions they wrote. I report convention deliberations and identify the determinants of constitutional provisions. I argue that constitutional conventions were distinctive institutions, more alert and responsive to public sentiment than territorial or state legislatures. Delegates represented much of territorial societies and saw themselves as "select committees of the people" writing documents in hopes of endorsement of their work by popular vote. They did not, like the federal Founders, attempt to write a document that would remain unchanged, but rather felt duty-bound to include innovations of demonstrated utility, the products of generations of political learning. At the same time, frequently the issues delegates faced were without precedent, new to their time and place. Delegates were industrious, pragmatic, and creative in devising policies and institutions in response. They were not citizens of island communities. Rather, in identity, worldview, getting and spending, and politics, they were very much part of the United States, and proudly so. I show that at each convention there are two conversations, one national and one territorial, and that these two histories draw attention to the roles of time and place. Constitutional conventions were not continuous but met at discrete times in selected places. For that reason they do not present a narrative of western history. Nevertheless, as delegates to the conventions discussed their constituents and their aspirations, acknowledged the strengths and difficulties of their territories, worked to manage their territories' relations with distant investors and the national government, and engaged the central controversies of each American generation, their deliberations, and my report of them here, trace the arc of western development from the last antebellum decade to the height of the Progressive Era.

2. Frontier Foundings

The first three western territories to become states were California in 1850, Oregon in 1859, and Nevada in 1864. As California, Oregon, and Nevada held their constitutional conventions, the initial settlements of US citizens in the Far West territories were just behind them. The three territories traveled a very fast track to statehood; western states admitted later spent decades as territories before they became states (see table 2.1). For settlers in the far western territories, recognition of the immense distance between themselves and the nation's capital, as well as the established states to their east, pervades reports from the territories and provides a subtext for deliberations in the constitutional conventions. Worry about distance from Washington, DC, was not ungrounded. Following the passage of the Homestead Act, a federal enabling act was meant to allow a territory to organize to be admitted to the Union. The act specified various requirements for the constitution, and sometimes also for the convention.[1] Yet three of the eleven western states—California, Idaho, and Wyoming—wrote constitutions and successfully requested admission without that legal invitation. Californians called their constitutional convention because the federal government failed to provide a functioning government for them, or even to draw boundaries and declare California a territory. The same distance reinforced settlers' worries about constructing political and social communities in their territories and increased their sense of vulnerability to Native Americans, or slaveholders who might bring and free their slaves in the West, or the challenges of attracting settlers and establishing viable economies. In Oregon farmers worried about their dependence on outsiders for supplies. In Nevada, even after the discovery of the Comstock Lode, residents referred to their community as "little sagebrush Nevada."

Although the settlers in the small societies of the western territories lived quite different lives from those they left behind, the constitutions

Table 2.1 Western Territories, Conventions, and Statehood

	Territory Created	Constitutional Convention	Years as Territory	Statehood
California	—	1849	—	1850
Oregon	1848	1857	9	1859
Nevada	1861	1864	3	1864
Colorado	1861	1875	14	1876
Montana	1864	1889	25	1889
Washington	1853	1889	36	1889
Wyoming	1868	1889	21	1890
Idaho	1863	1889	26	1890
Utah	1850	1895	45	1896
New Mexico	1850	1910	60	1912
Arizona	1863	1910	47	1912

Source: Dates for territorial status, convention date, and statehood are from Franklin Van Zandt, *Boundaries of the United States and the Several States*, Geological Survey Professional Paper 909 (Washington, DC: Government Printing Office, 1976). Convention dates are found in table 1.1.

California: never given territorial status, statehood, 151
Oregon: territory, statehood, 158
Nevada: territory, statehood, 158
Colorado: territory, statehood, 131
Montana: territory, statehood, 145
Washington: territory, statehood, 155
Wyoming: territory, statehood, 144
Idaho: territory, statehood, 156
Utah: territory, statehood, 159
New Mexico: territory, statehood, 160
Arizona: territory, statehood, 165

written in the West differed little, on issues common to all, from contemporary constitutions in other states. This result is not surprising; as David Johnson argued, the residents of the Far West shared, at midcentury, "the common ante-bellum political inheritance ... providing a framework of precedents and ideas that shaped state-making at every turn."[2] Although Johnson insists on the centrality of antebellum political principles, he does not explain to the reader what they were. In this chapter I describe the shared values and concerns of antebellum Americans, introduce the three territories that elected delegates to constitutional conventions, and present delegates' debates and decisions as they wrote founding constitutions for California, Oregon, and Nevada. For California and Oregon, banks and limited liability corporations presented worrying puzzles. Nevada faced, from its beginning, the dilemmas railroads and industry posed in western societies. For this first generation of western conventions I focus, as delegates did, on suffrage, corporations, and issues of growth.

Political Premises

The shared views of the antebellum years were forged in the eastern states, beginning before Andrew Jackson's first term. Two key beliefs were an agreement on the importance of citizen character in a republic and wariness of limited liability corporations. Before the Civil War, Americans were most conscious of their status as citizens of a republic, a new country, where financial and military resources were scarce. They understood the US experiment in republican government as a threat to the crowned heads of Europe who, Americans imagined, devoutly wished our failure. Residents of the United States thought it important that, unlike the citizens of European countries who exercised little if any influence on politics or policy, they, as citizens of the United States, were the source of government strength, and their character the bedrock of republican government. Workingmen's Party leader Ely Moore made the argument this way: "Other systems of government are susceptible of renovation—possess, within themselves certain recuperative powers or principles; and though failed today may rise again tomorrow—renewed and invigorated. But when a *moral pestillence* shall have seized upon the vitals of a republic ... then have Despair and Death already marked it for their own."[3] In the antebellum years, character and morality were prominent in politicians' rhetoric, partisan appeals, temperance campaigns, nativist organizing, worker activism, and newspaper discussions of contemporary issues. At the founding conventions of California, Oregon, and Nevada, citizen character was key to decisions about who might vote; the targets of worry were people of color and, in Nevada, veterans of the Confederacy.

Wariness of limited liability corporations was a second shared sentiment. Concern about corporations stemmed from corporate inducement of political corruption and corporations' ambiguous morality and destructive economic activity. The political effects were found in the provision of charters. Many corporations were chartered by special laws, either as favors to prominent citizens or as the result of corruption. John Wallis reported that the "numerous examples of truly special privileges created by state legislatures gave substance to concerns about corruption.... In New York, the Albany Regency ... granted bank charters only to its political allies. In Arkansas, the state chartered a bank and capitalized it by issuing state bonds, and then allowed the bank to be controlled by two powerful families."[4] George Williams explained in Oregon's convention, "Out of this system of special legislation for corporations has grown all those evils" of which there are complaints.[5] The most offensive special charters were those that created banks. Banks were objectionable because bankers did not produce wealth but simply arranged the transfer of wealth to their vaults by collecting interest on loans ("usury"), discounting paper, and issuing depreciated or even worthless notes.[6] Banks corrupted state legislators; bank charters were a result of special favors to clients who paid for them. As a result, corporations were anathema to those who believed, with Jackson, that government should, "like heaven, shower its blessings alike on high and low."[7] These thoughts underlay constitutional injunctions that corporate charters be issued only by general laws, a provision widespread in constitutions written between 1842 and 1852 and also common thereafter.[8]

A second reason to be wary of corporations was the affront to morals of limited liability, the very characteristic that made the corporation an attractive investment. At a time when people might be imprisoned for debt, how could it be that investors were spared the costs of their errors?[9] Although those who purchased stock saw themselves as investors, delegates to the California, Oregon, and Nevada conventions were more likely to think of them as speculators or gamblers. Banks were on particularly weak moral ground, as bankers seemed neither to labor nor to contribute to the common good. Corporations were suspect because they contributed little to government and because their interests were not necessarily aligned with the interest of the territory in which they operated. By the time of Nevada's convention, in addition to the issues of special charters and the dubious moral character of their enterprise, banks aroused hostility by offering currency of uncertain value. Weak currency was ruinous for those who held it, and it imposed havoc on the communities in which it circulated. At the California convention, Charles Botts reminded delegates that Daniel Webster proclaimed that currency not backed by specie was "the greatest evil with which the country could be afflicted."[10] These judgments underlay hostility to corporations and banks for decades beyond the Civil War.

Conversation at these conventions also foreshadowed a central issue of the Gilded Age. At the Oregon and Nevada conventions, delegates considered the difficulties caused by their dependence on corporate investors, most residing elsewhere and managing their businesses from outside the territories. Rather like Dorothy Parker's reflections on men, delegates thought investors were hard to live with and impossible to live without. California was, from the perspective of Oregon and Nevada, very soon to be a powerful source of investment, about which its targets had mixed feelings, and from which California reaped great rewards. Fifteen years after California's constitutional convention, the octopus had already appeared; Leland Stanford traveled to Nevada's founding convention seeking assistance for the Central Pacific. For Oregon this was a worry for the future; for Nevada it was a reality of the present. Convention debates about corporations in Oregon anticipated, and in Nevada recognized, the role of outside investors in the prosperity of their future states.

Three Territories

Beyond the first thirteen states, settlement of the territories followed one of three paths. In the first path, presented by Frederick Jackson Turner, explorers and adventurers, followed by trappers and traders, initiated settlement. In Turner's telling, "the fur hunters were followed by pioneer farmers, then substantial farmers, and finally town builders." That was the path of settlement in the Appalachians, on the Great Plains, and to some extent in Oregon and Washington. Not so in the West. There, the discoveries of trappers and explorers led only to small numbers of farmers in a few places. Rodman Paul argued that across the West "prospectors and miners were the pioneers," followed by "merchants, packers, teamsters, [and] stagecoach lines . . . well after the saloonkeepers and gamblers."[11] This was the path of northern California, Nevada, Colorado, Idaho, Montana, and Arizona. Mining marked the beginning of large-scale US settlement in California and Nevada; California mining generated the growth of

Oregon. California's gold rush was key to much that followed not only in California but also in Oregon and Utah Territories (which included the area that became Nevada). The gold rush brought thousands of people west, many of them overland to the coast and later, to Nevada. Both the travelers and the immense growth of the population in the coastal region provoked the creation of trading posts and towns, farms, and ranches.

Before the whole array of settlers arrived at mining sites, small communities arose along the trails to the West to supply travelers on their way to hoped-for fortunes. This happened in Oregon, Nevada, and Utah. In Oregon, British (Hudson's Bay Co.), US (J. J. Astor), and Russian hunters competed for the Chinese market in beaver and sea otter pelts. In Oregon Methodist missionaries settled next. The area that became Nevada was initially a part of Utah Territory, governed by Mormons from the capital at Salt Lake. The first US Anglo settlements in Nevada were in Carson Valley, established by Mormons both as part of their own westward spread and positioned to provide supplies to migrants to California. Not long after, Mormons were called back east toward what became the state of Utah, leaving 200 mostly gentile settlers behind in Carson and smaller settlements elsewhere.[12] Carson residents organized to hold elections and petition Washington to establish a separate territory; they were not successful. When the Comstock Lode was discovered in 1859, Nevada's population was about 250, and it doubled by the end of the year. A year later the populace numbered 7,000, and the small settlement near the strike, christened Virginia City, had become a small metropolis.

The third path of development was conquest of well-settled territory, the path of the Southwest territories formerly part of Mexico, the most important being southern California, New Mexico, Texas, and Arizona (although Arizona had fewer settlers). David Montejano has written that for each territory new to the United States, a "peace structure" was created. The peace structure might mean anything from annihilation or subjugation of initial residents, to evolution toward a single society with more or less equality. The appearance of Europeans in the West decimated Native American communities. Whether from diseases brought from Europe, or by violent extermination—brought to the Florida Seminoles by Andrew Jackson or to frontier Native Americans by the hunting parties of northern California, or by exhaustion along the Trail of Tears march to the west—there was little accommodation for Native American communities.[13] When the Spanish began settlement in California, there were likely 300,000 Native Americans in California; by 1850 there were 150,000, and by 1870, only 30,000.[14] By contrast, in the Mexican territories that became part of the United States in 1848, "Mexicanized" Anglos joined existing communities, married in, learned Spanish, converted to Catholicism, and acquired land (not incidentally the land of their fathers-in-law). This was what happened in southern California and New Mexico, as it did in Texas. As in much of the territory that was once Mexico, the driving forces of development were trade and land; "the old Spanish-Mexican society of *hacendados,* merchants, villagers, and *peones*" was displaced.[15] The new society was dominated by Mexicanized and other Anglos, and their lawyers. In New Mexico, "as much as eighty percent of Hispanic land grants were lost by 1900."[16]

Americans were slow to migrate to the Far West. The trip was long, dangerous, and very expensive. Reports from early travelers were uniformly discouraging. Of Oregon, for example, the "earliest visitors were fur traders and explorers who ... sent back reports of heavy forests, incessant rain, and difficult and dangerous approaches by land or sea." Lewis and Clark fared no better, reporting they were "cold and wet, our clothes and bedding rotten"; over ten days there were only two hours without rain. And the leader of the US Exploring Expedition to California in 1841 (a dry year) saw "cattle ... starving in the fields."[17]

Whatever California, Oregon, and Nevada had in common, they were quite different societies. This was of great importance in their constitutional deliberations. At their conventions much of the conversation was to clarify territorial identity: who the residents were, what they did, and what they expected for the future. California was an extensive territory with marked regional differences. The southern portion was a populous Mexican society, which, in 1848, counted about 6,500 residents, denominated by contemporaries Californios. Residents born elsewhere in the United States lived mostly in northern California in 1848 and were counted in a contemporary census as 700 "foreigners." Californio delegates were thirteen of the thirty-nine who attended the convention.[18] Although they often voted in unison, they remained a minority with few allies and were treated with disregard and open disrespect by US-born Anglos. California was also home to 150,000 Native Americans, who were not represented at the convention and whose numbers were already in swift decline. By the time of the convention, the gold rush had swollen the number of US-born residents considerably; in 1850 the US census counted 62,601 US-born migrants in California. The war with Mexico and the gold rush brought thousands of single young men to California, and Nevada was not very different, both territories contrasting with Oregon's population of overland migrant families.[19]

At the California convention, Rodman Price and other delegates routinely referred to the territory as one of laboring men, of whom there were two sorts. On one hand there were the placer miners, who dominated mining for some few years after the gold rush. "Placers" refers to gold on the surface, or often in a streambed, relatively easy to extract. The presence of placers suggests that there are significant veins or lodes nearby; however, that was not always so, in which case itinerant miners left to search for another area of placers. "The people of California are peculiarly a laboring people," Price explained. "They are miners, sir, who live by the pick and shovel, and 'by the sweat of their brow, earn their bread.'" California's placer miners birthed many service industries, and these employed yet more workers. Price recognized small entrepreneurs as well as the territory's workers. "We have another large class of citizens," he argued. "I mean those engaged in commercial pursuits, who are characterized by the greatest enterprise."[20] Earl Pomeroy reported that "large profits came to some who served the miners directly: cooks, physicians, gamblers, stagecoach operators, and saloonkeepers in mining towns." The miners' presence was also an immediate stimulus to businessmen who invested in city lots, hardware, groceries, or jewelry. Their businesses employed many working residents of San Francisco, equally a product of the gold rush. The same market spurred a growing farming sector:

> The profits of farming and especially of selling fresh produce increased so spectacularly that [new residents] overcame prejudices against Californian soil and the Californian climate, and men gambled by planting peas or potatoes as they gambled by digging mines and ditches.... The declining California cattle industry, which had been no more than an undependable outlet for hides, quickly reacted to a spectacular demand for beef, and the ranchers found ... ready markets at the mines.[21]

San Francisco's population increased from a few hundred in 1846 to 36,000 in 1850 and 56,802 in 1860. By that date mining was already quite different than it had been in 1849. Mining was becoming an industry, requiring elaborate equipment and substantial capital. It followed that the most important residents in mining settlements were not miners but "merchants and lawyers . . . men with a shrewdly calculating sense of the abstract realities of economic and political interest and capital gains. . . . [They, along with] grocers, bankers, and professional politicians" shaped the government and economy of the territory.[22] Nevertheless, deliberations in Monterey give little hint of California's status, within a decade, as the region's economic headquarters, much less its future as regional hegemon, which was close at hand. Henry George wrote in 1868, "Not a settler in all the Pacific States and Territories but must pay San Francisco tribute . . . not an ounce of gold dug, a pound of ore smelted, and field gleaned, or a tree felled . . . but must . . . add to her wealth."[23]

Oregon's population grew very slowly; for decades migration to Oregon was just a trickle. The first US citizens in the Northwest were trappers, competing with Britons and Russians for the trade in beaver pelts with China. Methodist missionaries succeeded them. Their goal was to teach and convert Native Americans. Efforts to save and tutor the territory's Native American population came to little.[24] The more successful and enduring contribution of the missionaries was their provision for migrants from the Midwest. Missionaries assisted US settlers in "the organization of schools and colleges, as well as the creation of provisional government." When a group of 800 migrants departed St. Louis in 1843, missionaries were scattered from the Mississippi valley to the Pacific.[25] In 1848, Oregon welcomed 3,000 migrants, the largest group yet; the next year a party of refugees from California, disappointed by the slim rewards of prospecting, moved to Oregon to become farmers—even as others were deserting Oregon Territory to seek their fortunes in California's mines.

In the same year, newly settled farmers in Oregon began to ship produce to working miners to their south. The gold rush transformed Oregon Territory. "It is no exaggeration to say," Charles Carey wrote,

> that nothing in the history of the colony . . . so influenced its destiny. . . . From an agricultural community, content with the production of its

own primary necessities, Oregon was transformed into an ambitious, enterprising and efficient source of supply for those who were too busy hunting for and mining gold to take the necessary time to produce the prosaic foodstuffs they required.... Those who remained at home found opportunity to organize agricultural and industrial production on a new and better basis.[26]

The population grew apace. In 1848 Oregon was home to 10,000 to 12,000 migrants; its 1850 population was 12,093. By 1860 the population had more than quadrupled, to 52,465. The great majority of the territory's settlers were farm families in the Willamette valley; a majority of delegates to the constitutional convention were farmers too, thirty-nine of sixty.[27] The centrality of farmers to Oregon's society and economy was a sustained theme in constitutional deliberations. Oregon was settled by a strikingly homogeneous population. That was surely a preference settlers hoped to maintain and did, well after World War I. The dominant sentiment at the convention was satisfaction with Oregon as it was, and a desire to preserve its most valued components.

Conflict between North and South in the nation created bitter divisions in Oregon, especially among Democrats. For a while, patronage and the personal popularity of Joseph Lane helped to keep both Lane and the Democrats in office.[28] Lane was appointed territorial governor in 1848; in the 1850s he was among the many Oregon politicians who were openly supportive of slavery. The 1858 elections resulted in "complete victory for the ... pro-slavery faction of the Democrats."[29] The Democracy in Oregon, like Tammany's majority in New York City, served both as the arena of public life and as a partisan choice.[30] The coming crisis transformed all of that; Lincoln took both Oregon and California in 1860. Very quickly "secesh" sentiment was denounced in Oregon, and the Union supported.[31] At the outbreak of the Civil War the division in Oregon was "union and loyalty vs. treason." Most Democrats quickly chose union and loyalty, and over the course of the war many became Republicans.[32]

In Nevada, the discovery of the Comstock Lode transformed the territory, much as the gold rush changed northern California. In 1860, J. Ross Browne described Virginia City as a rise "speckled with snow, sage bushes, and mounds of upturned earth" and ramshackle structures—"frame shanties, tents of canvas or blankets, ... of potato-sacks and old shirts

... coyote holes in the mountainside, pits and shafts with smoke issuing from every crevice." There and beyond were hills and fields with thousands of prospectors' claims.[33] By 1863 the thousands of claims had been replaced by limited liability corporations conducting advanced mining operations, and Browne saw, in place of ramshackle structures, "substantial brick houses, three or four stories high ... and many more ... still in progress."[34] In 1864, Carson City too was a small metropolis, even as it remained an overgrown mining camp: well over half of its residents were men, and the town boasted nineteen boardinghouses. Mines brought miners, and also the service industries mining spawned, and with them waiters, cooks, and clerks. Carson City was also the territory's capital; many white-collar workers lived in the city, as well as the territory's major officials and merchants. Its fast growth drew many craftsmen too, half of them in the building trades.[35]

Just as California's gold rush brought about investment in agriculture and ranching in California and Oregon, so the discovery of the Comstock Lode led to growth in farming and ranching in Nevada. Mineral discoveries nearby amplified demand and ambition. Farming acreage grew. Crops and farm products became more diverse, with production of milk, flour, butter, cheese, livestock feed, vegetables, and fruit—berries, apples, and peaches. Between 1860 and 1870, Nevada's population grew from about 7,000 to 42,491. Raising livestock too became important; the same decade saw the creation of a large ranch in Ruby Valley and "the beginning of four other important cattle and sheep empires" in the state.[36]

In Nevada mining was only very briefly a project of itinerant prospectors. There mining was very nearly born as an industrial enterprise; even early on, a large firm might have 500 or more employees. Miners in Nevada were skilled employees, and they were a diverse group. In the early 1860s, there were many foreign-born residents. The majority of mineworkers were immigrants; in 1880 US-born miners in Nevada numbered only 770 of 2,770.[37] Miners were also organized; in 1863 the Miners' Protective Association was founded in Virginia City. Miners were remarkably successful, maintaining the comparatively high wage of $4 per day for underground work. When production fell in 1865, wages were reduced to $3.50 per day. A new organization, the Miners' Union, formed in 1867, reestablished the $4 per day wage and maintained it despite lower wages elsewhere. In 1872 the union succeeded in establishing an eight-hour day.[38] These outcomes rested on ongoing and civil relationships between working miners and industry owners; these were the earliest miners' unions in the West.

Possibly more than Californians themselves, residents of Nevada were keenly aware of the resources and power of San Francisco. For one thing, after the discovery of the Comstock Lode, a large proportion of Nevada residents had crossed the mountains from California; at the constitutional convention all but two of the thirty-five delegates who attended were migrants from California. The difference between California's army of itinerant prospectors and Nevada's corporate mining underlay historian Gilman Ostrander's observation that "geology made California democratic and Nevada autocratic."[39] Large-scale organization and investment in mining created the small circle of investors, executives, and bankers who managed Nevada's industry; they were the territory's autocracy. The same economy that made Nevada autocratic made it a vassal of California:

> Capitalists in San Francisco, Portland, and the East were increasingly to control the newer mines of Nevada and the Northwest. This was partly because San Franciscans caught the speculative fever in the 1860s and 1870s.... More fundamentally, it was because by degrees the process of extraction became too complex for local technology and local capital.... Gold quartz and the silver of the Comstock ... [in] a major lode or vein required lawyers to defend it, shafts and tunnels on a new scale to reach it, and with them, systems of ventilators, hoists, drains, and railroads.[40]

The *Territorial Enterprise* explained their relation: "The interest of no parent country and colony could possibly be more closely united than are those of California and Nevada. The colony has untold wealth of gold and silver, and the mother country manages ... to get it all as fast as it is dug out."[41] Vassal or not, the size and buried wealth of the Comstock Lode encouraged Nevadans to be optimistic—and sometimes defiant—about attracting investors.

The Conventions

Delegates' debates in some ways paralleled discussions at constitutional conventions in other regions and decades. Here as elsewhere, delegates voiced a clear sense of purpose or mission; deliberations exhibited self-interested competition among industries, demographic groups, and regions within their territory, as well as principled claims, high-minded visions, legal expertise, and clarity of argument alternating with doubt, lack of understanding, and confusion.

Delegates in California and Oregon were clear about their obligations. In California, convention president Robert Semple explained, "We are now, fellow citizens, occupying a position to which all eyes are turned.... This is the preliminary movement for the organization of a civil government, and the establishment of social institutions. You are called upon, by your fellow citizens, to exert all your influence and power to secure to them all the blessings that good government can bestow upon a free people."[42] In Oregon one delegate declared, "This convention, as I take it, is a select committee of the people of Oregon appointed to draw up the frame-work of a constitution to be reported back for their acceptance or rejection." Delazon Smith agreed and described the possible outcomes: "If [the people] accept it, well and good; if not, that's the end of it."[43] Nevada delegates declared no such high purpose. On the first day, some delegates suggested that the territory respond to the enabling act by telling Congress they were not interested; in their view, statehood was not a demand of the people but a design of self-interested politicians. Agreeing to write a constitution nevertheless, delegates spent the second day debating where to begin, possibly with the first, rejected, constitution written for Nevada in 1863. Or perhaps with California's constitution, since so many Nevadans and certainly nearly all of the delegates were Californians to whom the text would be familiar. And again where to begin—the beginning, the middle, or the end of the chosen text? On day three delegates began at the beginning of the first constitution proposed for Nevada. Later, J. Neely Johnson insisted on their higher collective purpose:

> We have come here from all parts of the Territory, and ... we have come here for a noble purpose, without reward, or hope of reward, but honestly to represent the constituents who have sent us here.... I attribute to every member the holier and nobler purpose of desiring to construct the framework of a State Government which shall be the best that can be devised, and which shall exist after we shall cease to be.[44]

Delegates were in some ways deferential to the older states: much in these constitutions was taken from Iowa or New York.[45] There were also occasional statements of defiance. For example, discussing suffrage at the California convention, it was pointed out that the Treaty of Guadalupe Hidalgo promised voting rights to all those who voted when the territory was part of Mexico. Charles Botts was a vocal participant in the convention, especially on the issue of suffrage. Born in Virginia, Botts admired the ambition and energy of the northern states, claiming that "in economy and management we are in many respects inferior to our northern brethren." On the question of suffrage Botts was "astonished" by the doctrine that "the treaty of peace [with Mexico] ... could prescribe to this convention what persons it should make voters in the state of California!" In his view the "states of the Union are free and sovereign. They prescribe for themselves the right of suffrage."[46] Of course the treaty *did* bind the convention and California.

More broadly, delegates objected to the idea that all wisdom was a product of the past. Rejecting the rule that all juries should be staffed by twelve men, a delegate at Nevada's convention explained, "I do not believe in sacrificing to any time-honored evil, simply because it has the sanction of time."[47] By contrast, there was endorsement of the idea that recent improvements in policy should be adopted. In California, William Gwin was a veteran of the Bear Flag insurgency. His ambition for California and the delegates is clear in this statement: "We are a new people, creating from chaos a government; left free as air to select what is good, from all republican forms of government. Our country is like a blank sheet of paper, upon which we are required to write a system of fundamental laws."[48]

In Oregon, Delazon Smith, an ardent Democrat and old-fashioned republican, explained that he remembered when the oaths of nonbelievers were not considered trustworthy, and "when a poor man, because he hadn't a dollar in his pockets, was sent to ... jail." Smith continued that he remembered many things once thought to be perfectly republican and correct, now recognized as "blots upon our national escutcheon." Smith found an example of learning leading to new constitutional provisions in Indiana's Bill of Rights. For Smith, that Bill of Rights was a textbook of contemporary democracy, including "the civil rights as ascertained in those seventy years of progress."[49]

Deliberations at the three conventions were conducted in the shadow of competition and then conflict between North and South. In California, debate about the boundary of the future state was informed by the national preoccupation with the country's division between slave and free states. One proposal was for a boundary far to the east of the Sierra Nevada to the Gila River. In that vision, California took nearly all of the remaining open territory in what became Nevada and Utah, most of Arizona, and also slices of New Mexico and Colorado. The proposal had the advantage of foreclosing further debate about slave or free states in a large portion of remaining territorial lands.[50] Botts countered by opposing "the idea that we can or ought to solve the slavery question for the whole country, or the West, which that great extent of territory would do."[51] In Oregon, as already described, strong support of the South among the territory's majority Democrats soon succumbed to support of the Union and, for some, the Republican Party.

Nevada became a state despite its tiny population because Nevada statehood promised to help the Republican Party in several ways. The 1864 election was sure to be close, threatening to throw selection of the president to the House of Representatives. Adding Nevada as a state provided Lincoln with three new Republican votes in the Electoral College. For their part, Radical Republicans looked to Nevada to provide a precedent by rejecting states' rights in its constitution, which it did, anticipating similar statements in southern states after the Civil War.[52] At Nevada's constitutional convention debates about suffrage were in large measure devoted to the question of whether Confederate veterans might enjoy the franchise, or perhaps be required to take loyalty oaths. Debates about voting by Confederate veterans were powered by memories, still raw, of military service for the Union and the losses of colleagues, family, and friends in the Civil War, and amplified worries about those still fighting.[53]

Suffrage

Every state constitutional convention wrote provisions about who might vote; age and residence requirements varied only at the margin, and race was always on the agenda. At the three earliest Far West conventions the issue of women voting was not raised,[54] but questions about voting by people of color were considered, and in Nevada there was impassioned discussion about the possibility of veterans of the Confederacy voting. Conversations about voting rules were halting and complicated because delegates were unsure about many things. For example, there was the problem of whether or how to implement California's obligations to allow Mexican Americans to vote under the Treaty of Guadalupe Hidalgo.

When the discussion of suffrage began at the California convention, the treaty was the first issue raised. It provided that all those who had been enfranchised when the territory was part of Mexico would maintain their right to vote in California. The rub was that "according to Mexican law, no race of any kind is excluded from voting."[55] The treaty was contentious in two ways. One was the presumption, on the part of the federal government, to set voting rules for states. Edward Gilbert, editor of the *San Francisco Alta,* stanched all doubt by reading from the sixth article of the US Constitution: "This Constitution . . . and all treaties made or which shall be made, under the authority of the United States shall be the supreme law of the land.[56] Although other considerations were raised (what happened in Texas? Louisiana?), delegates turned away from the treaty itself to the scope of the franchise in Mexico. There was resistance to acknowledging that in Mexico men of all races voted. Even if that were the case, there was tremendous resistance to making the rule operative in California. The first section of the article on suffrage, as proposed, began, "Every white male citizen of the United States"; it was proposed that "and every male citizen of Mexico, who shall have elected to become a citizen of the United States" be added. Immediately the revision was proposed to add "white" before "male citizen of Mexico." De la Guerra objected, saying,

> It should be perfectly understood in the first place, what is the true signification of the word "white." Many citizens of California have received from nature a very dark skin; nevertheless, there are among them men who have heretofore been allowed to vote, and not only that, but to fill the highest public offices. It would be very unjust to deprive them of the privilege of citizens merely because nature had not made them white. But if, by the word "white" it was intended to exclude the African race, then it was correct and satisfactory.[57]

It was this speech that occasioned Charles Botts's frequently cited remark that "he had no objection to color, except so far as it indicated the inferior races of mankind," as neat a statement of white supremacy as one might find. There was considerable further discussion of "inferior races" despite the presence of Californios among the delegates. The final text, "Every white male citizen of the United States, and every male citizen of Mexico (Indians, Africans, and descendants of Africans excepted) who has elected to become a citizen of the United States" might vote,[58] was well short of the promise in the treaty, that all who had voted when the territory was part of Mexico would vote in the United States.

In California, discussions about African Americans were powered by fears of the possible migration of slave owners and their slaves, and the migration of free African Americans, to the West. The prospect of slave owners bringing their slaves west, having them work a few years, and then freeing them, was raised with surprising certainty. Oliver Wozencraft, newly arrived in California from the South, supported banning migration of any African Americans to California. The presence of many African Americans in California, he said, would pose a serious competitive threat to Anglo workers, particularly miners.[59] The proposal was dropped without a vote.

In Oregon too there were proposals to ban African Americans from migrating to the territory. There were also objections to the Chinese; the claim was that Chinese employees, like African Americans, posed unfair competitive threats to Anglo workers. Compensation of the Chinese was so low they were "practically slaves.... If Chinese emigration continued in this country no white men would inhabit it." There was agreement that the presence of many African Americans in the territories threatened unfair competition with Anglo workers; in Oregon it was argued, similarly, that white men could not compete with the Chinese.[60] Oregon considered banning migration into its territory of not only blacks but also Chinese, Indians, and Kanakas, arguing that "the association of these races with the white was demoralization of the latter."[61] In Oregon, Section 6 of the article on suffrage provided that "no Negro, Chinaman, or Mulatto shall have the right of suffrage." Similarly, in Nevada it was asked, if African Americans were barred from voting, why "should we condescend to make any of the inferior races our equal?"[62] In Oregon the question of not allowing African Americans to settle in the state, and the issue of whether Oregon should be free of slavery, were submitted to popular vote. The propositions passed, making popular commitment to homogeneity perfectly clear. The prohibition of migration of African Americans into Oregon was repealed in 1926.[63]

At each convention there were a very few delegates who objected to denying residence or—less frequently—denying votes to people of color. In California, Kimball Edward Dimmick, editor of the *San Francisco Alta,* opposed banning African Americans from the state: "I am most decidedly opposed, sir, to the introduction of any thing of this kind in the Constitution, because I do contend that free men of color have just as good a right, and ought to have, to emigrate here as white men."[64] In Oregon, William Watkins objected to the vote to ban in-migration of African Americans. He spoke to "protest the right of any man or set of men to place any other man or set of men, be he white or black, without the pale of the law." Watkins thought slavery "wrong in morals as in policy" and insisted "the free Negro has claims on us which we can neither ignore nor destroy."[65] Watkins, like Dimmick, nevertheless opposed granting suffrage to people of color. In this the western states were among the great majority of states that prohibited voting by African Americans and Native Americans. The overwhelming consensus that Anglos were superior in intelligence and character meant the issue of voting by others was not open to debate. In 1855 only five of thirty-one states did not modify manhood suffrage by prefacing it with "white." Two years later the Supreme Court declared that African Americans, "free or slave, could not be citizens of the United States," thereby disfranchising them in the five states where they were able to vote.[66]

At the Nevada convention delegates debated whether soldiers who fought for the Confederate states should have the privilege of voting. Many delegates had served; more had lost friends or relatives in the conflict. The provision agreed upon was that "no person who, after . . . the age of eighteen years, shall have voluntarily borne arms against the United States, or held civil or military office under the so-called Confederate states" might vote, unless the federal government enacted an amnesty.[67] The Civil War was ongoing as Nevada delegates wrote their constitution. The bloody flag was raised with recollections of those lost. Fitch listed men known to delegates, who "leaped into the yawning gulf which closed upon him forever ... [and] the grand devotion of the noble soldiers in the West, and how every banner in Missouri is draped in sable, and every bird seems to sing a song of sorrow ... how in Kentucky the streams today runs darker with ... blood" and "hundreds of other brave men have fallen and died ... the whole land has been filled with wailing and woe ... for the thousands and thousands of unrecorded dead."[68] Reminding colleagues of the human costs of the war, the terrible losses of sons, fathers, and friends, the perfidy of the Confederacy and the traitors who defended it, was the rallying cry of disfranchisement. Worse, Nevada "is the place sought out already as the home of rebels from Missouri, from Kentucky, from Alabama." Warwick vowed, "No disloyal man, tainted with treason ... shall be allowed to share in the elective franchise."[69] Debate in the convention rested with a decision to bar all those who, eighteen and older, chose to fight with the Confederate forces. Nevadans expected the federal government to grant amnesty to Confederate veterans, but in the meantime they wrote provisions for suffrage consistent with their anguish and their principles.

Corporations, Banks, and Railroads

Delegates' discussions of corporations, banks, and railroads revealed strongly held principles and sizable economic stakes. As they reached consensus and wrote constitutional provisions, delegates recognized that they had fallen short of resolving the dilemmas and challenges they faced. The documents nevertheless expressed such agreement as delegates were able to negotiate among themselves. When California and Nevada projected a bright future shorn of the challenges of banks and paper currency, it was for the most part in anticipation of the federal mint's provision of coin and bills, sure to supply currency of certain value. Delegates at Oregon's convention agreed to an appealing collective vision of "associations," popularly funded corporations.

Delegates at the constitutional conventions of all three territories wrote into their constitutions that corporations were to be drafted under general laws, not as favors granted in special legislation. One reason was commitment to Jacksonian evenhandedness; another was that charters granted by special legislation were often products of bribes to legislators; general laws for creating corporations eliminated that source of corruption.[70]

Paul Johnson presents Californians as fully persuaded that resources, talent, and energy, in the presence of a free market, would propel individuals and the territory to prosperity. Hence, the "widest range of freedom that could be afforded the individual in pursuit of self interest was indistinguishable from the public good."[71] As they discussed corporations and banks, however, delegates expressed the economic reservations and moral disquiet of corporations and bankers common to antebellum Americans. California's discussion of constitutional provisions for corporations was met with objections the moment the first section on corporations was read. This section provided that the legislature was to form corporations "by general laws, but . . . not by special act except . . . in cases where, in the judgment of the legislature, the object of the corporation cannot be obtained by general law."[72] In this the delegates freed the legislature with one hand from the key constraint they had imposed with the other, creating a loophole broader than the initial grant of power. Moreover, the loophole contravened the Jacksonian principle opposing special privileges. Earl reminded the delegates that they should ensure the government avoided special legislation. The first section also prohibited the legislature from chartering banks,[73] yet that injunction failed to preclude all banking functions. The section allowed the creation of organizations that might accept deposits of gold or silver, for which the customer would be issued a certificate of deposit, and these might circulate as currency. James McHall Jones presented the threat these organizations would pose:

> What was the purpose of these associations, if not for banking purposes? Would they do nothing more than receive the deposits and take their four or five percent for the purpose of keeping it safe, and counting it over and seeing that it was all right? No! . . . They would take the money deposited—they would enrich themselves with its use. But suppose their speculations failed, what would become of the poor man, who, after months of hard toil in the mines, had deposited his little earning in the coffers of the association! . . . he would lose every thing.[74]

Although on several counts the corporations organized under this umbrella were going to operate as banks, they were to be secured by "none of the usual guards of the banking system." The provision left Californians prey to the worst products of a banking system, currency of uncertain value, without the guarantees of most banks.

Banks were at the root of all sorts of troubles. Botts cited high authority for these views, reporting that the "greatest genius of the age," Daniel Webster, "a bank man of the very purest water, declared upon the floor of the Senate that the greatest evil with which the country could be afflicted was an irredeemable circulating paper medium."[75] Price argued that surely this was in opposition to the delegates' mission: "The people expect this convention will interpose its power as a shield to protect the commercial and laboring classes from the frauds and abuses resulting from the substitution of the credit and paper money of legalized banking associations."[76] Possibly banks were unnecessary. Gwin reminded his colleagues that he had seen

> our countrymen as wild on the subject of banking, as they now are about your gold mines. I have seen the people going by thousands to get loans from the banks, as they are now rushing to our banks of gold. Misery, ruin, and destruction to the citizens, and prostration of the public credit follows the banking era of 1834, '35, '36, and '37. The private wealth and public prosperity which it was predicted would result from the system, like dead sea fruit, burned to ashes on the lips, while our banks of gold, if left unrestricted by improper legislation, will yield a rich reward to the laborer for his toil, and ensure to the country a permanent prosperity.[77]

Price argued that there was profitable commerce going on in California, and no one had asked for a bank; "I am opposed," he said, "to the granting of any privileges here which are not required by the community, and which can only have the effect of consolidating capital." Nevertheless, Botts pointed out, "in a mercantile community, some circulating medium more portable than gold and silver" was absolutely necessary, and so his colleagues "may find bank men in this Country, and they are the sharpest and cunningest of men."[78] This dilemma—that delegates and their constituents opposed risky paper currency, but California could not manage without it—could only be solved by the federal government. Delegates placed their hopes on a federal mint they were confident was soon to be provided. Gwin explained, "The great depository for California must be the Mint, which will no doubt next winter, be located at some commercial point, probably with branches in the mines. It is the true policy of the United States to coin every dollar of gold taken from the mines." Nevada's decision was much the same, banning all paper currency except that provided by the federal government.[79] A mint was established in California in 1854; after 1866 state banks ceased issuing notes that served as currency, giving the federal government a monopoly on legal tender.[80]

Worries about limited liability corporations remained. The California convention attacked the moral hazard evil directly, adopting a provision that stated, "Each stockholder of a corporation or joint stock association shall be individually and personally liable for his proportion of all its debts and liabilities,"[81] a section repeated in California's second constitution (1878). Several states passed laws imposing double liability for holders of bank stock.[82] Oregon and Nevada, however, were too worried that potential investors would turn away from them to adopt so punitive a constitutional provision.

Oregon's constitution too enjoined the legislature to create private corporations by general laws and forbade the legislature from creating any bank corporation or any other corporation by special legislation.[83] In Oregon, it was argued, "It is not for the stockholder specially that I would offer a guard.... If they choose to contract debts, let them abide by the effects of their folly."[84] For example, if a man "could be induced to put his $100 into so transparent a humbug as the telegraph line [in Oregon] he ought to lose it."[85] Those who sold stock played on the naïveté of buyers, buyers' lack of information, and buyers' reprehensible hopes for gain without labor.

Oregon delegates had a long and thoughtful conversation about the need for corporations and outside investments, and the threats they posed. For one thing, the price of discouraging corporations and outside investment might be high. Here, Missouri offered a sad example; it "lagged behind sister states because corporations cannot be formed there" because its constitution forbade the creation of corporations.[86] Failure of outsiders to invest would especially hurt Oregon since "the means for this enterprise are not in Oregon; stockholders will be spread to New York and elsewhere; if they read this in the constitution, will they not hesitate?"[87] On the other hand, it was possible that no benefit would be gained for territory or state from the presence of corporations. Massachusetts offered a threatening example of the reign of corporate employers. Looking to the past, Cyrus Olney argued that a safer path for the new states would be to welcome businesses owned without limited liability safeguards and "to trust them to individual enterprise and responsibility, when men are responsible for their acts."[88]

Were Oregon to take the corporate path, much that was valuable in the Oregon way of life would be lost. Even more than Olney, Matthew Deady was an ardent proponent of maintaining Oregon society just as it was. Johnson reports that Deady strove to be a man who gained "fame and honor . . . through disinterested public service."[89] Deady grew up in the South and remained a supporter of the South and slavery well after the constitutional convention. George Williams thought the great majority of Democrats (who were a majority of Oregon voters) shared Deady's views. Deady moved to Oregon in 1849. He quickly became active in politics, successfully running for the state legislature as a Democrat, and later was appointed to the territorial supreme court. Deady sang the praises of Oregon as he knew it, where residents were "breathing the pure air, with the canopy of heaven for a ventilator. . . . we yet retain our individual independence. . . . We have an agricultural community, and the domestic virtues incident to an agricultural people; and there is where you look for the true and solid wealth and happiness of a people."[90]

Most delegates recognized the necessity of investment for Oregon's development. Oregon farmers were without local suppliers for almost all their needs. George Williams artfully provided a vision of a more modern Oregon without the oppression some saw in Massachusetts. Williams reminded his fellow delegates, "Do we not hear the complaint everywhere that the farmers are compelled to import everything which they consume — the fabrics of every description, their clothes, blankets, pants, shoes, and everything of that kind?" This drained the territory of "a vast amount of money"; "the only way to retain [that money] here is by the association of men who can engage in manufacturing." "Associated wealth" was a recasting of the corporation, from an organization that might "suck the wealth of the country from the vitals of the people" into a Lockean compact among equals for the common good. "With liberal provisions in the constitution," Williams explained, "those little farmers throughout the country can put their capital together, as they have . . .

in the woolen factory now in this city. Then a man can put in $250, and another $500, and another $1,000, the prospect is that there will be a fine and flourishing manufactory established in the territory of Oregon." Despite the fact that Williams chaired the board of the mill, his argument was persuasive in part because he had earlier established his anticorporate bona fides by dismissing the idea that delegates needed "to be careful and protect the ... corporations," since history showed "that all corporations take care of themselves ... soulless and irresponsible."[91]

Oregon was not to be the corporation-ridden state inhabited by "millions of poor human beings degraded into the condition of mere servants of machinery." Rather, Williams's portrait of Oregon corporations as associations of farmer-citizens was simply a more prosperous Oregon, much like the one delegates enjoyed, the arcadia described by Matthew Deady. The arcadian vision of George Williams calmed the opposition of Deady and other delegates most attached to Oregon as they knew it, enabling delegates to reconcile themselves and their state to the limited liability corporation.

Like their predecessors, Nevada delegates allowed incorporation only by general laws. The question of benefits provoked debate when corporations pressed state governments for subsidies. Oregon and California forbade their state legislatures and their county and municipal governments from making any investment in or assuming any debt of corporations.[92] At Nevada's convention delegates engaged in heated debate about just this issue in response to a request from Leland Stanford. Stanford came from California to speak to the convention, asking for assistance building the Central Pacific. In support of the request, Thomas Fitch argued at great (nearly interminable, even) length that he

> should be very sorry, that this road shall be finished across the mountains, when the traveler shall start in Sacramento in the morning, dine at Reese River, breakfast at Salt Lake, and watch the lengthening shadows of that day as they decline along the valley of the Platte. . . . I should be sorry . . . if it should be said . . . that in the community which most benefitted by it . . . had absolutely declared that the people of Nevada . . . should not be allowed to aid that road in the hour of its direst necessity.[93]

Although in response to questions Stanford spoke with great confidence about building the railroad, delegates found him unpersuasive. Charles DeLong, a veteran of the gold rush (which brought him no treasure) a self-educated and self-made man who became a successful lawyer, was unmoved by Stanford's request. DeLong responded with an account—totaling $21,600,400—of the aid already granted the Central Pacific and asked, "How in the face of all this, how can they ask our little ... sage-brush Nevada to burden itself by giving more aid, when it would be of little or no practical benefit to the road?"[94] Although DeLong was rhetorically superior, and his argument more solidly grounded in fact, the convention voted to subsidize the railroad. That vote was consistent with the long history of state governments and railroads—that those communities without railroads were likely to stop at nothing to be sure railroads were built in their territory, while those blessed with ample miles of track cursed the railroads, strove to regulate them, and bemoaned their fallen hopes for shared prosperity.[95] As a state in which mining was the main industry, Nevada was certainly very much in need of railroads.

There were other arguments against assisting the Central Pacific. George Nourse told the story of impatient Minnesota, which suffered $2.5 million of debt and yet had no railroads to show for it: "If you pass this they will hang back until we lend up to the limit"; "for my part, I do not believe that this system of state loans is a good system anywhere."[96] In favor of corporations, Albert Hawley looked to Georgia, "the empire state of the South," asking, "What raised her to this position? What, but the liberal aid which the state government gave to measures of this sort."[97] Nevertheless, delegates in Nevada dreaded "the building up of foreign monopolies with no direct interest in the Territory, but whose object is to extract the precious metals from the mines and convey it [elsewhere, which would] greatly retard the progress, cripple the enterprise and otherwise hinder the development of the resources of the territory by its own citizens."[98]

The decision to assist the railroad was rescinded before the convention adjourned. Nevada joined its western colleagues by resolving that the state would "not donate or loan money or its credit" to for-profit corporations.[99] Possibly here delegates were responding to their constituents; one delegate threatened, "If you incorporate [providing a subsidy to the railroad] into your Constitution, it will call for more earnest opposition to the entire instrument than any other clause . . . yet incorporated. . . . Poor men, struggling here to build a state in the sand, in the bosom of the desert, cannot consent to lend or give to a railroad company, which has more money than it needs."[100] For a variety of reasons, then, Nevada declined Stanford's request, and delegates wrote provisions denying state subsidies to corporations in the future. Delegates believed the railroad would be built anyway, and just as quickly without public subsidy as with Nevada's help.

The presence of mining corporations raised the contentious issue of how they might be taxed. In later years an important argument for statehood was that states would be better able than territories to impose taxes on corporations. In Arizona and Montana territories, for example, delegates to founding constitutional conventions counted the authority to tax mines as a major advantage of statehood. Nevada in 1864 was already home to large mining corporations. Moreover, there was no question that Nevada was the target of, and its development almost wholly dependent on, California investors, as well as investors even farther away. Dependence on outsiders cautioned delegates to be wary of imposing taxes and, so, alienating investors. Delegates were invited to recall "the effect produced simply by the talk there was ... of levying a tax on our mines.... In New York, in Philadelphia and elsewhere, where men had shown [an interest] in our mines they began to stand aloof."[101] Others were more confident. John A. Collins argued that Nevada had no need to woo corporations. "I admit," he said,

> that every interest needs encouragement. But the mines of this territory have challenged the avarice and cupidity of the capital of the world and you might as well attempt to knock the dong out of a bell as to prevent these mines from being known and prospected. The world will come here, capital will come here, and though capitalists may be defeated in one operation, they will nevertheless make their investments in another.[102]

Despite Collins's confidence, delegates were worried enough about investors to decline to tax the mines. Delegates also expressed resentment that Californians seemed to benefit more from Nevada mining than the territory's own residents, resulting in resolve that the mines be taxed. A. J. Lockwood, for example, said, "I am in favor of taxing the mines because I want to make those gentlemen who are rolling in wealth in San Francisco, pay something for the support of our government, [and] our common schools, and ... the courts."[103] There was also, of course, Jackson's principle of evenhandedness, recognized in Johnson's proposed text: "The legislature shall provide by law for the assessment and collection of taxes by a uniform rule, so that taxes shall be assessed and collected on all property, possessory rights and claims according to their true value in money.... When this is done we shall have recognized a principle founded in truth and justice."[104]

There were several possibilities for taxing mines. They might be wholly exempted from taxation, the first proposal before the convention. Delegates responded with a hail of objections. Exemption of mines and mining claims contravened a central tenet of taxation common to state constitutions even well before Andrew Jackson's presidency,[105] and certainly ran afoul of Jackson's insistence that government's action fall alike on all citizens. Delegates thought the public felt the same way. One insisted, "My constituents never will consent to be taxed for a State Government, unless the tax shall be uniform and equal."[106] Others endorsed the thought. George Nourse, for example, pointed out that "in accordance with a well known principle of law, does not this exemption [of all mining property but proceeds] take them entirely out of the operation of the principle or rule of a uniform and equal rate of taxation?[107] Albert Hawley described the ordinary emigrant who came to Nevada to farm and was soon "visited by the Assessor when he makes his round." Both his few acres and his cabin would be taxed. There was "no justice in exempting" the "mines ... which have raised men to princely fortunes."[108]

There were other objections. One was that mining corporations were particularly dependent on, and the largest consumers of, the territory's government, especially its courts. It followed that miners should contribute substantially to the government's support. Fitch, among others, made this argument:

> The time of the courts in this State ... will be occupied, to a very great extent in trying mining suits; as three-fourths of the litigation of the State will be on the subject of mines; as the expenses of the Government for the protection of the mining interest will be greater than for all the other property in the State, I can see no good reason why the mines should not bear a just proportion of the public expenses.[109]

Mines accounted for the lion's share of the territory's wealth. In 1863 the value of the mines was estimated at $60 or $70 million, and property other than mining at $25 million.[110] It was generally agreed that the taxes on property other than the mines were insufficient to sustain a state government.[111]

A second proposal was that mining corporations be taxed on their gross or net proceeds. These proposals brought forth vociferous denunciation of mine owners. Revenues were not subject to government oversight, and manipulation of estimates by management was legendarily unreliable, self-serving, and dishonest. Not uncommonly, firms paid dividends suggesting considerable profits, yet the same firms reported scant earnings to territorial and state governments. Collins wondered, "How are you going to get at the gross proceeds, when the Gould & Curry declares over two hundred and fifty thousand dollars in dividends, and returns its gross proceeds at only seven hundred and fifty thousand dollars? How is that to be determined?" Providing further evidence of the problem, another delegate responded that Collins was mistaken, and that the gross proceeds were "a little over four millions for the last year."[112] A third delegate added that he expected that if the provision were to tax net proceeds, "there would be found no net proceeds of the mines, if the State should last a thousand years." Manifest discrimination in favor of the mines provoked Nourse to comment that "if we will add that farms, and saw-mills, and other property shall be taxed only on their net proceeds, there will be some degree of fairness in his proposition."[113] Cornelius Brosnan lamented that deliberations about taxation "had taken so wide a range." The delegates' duty was, he thought, "barely to define a rule, clear and positive, as to the aggregate of property, without making any specification of the class or classes of property which shall be taxed—that we are here to establish a rule which shall be uniform, and which, within the State, shall be universal."[114]

Not only were the mines the greater part of the territory's wealth, they were also the source of the prosperity for its other residents. Representatives of stock-growing counties recognized this. Nelson Murdock, for one, made this argument: "Now I represent Churchill County, which is in partly an agricultural county, and the agriculture of that county depends wholly on the mines to the east of us. As to whether our agricultural lands shall be valuable or not, depends altogether upon the development of those mines. Hundreds of men are there now, hard at work, living on pork and beans."[115] As a result, cow county delegates understood that it could "not be the case" that the cow counties would "be helped by any course that will injure the mines."[116]

Others made the point more elaborately, to the end that relieving the mines of taxation might serve the collective good. Rejecting the claim that investors from San Francisco and elsewhere reaped all the rewards of mining, Charles DeLong argued that the money "has been paid out to the operatives here. It has been paid to the farmer for the products he has taken to the city of Virginia, to feed the laboring men working in the Chollar mine. It has been paid to the mill-owners . . . to the teamster . . . the mechanic; it has been paid for improving the streets. . . . That money has been dispersed throughout the community."[117] Murdock argued similarly, "When business is good in the mines, business is good with the agriculturalists; and just as the mines pay and flourish, just in the proportion the whole country will prosper."[118] The argument was a rhetorical coup, a simple, practical, and straightforward case for hegemony. Were Murdock to return to his constituents and explain that the constitution mandated taxing mines, "Then they will say, 'Very well; away goes your Constitution.'" And, he confessed, "I would help them." Banks reinforced the case against taxing the mines, attributing the defeat of the constitution of 1863 to that provision: "After the experiment of last year, and what we have since learned of public sentiment on this subject, it is the worst of folly for us to undertake to tax the mines . . . and still hope to prevail among the people."[119]

The provisions in Nevada's constitution were not fair if measured by the standard of Jacksonian evenhandedness, or the even older standard that all species of property be taxed alike. Johnson and Brosnan most consistently reminded delegates that following those rules should set the burdens of government. Many delegates recognized the health of Nevada depended on the health of the mining industry. Even were a universal standard proposed for taxes, Nevada government did not have access to corporate records to determine proceeds or profits, and it was hardly likely that mining corporations would faithfully report their profits to the state, so mines were relieved of taxes. In this Nevada provided a model to be repeated in the future of mining and taxation across the western states.

Delegates to the founding constitutional conventions of California, Oregon, and Nevada saw themselves as select committees of the people, and they pursued their deliberations to the end of securing collective well-being and winning endorsement of their work by popular vote. Provisions in the first generation of western state constitutions paralleled the choices of their contemporaries. Whatever sympathies some may have had for states' rights and the South, their primary allegiance was to the Union. For the overwhelming majority of delegates, the superiority of Anglos to others in intelligence and character was not questioned. Wary of limited liability corporations, delegates accommodated their presence by fealty to Jacksonian principles of evenhanded government without special favors. Beyond that agreement, conversations in each convention displayed their own character and reached their own consensus.

California delegates, perhaps because their territory was farthest away from Washington and the settled states, or perhaps because their territory was the first in the Far West, or perhaps because Californians felt abandoned by Washington, which traced no boundaries for them and did not allow them a territorial government, or perhaps because they did not anticipate—and certainly did not discuss—depending on outsiders for investment, or perhaps because in the initial headiness and exhilaration of the gold rush they felt empowered ("a virgin territory... whose great wealth is unparalleled"), and so declared themselves most free to write the document of their choice ("free as air... to select what is good, from all republican forms"), were most defiant of tradition ("what has New York's experience to do with us?" when it came to banks) and the federal government (rejecting the constraints of the Treaty of Guadalupe Hidalgo on who might vote in California), and most openly hostile to the limited liability corporation (putting double liability for holders of bank stock into their constitution). The provisions of California's constitution followed from these declarations.

Oregon delegates reconciled themselves to corporations by recasting them as "associations," popularly owned. Oregon delegates were focused on tending their own garden, and they resolved to do exactly that. As George Williams presented the association, and delegates accepted his vision, one wonders how many of them thought this possible. In the moment the strongest incentive for Williams to design this arcadian vision was to calm the anxieties and quiet the objections of Matthew Deady for two reasons: first, because it was certain Deady's sentiments were shared by other delegates, and very likely by many territorial residents as well; second, because Deady, as leader of the territory's Democrats, was a very powerful politician. For the convention to close with a sense of accomplishment and consensus, and for the constitution to win majority approval from the public, it was crucial that Deady, like-minded colleagues, and Oregon voters who shared his opinions support the document as written.

Nevada's delegates had the clearest understanding of their situation, and they were rational and pragmatic. They understood the critical features of their economy, even to the demise of the Comstock Lode in the not too distant future. We see this in the many delegates repeating the claim that mining was the key to prosperity for all. Beyond an initial exuberance about the likelihood of investors to flock to the territory ("the world will come here"), and despite agreement that evenhandedness was a fine Jacksonian principle, evenhandedness was not the rule in taxation. Mines were exempted from taxes in Nevada, or their taxes were minimized, as they were, later, across the western mining states.

In the Far West as in the nation as a whole, citizens agreed on the importance of citizen character in a republic and were wary of limited liability corporations. There was consensus, too, about the superiority of Anglos in intelligence and character. The conversation that brought delegates beyond these premises to practical compromises, working political institutions, and an understanding of the dynamics of their nascent state economies was the work of the constitutional conventions, revealed in the constitutions they wrote. Where they were without precedent they were creative. For these tasks each territory took its own path through argument, compromise, invention, and bargaining to consensus written in their founding constitution.

3. Managing the Periphery

In the late nineteenth century citizens in the West resented the neglect of the federal government, which they hoped would assist them with irrigation, transportation, corporate regulation, and keeping the peace. They expected even more of their state governments: to be the voice of the West in Congress, the enforcing arm of popular will, a peacemaker between labor and capital, the protector of residents from the irrigation company, railroad, or mine, and of the many from the distant, indifferent, and predatory few. At constitutional conventions held in the transition from territory to statehood, delegates designed state governments with these goals in mind. As in every chapter, my sources for these claims are the proceedings of the constitutional conventions held in the last quarter of the nineteenth century: Colorado (1876), California (1879), Montana (1888), Idaho (1888), and Wyoming (1889), and the texts of the constitutions written in the same years, Washington (1890) and Utah (1895). In each of these territories, save California, the delegates wrote the founding constitution for statehood.[1]

Compared with conventions and constitutions written at the same time in other regions, and in the West earlier in the nineteenth century, those of late nineteenth century in the West have three distinctive features. First, law and institutions were designed to facilitate growth and prosperity, a task I call "managing the periphery." Since it was a leading and distinctive concern in the western territories, managing the periphery is my focus in this chapter. It is surprising that despite the energy, effort, and many days convention delegates devoted to managing the periphery, scholars of state constitutions have paid remarkably little attention to their efforts.[2] Even as they desired settlement, prosperity, and growth, delegates to constitutional conventions saw their territories as prey to "foreign" investors and suffering from the indifference of the federal government. Their understanding was much like Immanuel Wallerstein's, although without the social science language. Delegates to state constitutional conventions hoped the state governments they created would protect their communities from the worst potential outcomes of these relations and foster the best ones. Second, the conventions repeatedly asserted the authority and expanded the scope of state government. To enable state governments to exercise their prerogatives, delegates created new institutions, mine inspectors and departments of labor among them. To the same end, delegates expanded the responsibilities of existing institutions, for example, county governments and lower courts.

Third, delegates to western conventions wrote ever longer bills of rights. Bills of rights in state constitutions grew as the century progressed. The California Bill of Rights in 1849 had twenty-one sections, the Idaho Bill of Rights had twenty-three sections, there were twenty-seven sections in Utah's bill of rights, Colorado's bill of rights listed twenty-eight, and there were thirty-seven sections in Wyoming's bill of rights. Sprinkled among these many rights were affirmations of state authority. Some of the sections were elaborations of the initial federal rights. There were, for example, elaborations of freedom of religion. And there were new rights. There were reforms of the criminal justice system. Rights of victims, rights of persons arrested (to counsel, and freedom from harsh interrogation), and those convicted (to humane treatment, to reformative rather than vindictive justice). Unlike the federal Bill of Rights, written to protect liberty by limiting government (hence, "negative rights"), many Gilded Age additions to bills of rights were "positive rights" prohibiting private behaviors and requiring enforcement by state government, or creating new obligations for state government. Among positive rights were education. Finally, there were broad guarantees. Wyoming's bill of rights elaborated the right to equality, promising "the laws of this state affecting the political rights and privileges of its citizens shall be without distinction of race, color, sex, or any condition or circumstance whatsoever."[3] Western state constitutions created state governments; in addition, their bills of rights have national importance. Alan Tarr and Robert F. Williams have argued, "The new judicial federalism was in many ways fueled from the West, with California and Oregon making early and sustained contributions to the increase in state constitutional rights protections."[4]

The Territories

By the time the constitutional conventions met, the territories had well-developed economies. Of the six territories writing founding constitutions, Colorado, Montana, Idaho, and to some extent Utah followed the western path to settlement and growth presented by Rodman Paul. This path began with the arrival of itinerant prospectors working at placer deposits of gold; news of their discoveries brought a larger immigration of hopefuls, and in time industrial mining, in some places of gold but more often of silver alloyed with a base metal, fostering agriculture, ranching, and settlement. Each of the four territories developed mining industries; in Colorado, Idaho, and Montana, mining dominated their territorial, and later their state, economies, and in Utah, mining was prominent in territorial and state economies.

Not one of these territories, however, had the easy and direct path from the initial discovery of placers to successful mining followed by California and Nevada. Colorado's initial gold rush was in 1848, a few months before California's; the next occurred in 1859. Gold was discovered at Coeur d'Alene, Idaho, in 1860, and in Montana in 1858, but the settlements were brief, and by 1870 the population in both territories had declined.[5] The two far northwestern territories, Idaho and Montana, faced additional obstacles. First, some finds were distant from larger settlements and so, isolated. One traveler remarked of Montana, "There is frequently a surprising ignorance of what has been done elsewhere in the way of determining the best machinery and processes, and the miner frequently wastes his time and money in experiments which have long ago been rendered unnecessary."[6] In addition, Idaho and Montana, where large strikes were farther north, also suffered from challenging topography and brutal winter weather.

The second challenge was that the ores were "refractory" or "rebellious," descriptors of precious metals difficult to extract from the surrounding rock. In California and Nevada, simple processes of grinding, stamp mills, and washing were sufficient; the same methods sustained the early gold camps in Idaho and Montana. For the refractory ores, these artisanal methods were not sufficient. Worse, the knowledge of geology, engineering, and science required to construct smelters that would work to isolate the precious (gold, silver) or industrial (copper, lead, zinc) metal was not to be found in the United States. In 1870 a group of eastern industrialists hired Nathan Hill, a teacher at Brown University, to work in Colorado on the difficulties of processing ore. His route to test the ore shows the strenuous effort required, and the paucity of expertise in the United States. Hill had "several tons of Gilpin County ores hauled across the plains to Missouri, thence by steamboat down the Missouri and Mississippi rivers to New Orleans, and then across the ocean to the great Welsh smelting center of Swansea."[7] The eventual result of Hill's efforts was a working smelter, the first of many. This work, and continuing developments in Colorado, transformed the practices of mining and processing. Yet because ores were different, it was not the case that Colorado's smelters were adequate to every instance; the process of seeking expertise, experiment, and discovery was repeated in each territory.

The third challenge was that the territories, especially Idaho and Montana, were distant from railroads. In 1875, Butte was 400 miles from the nearest railroad, which was in Utah. In Idaho's Boise Basin, more than 8,000 residents were mining gold in 1864. This placed them 300 miles from navigable rivers; hauling ore to the Columbia River meant three weeks' travel by pack train (mules), and the ore was still not where it might be sold or smelted.[8] Railroads were quick to respond once veins or lodes were discovered, and it was shown that they could be mined productively. That said, mining towns waited years for railroads. In Idaho, for example, gold was discovered at Coeur d'Alene in 1860, and the first real strike was in 1862; railroads did not reach southern mining areas until 1883, and the Coeur d'Alene region in the north a year later; from the key strike to the arrival of a railroad took more than twenty years.[9] In Montana the first placer discoveries may have been as early as 1857, and the great gold camps were thriving in the 1860s, yet once the placers and easily retrieved gold diminished, the population of the gold camps declined. The first large strikes, of silver and copper, with productive mining to follow, were in 1879. The Utah–Northern Pacific reached Silver Bow County, rich in silver and copper, in December 1881.[10] Once the railroad was in place, its effects were dramatic—the mining industry grew rapidly; farming, ranching, and population growth followed.

Colorado began mining, as California and Nevada had, with prospectors and gold. In Colorado gold marked the beginning of mining in many places, but it was not the mainstay of the mining industry that followed. More often gold placers gave way to silver and base metals—lead, copper, zinc—as happened in Telluride and Leadville. In Ludlow there was coal. Colorado's first bonanza began with the discovery of gold at Leadville, and the bonanza—Colorado's first major strike—was not gold but silver. In the fall of 1877, "Leadville was a hamlet of log huts. Its population may have been as large as 200"; its business district boasted one grocery store and two saloons. In 1880—only three years later—Leadville's population was 14,820. The mine was enormously productive. Rodman Paul reported that Leadville's "annual output of silver soon surpassed that of any foreign nation except Mexico, and its auxiliary production of lead was nearly equal to England's." Sometimes the discovery of gold placers did lead to sizable deposits of gold, as happened in Cripple Creek. Gold was discovered there in 1891; like Leadville, it grew very quickly and was home to 10,000 residents by 1894. As late as 1902, gold production in Cripple Creek was the largest of any gold district in the United States, almost a fifth of the gold produced in the United States that year. Colorado's ores were more diverse than the treasure found in other western states, and the state enjoyed a long history of profitable mining.[11]

In Idaho both gold mining and mining of silver in combination with lead were successful. Silver-lead mining posed the greater challenge and grew slowly. Silver-lead mining required tunnels, blasting solid rock, and separating waste rock from the precious or industrial metals. This required either a smelter or transportation of the ore to one, which, to be affordable, required railroads. More immediately, silver-lead deposits required corporate funding and organization; once the smelters, investors, and railroads were in place, the proliferation of mining camps followed. As elsewhere, the railroad was last; within two years of its arrival, "practically every lead-silver mine of any consequence in Coeur d'Alene was discovered and legally possessed."[12]

In Montana too the inability to retrieve precious and industrial metals from ore was a barrier. There William Andrews Clark himself, later one of the most successful mining executives in Montana, went to Columbia University School of Mines to learn about processing ore and built a smelter in Butte in 1879. The strikes in Butte produced silver and, in greater and more profitable quantities, copper. Butte, Helena, and Anaconda became the mining centers of Montana; their foundations were copper, silver, and lead. Anaconda Silver Mining was founded in 1880 and became more productive as a copper mine; a smelter was built nearby in 1884. By the end of 1892, Anaconda Silver Mining was the world's single largest producer of copper.[13] By the time Montana was admitted to the Union in 1889, its mineral production was second only to Colorado's. Although early in Montana's history mining and cattle ranching contributed equally to the territory's prosperity, by the time of the constitutional convention, losses to stock growers in the harsh winter of 1886–1887 and the subsequent decline of cattle ranching, on one hand, and the growth of mining, on the other, meant that mining dominated the "treasure state."[14]

One distinctive characteristic of the mining industries (and cattle ranching too) was that there always seemed to have been eager investors in the East, San Francisco, and Europe. Among them were the foolish and gullible; their most costly error was investing in the effectively but deceptively promoted Emma Mine, in Utah, which quickly collapsed.[15] Distant investors increasingly bought the mining companies in which they invested, or owned them outright from the start. As outside investors assumed management of the mines, relations with labor deteriorated, rapidly turning hostile and worse, violent. The Coeur d'Alene mining war, a violent, deadly confrontation between miners and management, began in July 1892, not three years after the Idaho Constitution was signed. After these territories became states, they were the scenes of serious conflicts between management and labor in the remaining years of the nineteenth century, and well into the twentieth.[16]

The other great enterprise of the western states was cattle ranching. In Wyoming cattlemen dominated both the economy and politics. The range cattle industry in Wyoming and Montana began with cattle raised locally and grew exponentially as a consequence of cattle drives from Texas north to their territories. Texas cattle, slimmed by their long walk north, were fattened in Wyoming, and on a smaller scale in Montana, for shipment and sale to the east. At the height of the range cattle industry, in 1885, there were 1.5 million head of cattle in Wyoming and 1.05 million in Montana.[17] Stock raising was termed the "range cattle industry" because cattle fed on the open range, to be retrieved and sorted by their owners twice a year. This system necessitated organization and monitoring by stock growers—the registration of brands with the state, passing laws making the sale of young calves illegal, and arranging for the management of stray cattle. The Wyoming Stock Growers Association was founded in 1870; the Montana Stockgrowers' Association in 1885.[18] Management of the industry required effective monitoring to control theft and, once Texas cattle appeared in the territories, disease. The result was that stock growers in both territories were well practiced in collective coordination, political leadership, and centralized direction. Despite their skilled management, stock growers needed the enforcing arm of the law, and cattle ranchers soon found their way into territorial government.[19] The Wyoming Stock Growers Association wielded tremendous power and authority in the state; in 1888 association members made up half of the Wyoming Council (the upper house of the legislature), and in 1890 eight of twelve councilmen were association members. In Wyoming their dominance easily outweighed the influence of the much smaller mining industry. That stock growers and territorial government in Wyoming were nearly equal partners is aptly symbolized by the presence, in Cheyenne, of both the territorial capital and the headquarters of the Stock Growers Association.[20]

The range cattle industry required enormous amounts of land, making cattle ranchers and farmers natural enemies.[21] Competition with stock growers for land was only one of farmers' problems. Farming was very difficult in each of these states, and in California as well, largely because of the scarcity of rain. In California the winter of 1876–1877 was a time of enormous losses of cattle and sheep not from cold but from starvation—there was so little rain that the state's grasses were insufficient to feed them.[22] Scarcity of rain in the region also made farmers insistent that politicians attend to irrigation. Irrigation could not be undertaken by the lone farmer; everywhere irrigation required collaboration among farmers, corporate provision of water, or government initiatives. In the early 1860s, Montana farmers "with much brawn and little capital" constructed ditches for irrigation. Land farther from rivers required both money and organization to build canals, and corporations did so. Water provided to farmers by corporations was fraught with disappointment even this early, and farmers arranged "mutual ditch companies" to provide irrigation for themselves. For this to work, Montana enacted legislation creating ditch districts, which could issue bonds to cover costs. With some assistance from the federal government, this system worked well into the twentieth century.[23] In Idaho irrigation and water monopoly were key concerns of the Farmers' Alliance, as they were in Oregon and Colorado.[24] In California, where irrigation was "prohibitively difficult and expensive," "thousands of acres of productive land [were] ready for cultivation, all ready except for water."[25] Farmers had additional discontents. In some areas farmers were ill-served by railroads; farmers across the West resented the interest and taxes they paid on their mortgages, and as debtors they desired relief from deflated currency. As their constitutional conventions met, Farmers' Alliances, precursors to the Populist mobilization immediately ahead, were already present in Idaho, Colorado, California, and Montana.

California at the writing of its second constitution was hardly the territory that wrote the first. For one thing, the state's population, more than 800,000 residents, was in 1880 seventeen times the size of the sum of the territory's scattered communities of 1849. In 1849 the territory was in the first exuberant years of the gold rush; a majority of northern California's Anglo population were single men. In 1878 the value of California's crops and industry (slaughtering and meatpacking, foundry and machine shop products, men's clothing and footwear, cigars, sugar, and molasses) was greater than the worth of the minerals retrieved from the state's mines. Despite this progress, California was suffering from the nation's economic malaise in the 1870s, and there was widespread discontent, disgruntlement, and anger. Within the state these were directed at the small number of men with outsize holdings of land who were in control of the economy, and even more prominently the railroads, corruption in the state legislature, and the Chinese population. The most important voices calling for a constitutional convention were from the Workingmen's Party, mobilized primarily by anti-Chinese sentiment but also by more generalized economic and political discontent.

It was for these states, with their growing mining industries and a variety of smaller industries, stock raising, struggling farmers and settlers organized, and politically active in each sector, that delegates met to write founding constitutions in the last quarter of the nineteenth century.

Designing Western States

Constitutional conventions offered unparalleled opportunities to shape the politics and character of the states. The character of the delegates and their sensitivity to public sentiment led to outcomes that were unlikely from ordinary politics. Primary among these outcomes were protections for labor. Workers, especially miners, were organized, labor leadership was articulate, they had a clear list of laws they desired, and workers voted. Yet in the political life of the territories, and later in the states as well, labor's political activism brought little reward. In Colorado, for example, "the demands of labor in the 1890s"—the eight-hour day, the abolition of scrip, and effective employers' liability—"were essentially the demands of labor in the 1880s," showing how little was achieved in the earlier decade. "The fact that all the political parties in Colorado had at one time or another included these same resolutions in their partisan platforms reflects the real gap between campaign rhetoric and statutory reality. . . . Few political candidates took an openly antilabor stance in their campaigning, but during the assembly sessions antilabor lobbying took its legislative toll."[26] In Montana labor leaders hoped for gains from the new state government. Governor John E. Rickards, a Republican, supported several progressive measures but not the eight-hour day.[27] In Colorado, Montana, Idaho, and Utah, only the appearance of the Populist Party enabled labor to effectively interrupt the consensus politics of the major parties.[28] Labor's advocates often fared better at constitutional conventions.

Delegates were elected, and they reflected the societies that elected them. More than other regions, the West enjoyed competitive party politics, and elections of delegates resulted, in most territories, in conventions without a predominant party. For example, Montana's convention seated thirty-five Republicans, thirty-eight Democrats, one independent, and one Labor delegate. In Colorado elections were as a rule particularly close, but in the election of delegates to the constitutional convention, low turnout in the southern part of the state meant a majority of delegates were Republican. Republicans claimed twenty-four seats, Democrats only fifteen.[29] In Idaho, in two counties citizens cast ballots, in ten counties the central committees of the parties selected the delegates, and in six counties the parties held conventions to elect delegates. By these various means, Idaho sent thirty-eight Republicans, thirty-three Democrats, and one Labor representative to its convention.[30] In Wyoming, Governor Carey "arranged for an election" ostensibly "on a nonpartisan basis." The results were consistent with the territory's usual party returns, as thirty-two Republicans and nineteen Democrats were seated.[31] In California the Workingmen's Party was at the forefront calling for the convention, and in response, some Democrats and Republicans collaborated to sponsor Nonpartisan candidates. Carl Swisher agreed with contemporary newspaper commentary that "the nonpartisan movement was itself partisan, and was a fusion to prevent reform." The Workingmen elected fifty-one candidates and the Nonpartisans, seventy-seven. Eleven unregenerate Republicans and ten adamant Democrats, as well as three independents, were seated.[32]

Among the delegates were men who had long lived in their territory, and migrants from other territories or states, some of whom had participated in a constitutional convention elsewhere. Henry Bromwell was one of several members of the Colorado convention with a long prior political career. Bromwell, leader of the Granger faction of Republicans at the convention, argued consistently for strong government. He had migrated from Illinois, where he was an active member of his party, and cast his electoral college vote for Fremont in 1856 and Lincoln in 1860. Bromwell was also a delegate to the Illinois constitutional convention in 1869. At the Colorado convention, Bromwell chaired the committees on commerce and public indebtedness.[33] Volney Howard could claim political seniority at the California convention. In the late 1830s, he served in the Mississippi legislature; in 1845 he moved to Texas and was almost immediately elected to its constitutional convention and subsequently to the House of Representatives. Howard, a Democrat, was elected to the California convention from Los Angeles.[34]

Every convention was attended by former territorial governors and future state governors. Although for decades there was unanimity in the press that presidential appointees, and governors among them, were carpetbaggers at best and incompetent and corrupt at worst, former governors were treated with great respect in every convention. In Wyoming Governor John W. Hoyt was appointed by President Hayes. At the convention he offered the incendiary proposal that merit, not politics, determines the appointment of lesser government officials; it did not pass.[35] There were future governors too. Joseph K. Toole, a Democrat from Missouri, was the first elected governor of Montana (1889–1893) and served as governor again from 1901 to 1908. In the convention Toole argued strongly for one-man-one-vote apportionment of the state legislature (as opposed to allocating seats by county). Toole was a strong supporter of direct democracy and protections for labor; in his later terms as governor Toole presided over the enactment of a series of progressive reforms.[36] Every convention hosted many lawyers, small businessmen, and representatives of larger interests.

There were as well Populist partisans, farmers' advocates, and workers from the mines. Peter Breen chaired the labor committee at the Montana convention. Breen, who left his midwestern home for the West at nineteen, worked as a locomotive fireman, drove a mule team in the mountains, moved to Leadville, and worked "at a smelting furnace in the winter and prospected in the summer." Breen was a member of the Knights of Labor and, later, a founder of the Western Federation of Miners. The peripatetic Breen was in Idaho during the Coeur d'Alene mining war and afterward was charged with murder. Found not guilty and back in Montana, Breen was elected as a Democrat to Montana's first and second legislatures, studied law, and was admitted to the bar. In 1900, Breen was serving as county attorney in Silver Bow, elected on a Populist ticket.[37] There were cattle ranchers, investors in railroads, and owners of irrigation companies and mines. At the Colorado convention, Henry Thatcher, an investor in railroads, insisted on the necessity of investor freedom and offered a doomsday scenario were the state to attempt to regulate the rails. Charles Burritt, a lawyer, cattle rancher, Democrat, and investor in irrigation systems, presented the proposal for Wyoming's water board to the delegates. Burritt was also a truculent defender of woman suffrage. Women in Wyoming were granted the vote in 1869, twenty years before statehood; when it was suggested that the territory might be denied admission if women were allowed to vote, Burritt declared, "If they will not let us in with this plank in our constitution we will stay out forever."[38] The convention approved woman suffrage in the constitution.[39]

Delegates represented the diversity of occupations in the West, but the demography was narrow. There were no women, Native Americans,

Chinese, or African Americans among the delegates. Mexican Americans were represented, not least because — following the Treaty of Guadalupe Hidalgo — they voted. In Colorado, Casimiro Barela, Jesus Maria Garcia, and Agipeto Vigil represented the Mexican American community. Barela had a long career in Colorado politics. At the convention he secured provisions important to his constituents. One was that laws be published in Spanish as well as English. Another was that there be no educational qualification for voting for twenty-five years. Barela also opposed the headless ballot (a ballot without party designations for candidates), known to his constituents as the "southern ballot."[40]

Managing the periphery placed great responsibilities on western state governments. Major tasks in managing the periphery included creating systems of water rights, the distribution of public lands, regulating and taxing corporations, and the protection of labor. These issues shared distinctive characteristics. First, they were issues new to the United States, arising from new industries (industrial mining), new legal challenges (writing law for property in water), and new dilemmas (the regulation of corporations; the need for the protection of labor). Here indeed were "great questions of government policy" arising from politics, "the field, and the forum," and not yet resolved. Each had enormous economic value, presenting opportunities, often realized, for corruption. Issues of managing the periphery also had widespread salience. These were not arcane debates but the stuff of community interest, likely to move citizens when constitutions were judged by popular vote. Managing the periphery required difficult moral and political choices, especially trying when the alternatives (as in the cases of water and land) appeared to be zero-sum. Finally, managing the periphery presented complex practical, political, and intellectual puzzles. For the states to perform these tasks, delegates to constitutional conventions created new institutions and added to the responsibilities of existing institutions, increasing the authority and reach of state government.

Water

Each of my claims about managing the periphery, and the inescapable centrality of state government to that effort, can be illustrated by convention discussions of water rights. Water rights posed issues with enormous economic stakes, high salience, difficult choices, and complex puzzles. Discussion of water and irrigation also brought to the fore western resentment of corporations and the region's wistful demands of the federal government. At the same time, water presented a particularly western problem. As one delegate from Montana remarked, "God does not sprinkle these plains, and so they are an absolutely barren waste, and without water can never be used."[41] At the first of the Gilded Age conventions, Colorado delegates pioneered writing rules for allocating water. Since Colorado was a western state, and enjoyed remarkable growth and prosperity in the years after its convention, delegates at other conventions built upon Colorado's work. They did not copy Colorado's system exactly; rather, each convention modified Colorado's arrangements to suit conditions specific to its own territory.

Not a territory in the West had enough water when and where it was needed, and the region was without a well-developed legal framework for water rights. Yet were the region properly irrigated, there was great potential for settlement and prosperity. In a typically optimistic appraisal of the region's prospects, a delegate to Montana's convention argued the territory "was capable of supporting a population of ten million people if a proper system of irrigation can be had there."[42] The shortfall between "barren waste" and prosperous settlement made water and irrigation important political issues. Delegates commonly expressed hostility to water and irrigation companies, both foreign and domestic. Farmers in Colorado were dissatisfied with private irrigation companies, supported state ownership of water companies, and endorsed demands for federal reclamation projects.[43]

In Montana too corporations did not have a good record for providing irrigation. When out-of-state companies invested in irrigation systems, they set extortionate rates for water. As one delegate explained, "The ... law that provides that the county commissioners shall regulate the price of water has been practically abrogated by the promoters of this enterprise going to the farmers themselves and exacting from them contracts" at "exorbitant" prices.[44] As a result, farmers in Montana were unhappy with private irrigation companies and pressed for federal assistance from the Populist era until the turn of the century.[45] In Idaho political agitation about irrigation was at the heart of Populist politics. Farmers' Alliances in Washington, Elmore, and Latah Counties denounced plans to "contribute a billion dollars to improve the rivers that could be navigated only by turtles and catfish" while they failed "to appropriate a cent to irrigate arid land in . . . South Idaho."[46] In these three states, then, as well as in California, there was broad mobilization around water issues before the conventions, and for decades after.

The management of water raised several issues. Convention delegates were called upon to create a legal framework for water rights and make decisions about eminent domain and its delegation, the reach of beneficial or public use, and the regulation of corporations that constructed irrigation systems or sold water. States founded elsewhere in the Union did not write constitutional provisions about property in water; this was a peculiarly western problem, and here as so often, delegates were writing without precedents. The organizing principles of water management were not well established, yet the raw material for writing provisions was close at hand. Delegates explained that in the Midwest and the East the common law of riparian rights provided adequate guides for the distribution of rights to water.[47] Riparian rights awarded use (although not exclusive use) of water to those whose lands were adjacent to the natural waters of rivers, streams, and lakes, although the flow of water was not to be substantially diminished. Where water was plentiful, riparian doctrine served as a practical general guide. Instances of dispute were resolved in court, not with reference to legislation but rather as matters of common law adjudicated by the presentation of facts and the exercise of the court's judgment. As practices in common law, these decisions were guided by principle, custom, fact, and considerations of equity. At the conventions, farmers championed riparian rights.

The doctrine of "first appropriation" or "first in claim, first in right" meant exactly what it said. First appropriation was a rule embraced in early days of mining to protect the discoveries of prospectors. By the Gilded Age, the day of the prospector was long over, and large companies, often incorporated and owned elsewhere, were beginning to dominate mining. Mining and smelting industries were ardent proponents of "first in claim." Unlike riparian rights, rights of first appropriation were unlimited. A mining company's claim near the headwaters of a river, for example, could deprive farmers downstream of water that ran through their property. Or water might be polluted with tailings and other detritus of mining, making it unsuitable for irrigating crops.

There were also community or pueblo rights, in some places legacies of Mexican settlement, reinforcing government's claim to water management. The details of convention deliberations should not obscure how fundamental the question of water rights—that is, property in water—was. At issue was not only to whom the water "belonged" but also whether ownership or right meant use alone, or the right to pollute or destroy the source of water. At the California convention, James Hale described the central puzzle of designing rights to water: "There are two distinct phases of this question.... One is the security of the rights of those parties who make these appropriations [of water], and the other to secure the public against oppression from their use."[48] Henry Bromwell's recollection was that finding compromises, or resolving these issues, was tough. "The irrigation committee, wherever found," he wrote, "is (to its members) a mild form of martyrdom."[49]

Delegates in Colorado confronted these difficulties immediately. The Committee on Irrigation, Agriculture, and Manufacture proposed a first section of the article on water innocently enough: "The water of every natural stream within the State of Colorado is hereby declared to be the property of the people of said State, and the same is dedicated to their use forever." It was quickly objected that "the section interfered with the rights of individuals under the old doctrine of riparian rights," to which another delegate responded, "There was no such thing as riparian rights in Colorado."[50]

The second section proposed that priority of appropriation should give priority of right. To priority of appropriation it was objected that although the principle may once have been drafted to protect "the poor man" (the prospector), in the present the provision "would operate to enable rich corporations to appropriate all the water of the streams, to the serious injury and grievous oppression of the poor." Surely all could agree that "when a man took up land in a valley adjoining the valley of a stream, he ought to have the right to secure water to irrigate it."[51] To repair the potential deficit to agriculture, two provisions were required. First, prior appropriation was modified by a hierarchy of uses, so that when water was insufficient for all purposes, domestic use would have first priority, then agriculture, and then manufacture. Of course, disputes about water rights continued; these were to be settled by lower courts. Second, county commissioners were empowered "to establish reasonable maximum rates to be charged for the use of water."[52]

Colorado's deliberations present the parameters of subsequent convention debates: riparian rights; right of prior appropriation; the hierarchy of domestic use, agriculture, industry; government price setting; and, at least implicitly, the courts. There were good reasons for this to be so. Colorado first created constitutional provisions for rights to water—Colorado was a western state—and in the twenty years between the writing of Colorado's constitution and the next western constitutional convention, Colorado flourished. Fifteen years after the Colorado Constitution was ratified, Bromwell wrote of the courts, "[Their judgments] have proved so satisfactory throughout the many water districts, that they have never found their way into the reports of Supreme Court decisions.... It may now be truly said that our courts have given to Colorado a far better system of adjudicated irrigation law, than could have been expected, under the scanty enactments of Congress, the Territorial legislature, [or] the constitution and statues of the State."[53] For Bromwell, this record was a vindication of common law processes.

Discussion of water rights at California's convention began with a long disquisition of which the lesson was that large-scale irrigation systems faced insurmountable hurdles. Wiley Tinnin, a merchant and banker, elected as a Nonpartisan delegate, argued that all the world's experience of large-scale irrigation was in autocratic countries. Egypt and India were cases in point. Their governments, unhindered by the rights of the people, imposed taxes and enlisted labor as they wished. According to Tinnin, "The use of water for irrigation and mining was, until the last twenty-five or thirty years, practically unknown to the American people.... When we attempt to ... place it under legislative control, we are embarking on a new era." The cost had only to be calculated to reveal that prospects for such grand projects in a democracy were poor. Large-scale irrigation systems were expensive, and who would be willing the pay the taxes necessary to build them? Estimating the cost at "three or four hundred millions of dollars to even start this great enterprise," Tinnin asked, "would the farmers of San Diego, Los Angeles, Santa Barbara, Ventura, Santa Clara,

Humboldt, Mendocino, and miners of the state of California, submit to such a tax? Certainly not."[54]

The subsequent discussion of water rights was acrimonious. Issues and conflicting interests common to water rights deliberations in other conventions were debated in California with strong statements, ad hominem aspersions, and little resolution. Three issues triggered debate. The first division provoking hostile debate was about the meaning of "rights" in water. Dennis Herrington, a lawyer (Santa Clara), explained that rights to water were only use: "There never has been any higher degree of proprietorship of the waters in this state than a use. That is all. And there is no one that can acquire any other different property in it, except he appropriate it, and the extent of that appropriation goes only to that which he uses personally."[55]

C. W. Cross agreed: "It is only the use of water that any man can have. No law in any country has ever intended to grant any man any interest in water, except the right to the use of water than any man can have."[56] Joseph Brown countered that "water is property, and it is not the use which is taken, but the water itself ... a man has a right to waste or destroy it, just the same as he has a right to kill his own horse if he chooses."[57] Volney Howard read a law text endorsing Brown's view: "A grant of land conveys to the grantee not only the 'field' ... but all the growing timber and water standing and being thereupon; and a stream of water is therefore as much the property of the owner of the soil over which it passes as the stones scattered over it."[58] At the second discussion of water, Brown objected again to the idea that property in water was simply use: "This idea that there can be no property in water is wrong.... These wild notions are all wrong.... We had better be guided by the decisions of the courts of the land, and by experience, and by a sense of justice than to launch out upon an unknown sea."[59]

The second contentious issue was the rights that might follow from appropriation. How extensive were the privileges justified by the doctrine "first in claim, first in right"? Herrington described the dangers of the rule:

> When they made these appropriations of the headwaters of the San Joaquin, who ever asked permission of the farmers along the banks of that stream? No man. And when the miners wanted water, which of them asked the farmers along the banks of the Sacramento and its branches? Never a

solitary instance.... No one has a right to take these waters unless it can be shown that it is taken for a public use, and for the benefit of the public. Anything else is robbery.[60]

Appropriation made no difference. "What different right do you acquire by sticking up a notice, and declaring that you take it? It is all nonsense."[61]

The villain here was the corporation. A delegate from San Francisco made the case most forcefully: "We find, all over the State, an attempt made to condemn and monopolize all the waters of the State by corporations. Especially, sir, this is the case in San Francisco, where the influence of these tremendous water companies is so manifest."[62] San Francisco had recently suffered the effort, by the Spring Valley Water Company, to sell its works to the city at a greatly inflated price; this provoked an effective if disorderly protest from Denis Kearny and other Workingmen's Party leaders.[63] The influence of the company—or suspicion of it—was also felt in the convention. "I am thoroughly convinced," observed Herrington, "that if this question had been managed and manipulated by the Spring Valley Waterworks, it could not have been managed more to suit their taste."[64]

The third division (also debated in Colorado, Idaho, and Montana) was about whether water users should have access to water if access were dependent on a path through land belonging to someone else. This privilege, were it granted, devolved the power of eminent domain to individuals whose takings were possibly for private use. Objection was immediately voiced. "This I look upon as only another mode of confiscation," one delegate declared. "This is simply an attempt to infringe upon the sacred right of private ownership where no public interest is involved."[65] In Colorado, Idaho, and Montana, devolution of eminent domain for the creation of ditches for irrigation or for functions related to mining was confirmed. In California, possibly because mining was not so important an industry as in the three mountain states, it was denied.[66]

At the California convention of 1878, debate about water was so heated and bitter that it was not possible to draft a set of water rights or rules that could gain majority support. The result was a minimalist article that nevertheless affirmed the role of government in managing water. The article specified, first, that all appropriated water was a public use, and so subject to state regulation; second, that the right to collect rates or compensation for water supplied to the public was a franchise, to be awarded and regulated by law; and, third, that boards of supervisors or other local governments should set water rates annually. To Colorado's deliberations California added a long and indecisive conversation about the meaning of property in water, and James Hale's reflections on the "two phases" of resolving conflicts about water (securing property in water and protection of the public from "oppression" by those rights). Following Colorado, the constitution placed the authority to set rates for water in local government.

Idaho and Montana repeated the conflicts and compromises of the Colorado convention, as well as arguments from California. At Idaho's convention there were repeated protests that prior appropriation "might exclude the riparian owner" and "overturn the common law."[67] The result, if "the water power of this country can be used to prevent irrigation, if it can be held by virtue of a prior right, good-bye to all the prosperity that we expect to come from the use of the water in irrigating our plains."[68] This was the very objection raised at California's convention, when corporations made first appropriation claims. Idaho and Montana followed the path cleared by Colorado. At Idaho's convention, Edgar Wilson explained:

> Colorado ... is generally conceded [to] have the best laws relating to the question of irrigation of anywhere in the United States. ... I have been over that state a little, ... particularly in the portions where they irrigate ... and I know to what perfection the country which was naturally an arid country has been redeemed by this until land is worth $100 an acre for agricultural purposes alone, and I don't think we can do very much better than to follow them.[69]

Territorial legislation from 1881 served as the starting point of deliberation. Territorial statute protected settlers along ditches, declaring their right to the amount of water "good husbandry shall require." The same law guaranteed all landowners near streams a right to use the water for irrigation. Having thereby endorsed riparian rights, Idaho's statute also endorsed the rule of prior appropriation. Leaving no legitimate claim unrecognized, the law required courts to recognize any existing custom and practice of common right. These were the provisions recommended by their use in Colorado.

Finally, in Idaho the law created water districts to select, by majority vote, water masters to supervise and distribute water.[70] The creation of water districts also served as a political settlement between farmers and miners, as mining areas and farming areas in Idaho were for the most part geographically distinct from one another. In Montana too the familiar set of articles was proposed: that all water not yet appropriated be declared a public use; that the right to divert unappropriated water to beneficial uses not be denied, that priority of appropriation gave the better right, and that county commissions should set "reasonable maximum rates" for water.[71]

Wyoming's constitutional convention built even more government. Article VIII, Irrigation and Water Rights, opened with the declaration "Water is state property. The water of all natural streams, springs, lakes, or other collections of still water . . . are hereby declared to be the property of the state." Subsequent sections provided for a board of control to "have the supervision of the waters of the state, and of their appropriation, distribution, and diversion" (although its decisions were subject to review in the courts) and for a state engineer. The state was to create four water divisions; their superintendents and the engineer would constitute the Board of Control. Priority of appropriation "gave the better right" to water.[72]

The declarations of Article VIII, presented to the convention by the Irrigation Committee on September 12, were met with confusion and protest. Did not the federal government have eminent domain over all the country's land? Would a settler need two titles, one to land and one to water? What of riparian rights? Might it not be best to declare all irrigation ditches common carriers? What of the large alternate tracts of land owned by the railroads? Would a settler on one of the public tracts have access to water from a railroad tract, or might the railroad sell the water at extortionate prices? Charles Burritt, chair of the Irrigation Committee, intervened to say that the territory's irrigation system was in a sorry condition. Elwood Mead, the territorial engineer, had written a report explaining "the evils of our present irrigation system, and the . . . state board of control [proposed] to reverse that system." Copies of the report were distributed, and discussion of Article VIII was postponed.

Nine days later, Burritt had succeeded at persuading the convention to adopt Article VIII. On the question of irrigation, he claimed, the article "is twenty-five years ahead" of California and Colorado, and hence of any area in the arid West. More, the system proposed "would give [Wyoming] the most perfect water system that has been tried in this country." In their haste to arrange for irrigation, many had lost sight of the other beneficial uses of water, other just claims—mining, manufacture, stock raising, and domestic purposes—"all of which, so far as our constitution is concerned, are entitled to equal protection and privileges." No one need worry about the small farmer, for if a man settled on his 160 acres, and a small stream ran through it, his "domestic and family purposes, should by all laws of nature give [him] the better right," even if the stream commenced a bit outside the boundaries of his farm.[73] Reassurance was rejected as disingenuous, which it surely was. Here as in the other conventions, vociferous objection to the doctrine of prior appropriation remained. Attempts to define "appropriation" were deterred by arguments against "putting definitions" in the constitution, "making this a dictionary." With only a few delegates dissenting, Article VIII was adopted at the next reading.[74]

Why did Wyoming adopt the Board of Control to manage water and water rights? Andrew Morriss has argued that Wyoming's system of water management by experts and bureaucrats was the system of choice of the territory's cattle ranchers.[75] As I suggested earlier, it was a system much like the arrangements cattle ranchers created in the Wyoming Stock Growers Association. There were cooperative agreements on rules for branding, limits on sales, and so on, and for those who violated those agreements there were fines; cooperation was balanced with centralized sanctions. In Wyoming farmers and mine owners were lesser players than in Montana, Colorado, and Idaho; in Wyoming cattle ranchers were dominant in the economy, in politics,[76] and at the constitutional convention. The same men invested in irrigation, another sizable business effort in the territory. The *Cheyenne Daily Leader* explained, "In every part of the territory are favorable locations for the investment of capital in the construction of irrigation works of great magnitude."[77] The new water law regime was a weapon in the long-running war of cattlemen and irrigation investors against farmers whose homesteads both interfered with their ability to control land and threatened their control of water.[78] If, in Colorado, Bromwell lionized the courts as providers of justice and equity, for those very reasons the courts in Wyoming were the bane of cattlemen's dominance.

For those who raised cattle, juries were "a 'vexatious' problem because they followed popular notions of justice rather than the letter of the law."[79]

From Wyoming's constitution, with the most elaborate provision for centralized public water management, through the three mountain states with their competing principles and hierarchy of uses, to California's constitution, with the most brief and minimal article on water rights, the single constant was the critical role of state government in the management of water. It was never proposed in any of the conventions that the market, left to its own devices, would deliver water to all who needed it. Private sector provision of water or water management was nowhere praised; hostility to corporate water management was the rule. One Montana delegate expressed resentment toward "foreign" corporations that might provide irrigation: "If you have got to coddle and fondle and caress these great capitalists in order to get them to come out here and invest their money in these enterprises, then I ... say that we don't want these entrepreneurs, for home capital will produce them; home capital will be invested in these enterprises just as fast as the demands of the people call for it."[80] In California it was domestic corporations that oppressed their fellow citizens. "We find, all over the State," one delegate claimed, "an attempt made to condemn and monopolize all the waters of the State by corporations. Especially, sir, this is the case in San Francisco, where the influence of these tremendous water companies is so manifest."[81] A delegate to Montana's convention expressed common sentiment about the ultimate resolution of disputes about irrigation: he looked to government. "I hope to see the day come," he said,

> when systems of irrigation shall be either under the control of the state or of the United States.... We are opposed to landlordism; we don't want any company or any corporation or any individual to own vast tracts of the land in which they may have tenants. But ... if the companies or individual or corporations are to own the vast water courses, that would be a species of landlordism of the worst kind.[82]

Another delegate endorsed the view that water and irrigation should be public functions. "Well now," he began,

> suppose heaven, in its infinite mercy, would bestow a little sense upon these men in Congress—it is devoutly to be hoped for, although

unreasonable to be expected — and those men would wake up to the interests of northern Dakota [Territory], that is capable of supporting a population of ten million people if a proper system of irrigation could be had there, and the waters that are now going to waste could be mixed with the soil of God's earth to bring forth its increase. Until that thing is done there is no reason for us to hope for a permanent dawn of prosperity.[83]

Even the Republican *Helena Daily Herald* agreed. "We hold that it is clearly the best policy," the editors wrote,

not to encourage the establishment of private companies interested in the ownership and supply of water.... The allowance of private corporations to monopolize and control the water supply will delay the attainment of the more desirable end of creating a public supply.... Of this we are certain, that if the nation does not carry out the irrigation system in detail, the State must do it, either directly or indirectly.[84]

Absent federal or state initiatives, and even in their presence, water issues remained a continuing source of conflict and adjudication across the West.

Railroads and Other Corporations

Corporations, especially corporations with out-of-state owners, were a most important concern in managing the periphery. In their Address to the People, the authors of Colorado's constitution wrote, "No subject has come before the convention causing more anxiety and concern than the troublesome and vexed question pertaining to corporations.... The Legislatures of other states have, in most cases, been found unequal to the task of preventing abuses and protecting the people from the grasping and monopolizing tendencies of railroads and other corporations." The prudent course, in the delegates' view, was to make provisions in the constitution to manage corporations, while placing "positive restrictions on the powers of the Legislature."[85] For western leaders, including delegates to constitutional conventions, foreign corporations brought both alluring possibilities of growth and prosperity, and threatening potential for exploitation, struggle, and disruption. No corporations presented these alternatives more forcefully than the railroads, in these Rocky Mountain states prosperity rested on the presence of railroads, and in no area did the western states so closely follow the path of the states that preceded them. As much as any other set of issues in managing the periphery, railroads and other corporations were weighted with tremendous economic stakes; were of great concern to mining industries, farmers, and all who desired more settlement; and posed difficult puzzles and choices for delegates.

The regulation of railroads was an issue across the United States. Debate about railroads moved from east to west with the rails. In regions without railroads, states and towns were eager to recruit them; by contrast, regions well crossed by railroads insisted on their regulation.[86] Early in the century, states and towns subsidized the growth of railroads—an experiment of which the unfortunate consequences were well known by the Civil War. The lessons of that experience were written into Gilded Age constitutions: states were not to own or subsidize corporations, and the debt of county and town governments was severely limited.

Changes in railroad organization after the Civil War magnified the divergence of railroads from community interests. If earlier, towns or counties might reasonably have imagined that their community and a small railroad shared prospects for growth, a decade after the Civil War it was clear that the enormous railroad corporations, with interests spanning whole regions, had their own goals and prospects independent of communities or states. Despite these experiences, after the Civil War areas without railroads remained anxious to recruit them. This was especially so in the West because its main exports—precious metals, lead, and coal—were very heavy, bound for distant markets, and so profitable only with rail transport. As a result, short of outright subsidy, communities without railroads were generous in offering freedom of action to railroad corporations. Yet in the West as in the East and on the plains, where railroads were well developed, citizens were most anxious to regulate them.[87] The impulse to regulate took institutional form in the 1870 constitution of Illinois and the legislation passed afterward to create a railroad commission.

At Colorado's constitutional convention, the familiar debate between regulation and welcome was between counties that had railroads and counties that did not, between investors and advocates of railroads and delegates with Granger views. After carefully counting votes at the convention, historian Donald Hensel declared, "Party affiliation meant nothing."[88] The argument for regulation was based on both experience and principle. George White, from Jefferson, voiced a bitter critique of railroads. By land grants and subsidy, the "government had built the railroads, and now the ... great cormorant power was reaching out and swallowing up all the railroads in the country. The counties of Jefferson and Boulder had been grievously wronged by these companies.... Should there not be placed in the constitution a clause for the protection of the people?"[89]

When Colorado's convention met in 1875, there were only 675 miles of track in a territory where all pinned their future on the mines, and none of the track served mining areas. Short as the lines were, many counties had gone far into debt offering subsidies in their efforts to lure railroads. Those sad experiences were a prime motive for constitutional limits on county debt (subsequently flouted). The outcome of this debate could hardly have been in doubt. The railroads were well represented among delegates and, according to Bromwell, the "siege upon the convention in the railroad matter was led by the most influential of the public men of the Territory."[90] Henry Thatcher, representative from Pueblo and an investor with large holdings in railroads, offered a doomsday scenario if rate regulation were placed in the constitution. Wisconsin and Minnesota regretted and repealed their regulatory legislation, he claimed, while Kansas and Iowa refused to countenance enacting it. And wherever railroad commissioners had been appointed, they concluded that setting rates was too complex a task for government. To the proposal that Colorado courts determine fair rates, Thatcher replied, "Enact these sections and not another mile of railroad will be built in Colorado. Capital, ever sensitive and timid, will find more secure investment elsewhere." Thatcher insisted, "Competition will do more to regulate and cheapen the rates of fare and freight than all the legislation of the country."[91] Although the constitution declared railroads common carriers (thereby requiring that they treat all passengers and shippers equally), delegates refused to appoint any agency to regulate rates and declined even to deny the use of free passes to state workers or politicians.

California wrote its second constitution just two years after Colorado wrote its first. As Colorado, with few railroads, was most reluctant to constrain them, so California, well traversed by railroads, was most aggressive at regulation. Of course delegates recognized the contribution of the railroads. "The railroads redeemed this State from a wilderness and made it what it is today," explained James M. Shafter. "The railroad property of the state today pays taxes on five hundred millions of dollars.... Take away these roads, tear up the rails, and the country would soon revert to savagedom."[92] Nevertheless, in California railroads provoked tremendous anger that was fully expressed at the constitutional convention. When the corporations article was discussed, several delegates reviewed the state's miserable experience with railroads. "Way back in eighteen hundred and sixty," one delegate recalled, "this railroad excitement commenced. There was not a man in the State who would not turn his pockets wrong side out to help build a railroad. The people were willing to give them all they asked and all they did was to take all the people gave them."[93]

Volney saw the same trajectory in Los Angeles, which had "contributed seven hundred and fifty thousand dollars to the railroad by way of subsidies, to enable the road to cut our own throats. They have not only bought up the landings and wharves they are virtually monopolizing the ocean, by driving off all competition."[94] Morris Estee,[95] who as a candidate criticized the Workingmen's Parties for insufficient commitment to their supporters, and who chaired the committee on corporations, drew the moral of this history: "I now lay down the doctrine that where combination is possible, competition is impossible, that in truth and fact there is no such thing as competition today in the great carrying trade of the country on land" "except by and through the sovereign will of the state."[96] Moreover, in the wake of *Munn v. Illinois* (1877), it was clear that it was legally proper for states to regulate railroads.

Little could be hoped for from the state legislature. James Hale voiced the common judgment. Although the state and federal governments agreed that regulation was legal and necessary, "this ... fact stares us in the face, that we have been attempting, through the medium of the Legislature, to exercise this control for the past fifteen years, and thus far all efforts ... have been abortive."[97] Charles O'Donnell claimed popular support for the convention to act, asking, "Who has any confidence in the legislature that have been in the state for the last fifteen or twenty years? Most of us members were sent here for the purpose of regulating freights and fares.... Now don't you leave this thing to the legislature."[98]

The committee proposed a railroad commission for the state. California was to be divided into three districts, each to elect a commissioner.

Together the three commissioners were to set rates and arbitrate claims. Were the convention to adopt the proposed commission, it would "mark a new era in the history of the state; it will stamp upon the organic law of California that right of . . . regulation of railroads necessary for the protection of our people."[99] The proposal for a commission recommended itself, both because regulating railroads was beyond the competence of the legislature (it was corrupt and only met "once in every two years") and, second, because the multiplicity of disputes and claims could not be resolved by legislation.[100]

Although there was agreement that railroads should be regulated, some delegates thought the commission would be even more vulnerable to corruption than the legislature. Marion Biggs made the case against the commission: "I am opposed to the Report of the Committee of the Whole; and I want gentlemen to understand that I do not wear the collar of the railroad, or the corporation, or anything else. I am opposed to this report. It gives too much power to these men. . . . There is no appeal. They are the lords of all California; they are the lords of everything."[101] William Dudley agreed. Insisting on his innocence of fealty to the railroads, Dudley argued, "Power over corporations is a power that belongs to the people of California. Now, it is proposed here, by one fell swoop, to take that power from the people and give it into the hands of a triumvirate. I believe it is a mistake."[102] Proponents of the commission countered that many states had created commissions to regulate railroads; Wisconsin and Illinois were happy with their commissions. Morris Estee offered an optimistic forecast: "I believe that you can trust the people to elect three men who will deal fairly with these great evils. . . . Great responsibilities always bring great attention to duty, and I believe that the very existence of such a Commission will have a most marked influence upon the future prosperity of this state."[103] Despite the qualms of some delegates, the commission carried the day.

Estee's optimistic forecast did not come true. At the first election of commissioners, the Democratic, Workingmen's, and Republican Parties, and their candidates, all pledged that the commission would protect the public by prescribing fair rates. One Democrat, one Republican, and one Workingman were elected, and each failed to keep his pledge. That disappointing outcome was repeated after every election. Writing about the commission in 1895, S. E. Moffett concluded, "A body created sixteen years ago for the sole purpose of curbing a single railroad corporation with a strong hand, was found to be uniformly, without a break, during all that period its apologist and defender. Not a single majority report has ever issued from the ... railroad Commission of a nature unsatisfactory to the company the Commission was established to control."[104]

By the time Idaho, Montana, and Wyoming held their conventions, federal actions had changed the law of regulation. *Munn v. Illinois* confirmed the authority of state governments to regulate business; the Interstate Commerce Commission (1887) was the institutional result of the judgment that regulation was required. Although *Munn* legitimated state regulation of the rails, and the federal commission confirmed the need for regulation, they failed to embolden Idaho, Montana, and Wyoming to follow the lead of Illinois. As in Colorado, the desire of the three territories for railroads, their lack of experience with railroads, the presence of railroad interests at the conventions, the recognition that the development of mining would be stymied without the presence of railroads, and dependence on outside investors stopped the creation of railroad commissions. The pressing need for railroads was often voiced. In Idaho, John Morgan, a Republican who had served on the territorial supreme court, declared, "The great need in this country, it seems to me, is railroad lines, and whether they are competing or not I do not care, so we can get the railroads."[105] William Clagett, a Republican and chair of the Convention, thought so as well, claiming, "We are a young country and what we want of all things is local lines of railway."[106] Surely "every sensible man sees at once that if we have railroads built here it will not be by our own people; we haven't the money; the money has to come from abroad."[107] Dependence suggested caution. In response to a proposal that the constitution ban consolidation of railroads, one delegate declared, "It seems to me that we are acting upon the theory that now is the time to keep railroads from coming here." Since only the Union Pacific operated in Idaho, discouraging other railroads would "leave our state for all time in the hands of this one corporation."[108]

Nevertheless, the constitutions of Montana, Idaho, and Wyoming stated clearly the states' prerogative to set rates. State authority followed from declaring railroads to be public highways and common carriers, hence "subject to legislative control." In each constitution the legislature was given "the power to regulate and control by law the rates of charges for the transportation of passengers and freight."[109] In Wyoming, former territorial governor John Hoyt provided the justification for exercising state authority: "I think every member appreciates the value of railroads, and we need more of them, and wishes to deal justly and fairly with them, but there are certain interests of the public, which the railroads themselves will concede, which should be preserved and protected, and the object of this proposition is to protect the ... interests of the entire public."[110]

As in California forty years earlier, and in Oregon thirty years earlier, the limited liability corporation remained morally suspect. Some delegates thought the corporation should be done away with, and business conducted by partnerships. In Colorado, S. J. Plumb, a Republican rancher, wanted to abolish limited liability.[111] For these delegates, as for their antebellum forebears, it seemed just plain immoral that, through the device of the corporation, men were not held accountable for the troubles, injuries, and deaths that occurred as consequences of the conduct of their businesses. One response was to expand the liability of corporate directors, making them more accountable. California's convention supported expanded stockholder liability, as it had in 1849, placing this section in the constitution: "Each stockholder of a corporation ... shall be individually and personally liable for such proportion of all its debts and liabilities contracted or incurred, during the time he was a stockholder, as the amount of stock or shares owned by him bears to the whole of the subscribed capital stock or shares of the corporation."[112] Of the other western states, only Utah also expanded the liability of stockholders to twice the value of their stock.[113]

There were other assertions of state authority over corporations. Every western state constitution made clear that the power of eminent domain was a power to regulate corporations. California's declaration is typical:

> The exercise of the right of eminent domain shall never be so abridged or construed as to prevent the legislature from taking the property and franchises of incorporated companies and subjecting them to public use, and the exercise of the police power of the state shall never be so abridged or construed as to permit corporations to conduct their business as to infringe on the rights of individuals or the general well-being of the state.[114]

Wyoming's constitution went further, affirming the status of corporations as creatures of the state:

> All powers and franchises of corporations are derived from the people, and are granted by their agent, the government, for the public good and general welfare, and the right and duty of the State to control and regulate them for these purposes is hereby declared. The power, rights and privileges of any and all corporations may be forfeited by willful neglect or abuse.... The police power of the State is supreme over all corporations as well as individuals.[115]

Delegates failed nevertheless to deny corporations their customary privileges. Only California and Idaho outlawed free railroad passes; only Utah banned blacklists, and although labor representatives hoped payment in scrip would be outlawed, the conventions failed to do so. For all their bravado about the authority of states over corporations, worry and recognition of the importance of railroads to their territories kept delegates, and later state governments, from effectively regulating them.

Protection of Labor

Every Gilded Age constitution in the West provided protections for labor. Table 3.1 displays protections for labor provided in state constitutions, both in the western states and in states from other regions, written between 1870 and 1899. Protections for labor hardly appeared in constitutions in other regions; they were for the most part confined to constitutions of the western states. The presence of workers among the delegates was critical to the passage of these protections. Suggested provisions puzzled some delegates. The testimony of workers, from their own experiences, persuaded colleagues the proposed sections were necessary. Delegates were also moved by the appearance of violent labor-management conflict in mining between the admission of Colorado (1876) and the conventions of the other western states. The same years saw the organization of the Populists, who were strongly supported by workers in the mountain states. Although western state constitutions contained more protections for labor than did other state constitutions, labor did not get all it wanted. Only Utah outlawed the blacklist; not a single convention forbade scrip or company stores or abrogated the fellow servant doctrine; Montana and Washington failed to include the eight-hour day for any workers. Some of these omissions were repaired by legislation before 1900. Delegates created mine commissioners and bureaus of labor, immigration, and agriculture; declared eight hours the working day for government employees and in mines; set minimum ages for the employment of young people; made recovery of compensation for injuries suffered at work more generous and more available; outlawed private militias; and provided mechanics' liens. Emily Zackin's analysis of constitutional labor rights over a longer period (1870–1940), and including amendments to state constitutions, also shows the greater number of positive rights granted to labor in the western states.[116]

The deliberations surrounding the adoption of protections for labor were not the same as the considerations leading to different outcomes in the courts. There were several grounds on which judges might find protections illegitimate. The courts' continuing fealty to Jacksonian even-handedness inclined judges to view labor protections as illegitimate "class legislation." In addition, "class legislation, discriminating against some and favoring others [was] prohibited by the fourteenth amendment."[117] A government might act under its police powers to serve a public purpose but not to transfer resources from one group to another out of sympathy for the latter. A state might properly intervene between employer and employee to protect public health or safety. Hours laws for women were necessary because of their weaker and more vulnerable status, and also justified by women's role as "mothers of the race."[118] It was sometimes argued that hours legislation unconstitutionally interfered with the liberty of an individual worker to negotiate his own contract with his employer. Both arguments were made in Colorado in 1895, when the state supreme court offered an advisory opinion on a proposed eight-hour law. The court declared that the law would be "class legislation" and would violate "the right of parties to make their own contracts."[119]

Over time, however, the liberty of workers was more and more recognized as illusory, given "the vulnerable, dependent status of wage earners."[120] As constitutional conventions deliberated proposals for protections for workers, these arguments were sometimes invoked clearly, sometimes echoed, sometimes implicit, or sometime absent altogether. Moreover, since delegates were writing constitutions, creating constitutional law for their states, they were not bound by territorial court

Table 3.1 Constitutional Provisions for the Protection of Labor, 1870–1899

	West							Northeast and Midwest								South							
	CA	CO	ID	MT	UT	WA	WY	DE	IL	MO	NE	ND	NY	PA	SD	AK	FL	GA	KY	LA	MS	TN	TX
Bureaucracy	X	X	X	X			X									X	X						
Mine Regulations		X		X	X	Xa	X		X							X							
Eight-Hour Laws Government	X		X		X																		
Mines							X																
Restrictions Women-No Mines					X		X																
Children-Age			X									X	X						X				
Children-No Mines			X		X		X																
Employer Liability					X	X	X						X	X					X				
Ironclad Contracts				X			X						X										
Private Militias				X			X																
Blacklist					X		X					X											
Chinese	X																						
Prison Labor		X	X		X	X		X					X						X		X		
Mechanic's Lien	X	X	X													X	X						X
Fellow Servant																					X		
Statement of Principle				Xc			Xd					Xe				Xb					Xf		

Sources: For all constitutions before 1894: George A. Glynn, ed., *Convention Manual of the Sixth New York State Constitutional Convention, 1894*, 2 vols. (Albany, NY: Argus, 1894). For New York: Francis Newton Thorpe, ed., *The Federal and State Constitutions of the United States of America*, vol. 5 (Washington, DC: Government Printing Office, 1909). For Utah: *Official Proceedings and Debates of the Convention: Assembled at Salt Lake City on the Fourth of March 1895* (Salt Lake City: Star Printing, 1898).

a. Washington Constitution art. II, sec. 34: "a bureau of statistics, agriculture and immigration" (Glynn, *Convention Manual*, 2:610).

b. Arkansas Constitution art. XIX, sec. 18: "The General Assembly by suitable enactments shall require such appliances and means to be provided and used as may be necessary to secure as far as possible the lives, health, and safety of persons employed in mining and of persons traveling upon railroads, and by other public conveyances, and shall provide for enforcing such enactments by adequate pains and penalties" (Glynn, *Convention Manual*, 1:147).

c. Utah Constitution art. XVI, sec. 1, "The rights of labor shall have just protection through laws calculated to promote the industrial welfare of the State"; sec. 3, "The Legislature shall prohibit ... [part 4] The Political and commercial control of employes [sic]"; sec. 6 "... the Legislature shall pass laws to provide for the health and safety of employes in factories, smelters, and mines" (Utah, *Official Proceedings*, 1878).

d. Wyoming Constitution art. I, sec. 22: "The rights of labor shall have just protection through laws calculated to secure to the laborer proper rewards for his service and to promote the industrial welfare of the State" (Glynn, *Convention Manual*, 2:764).

e. North Dakota Constitution art. I, sec. 23: "Every citizen of this State shall be free to obtain employment wherever possible, and any person, corporation, or agent thereof, maliciously interfering or hindering in any way any citizen from obtaining or enjoying employment already obtained, from any other corporation or person shall be deemed guilty of a misdemeanor" (Glynn, *Convention Manual*, vol. 2, pt. 2: 94).

f. Mississippi Constitution art. VII, sec. 191: "The legislature shall provide for the protection of the employes [sic] of all corporations doing business in this State from interference with their social, civil, or political rights by said corporations, their agents, or employes" (Glynn, *Convention Manual*, 1:1085). Art. VII, sec. 193: "Every employe [sic] of any railroad corporation shall have the same right and remedies for any injury suffered by him from the act or omission of said corporation or its employes as are allowed by law to other persons not employes." This article limits the use of the fellow servant doctrine by the railroads (Glynn, *Convention Manual*, 1:1086).

precedents and did not need to consider them. Conversations were centered on fairness to workers. In considering ironclad contracts, for example, Palmer commented in Wyoming that it was "nothing more than right" to abrogate contracts in which workers pledged never to sue their employers. In discussions of child labor the focus was on the well-being of young workers, as evidenced, for example, in the remark in Arizona's convention that if they worked as children, they would not be able to work as adults. Finally, the focus in conversations about assumption of risk and fellow servant doctrines was on their function, in practice, of denying compensation to workers.

Among the delegates at the Wyoming, Colorado, Montana, Idaho, and Utah conventions were both mine workers and mine owners. In California the Workingmen's Party was the leading force calling for the convention and a major presence in convention deliberations. From Colorado's constitutional convention in 1876 through Utah's in 1895, issues of concern to labor were discussed at every constitutional convention in the West. Deliberations at the Colorado convention anticipated many of the issues raised in subsequent western conventions. Colorado's constitution outlawed so-called ironclad contracts, provided for a commissioner of mines, specified that the legislature pass laws creating safety standards for the underground construction of mines, and allowed for boards of arbitration. Later conventions in other territories debated employers' liability for worker injuries, hours of labor, protection of women and children at work, competition with prison and Chinese labor, scrip, blacklists, and workmen's liens. As delegates considered these provisions, there were as well laws passed by state legislatures and judicial rulings on their appropriateness and constitutionality.

Colorado was the first state in the Union to ban the ironclad contract, which required employees to renounce any effort to hold their employers liable for injuries suffered at work, even when injuries were the direct consequence of employer negligence. Article XV Corporations, section 15, of Colorado's constitution declared, "It shall be unlawful for any person, company, or corporation to require of its servants or employes [sic], as a condition of their employment . . . any contract or agreement whereby [the employer] shall be released . . . from liability or responsibility on account of personal injury."[121]

Introduction of the same language at the Wyoming convention met with immediate resistance. Anthony Campbell argued that this "bill ... introduces a new element in the relation of master and servant, and ... if it is passed no corporation or person can afford to engage in any business whatever.... The doctrine of master and servant is pretty well defined, the courts are getting away from the rule further every year and giving it a more liberal construction in favor of the servant."[122] Thomas Reed, defending the provision, argued that Campbell's reading was far too broad, and explained the correct interpretation:

> This is to reach what we originally call the old ironclad agreement. I can see the object of this because I have worked on all the railroads west of Chicago ... and they have all adopted a policy that this here touches upon. It was called the ironclad agreement, by which a man when he entered the employ of the company agree to release the company from all liability for any accident that might occur to him, no matter whether the fault was directly traceable to the company or not.... I believe it should pass. It is to protect the poor man.[123]

George Baxter concurred, pointing out that the "answer to the objection that it will keep out capital, I have only to say this is found in the constitution of Colorado, and I doubt if any state in the union has received more rapid development and growth than that state."[124] George Smith tried to make the provision more expansive, offering an amendment that read, "And the rule of common law as to the negligence of fellow servants shall not prevail in the courts of Wyoming."[125] The amendment failed, not to appear in the West until Arizona wrote its founding constitution in 1910.[126] For the moment, the authoritative statement on the Wyoming article was Palmer's: "I believe it is nothing more than right for us [to] say that a railroad corporation, or any other corporation, cannot say to a man, if we employ you, you must take all the chances yourself, and this company will not be responsible to you for any damage that may result by reason of the negligence of ourselves or of any of our employes [sic]."[127] The provision was a middle ground, not abrogating the fellow servant rule but effectively obviating the doctrine of "acceptance of risk." Banning ironclad contracts passed unanimously. Wyoming and Utah passed in addition provisions that there were to be no limits to damages, nor a deadline by which injured workers or their survivors must file, for compensation for injuries suffered at work. California, Montana, and Utah too outlawed ironclad contracts. In Idaho the provision did not pass. Opponents argued, incorrectly but successfully, that any contract requiring workers to renounce their rights would be found invalid in the courts. The section was deleted.[128]

Colorado's constitution provides for a commissioner of mines. Subsequently Idaho, Montana, Wyoming, Utah, and Washington created (or provided for) public officials whose obligations in one way or another involved labor. In Idaho discussion of the article on labor began a proposal for the creation of a commissioner, and bureau, of labor. The bureau would be important as Idaho was soon to be admitted as a state, and so would "very soon be confronted with problems of a very difficult nature relating to labor." The legislature and governor would need information to act wisely. More, the bureau would, in its annual reports, give labor a voice. Of course, labor might petition the government, but "the trouble with petitions is ... when they come up nobody knows whether they are the result of careful inquiry ... or not," while "if you have a commission whose special object is ... to keep run of all these matters ... we have a collection of statistics which may prima facie be considered as reliable."[129]

The same argument was made in Montana.[130] Over time the bureaus did indeed become active and "effective advocates" for labor.[131]

Delegates created agencies to regulate and oversee working conditions in the mines. In Colorado and Wyoming, commissioners of mining were to devise safety standards for underground mines, both ventilation requirements and requirements for shoring up ceilings. Like state bureaucrats who assembled credible information, mining commissioners became important advocates for working miners. In Wyoming there was also to be an inspector of mines "to go about and see that the laws governing mines are carried out." Moreover, the inspector of mines was required to be certified by a board of engineers as competent to make those judgments.[132]

California, Idaho, Utah, and Wyoming declared eight hours to be the length of the working day in public employment and, in Wyoming, also for underground workers in mines. Proposals to limit the workday in public employment raised questions in Idaho. Why should a man be paid for a day's work of eight hours in public employment if in the private sector he has to work ten hours? William Clagett did not think the section should stand: "If that is so I am in favor of striking it out, for the reason that I do not believe the state should have any pets of any kind.... I believe that when that man works for the state he should give the state just as good and honest a day's work as when he gives it to the individual."[133] Clagett's objection to "pets of any kind" echoed judicial reasoning opposing protections enacted only to protect specific groups of workers. On the other hand, to declare eight hours a day's work for government would be consistent with general practice: "For all classes of labor there is a fixed and general price. For instance, a bricklayer receives so many dollars a day in the community; so with the carpenter or any other mechanic. And if a municipality employs a man by the day at these wages, they are required to work only eight hours."[134] Moreover, were the state to adopt the eight-hour day for public sector workers, it would set a powerful example. Hampton offered his reading:

> I take it that one object of this section is or should be a sort of entering wedge, as it were, to enforce or bring about the custom of eight hours of labor among laboring people. I believe this is enough for any man to work hard, and if the state will adopt the idea that eight hours is sufficient for a day's labor, it will have the effect of introducing such a custom among other people, and for that reason I am in favor of it.[135]

That reading being acceptable to the delegates, the provision passed without further debate.

Proposals to protect women and boys by restricting their employment were passed in Wyoming. There, prohibition of employment of boys under the age of fourteen was supported by argument that there was good evidence that underground work was "ruinous to their health." It was argued that minimum age requirements not only protected boys but also protected other workers from boys' immature judgments. There was brief resistance to prohibiting women from working underground; one delegate argued, "This convention has delegated to women the right to vote, she ought to have the right to dig coal if she wants to."[136] When it was suggested that limitations on work for women and boys were properly matters for the legislature, it was countered that "it is proper to restrict the legislature, it is proper to say right here that no boy shall be permitted to go into a coal mine to work, and there is nothing wrong about our putting it into the constitution that I can see. Colorado and

Nevada and other states have this same restriction, and I see no reason why we should not put it into our constitution."[137] The proposal passed.

Labor also brought demands to suppress competitors, in particular, prisoners and the Chinese. Conversations about prisoners began with supporters of labor claiming that it was degrading to honest workmen to ask them to work alongside (as in road construction) or to compete with prisoners. It was countered that to keep prisoners idle was cruel and unusual punishment, and that states should make efforts for the rehabilitation of prisoners. The compromise arrived at was the same everywhere. Delegates agreed that leasing prisoners to employers outside of prison grounds was forbidden; work to maintain the prison itself was both appropriate for inmates, and not threatening to labor.[138]

Demands that Chinese be kept from labor and residence were powered by racism as well as fear of competition. Anti-Chinese sentiment was the motive force of California's Workingmen's Party; as Harry Scheiber reported, "no single issue mobilized [the public] so effectively."[139] The California article on the Chinese enjoined the legislature to "protect" the state "from the burdens and evils" that might arise from the presence of some aliens in the state; forbade employment of Chinese workers in the private sector or by government; and required the legislature to discourage the immigration of Chinese and to assist cities and towns at expelling Chinese residents, or confining them to "prescribed portions" of city limits.[140] The article passed easily.[141] Its provisions were later declared unconstitutional.

Hostility to the Chinese was not exclusive to California, nor were anti-Chinese constitutional provisions passed only in that state. Only in California, however, was there a large proportion of delegates, a third, elected by a party of which the slogan was "The Chinese Must Go." The greater intensity and success of anti-Chinese activism in California is likely attributable to the size of the Chinese population. There were many more Chinese residents in California than in any other state, both in absolute numbers and as a proportion of the population, about 70,000 residents of 865,000 in 1880. Opposition to the Chinese was in addition powered by the presence of talented and ambitious political entrepreneurs, who were also very effective rabble-rousers.

In Wyoming and Colorado, as in California in the months preceding the convention and in years to come, there were attacks on Chinese residents, they were expelled from towns and cities, and their communities were burned down.[142] Nevertheless, no other state passed provisions like California's restricting the Chinese. A similar article was introduced at the Montana convention and sent to the Committee on Labor. Without explanation, the committee reported proposed sections back with a recommendation that they not pass.[143] A few delegates voiced qualms about losing Chinese labor. In Idaho the question of employing Chinese workers was finessed. Section 5 of the article on labor provided that "no person not a citizen, or who has not declared his intention to become such, shall be employed" in state or municipal work.[144] One delegate worried that this might apply to Chinese, "because we work 400 Chinamen here" building the streets. In Wyoming the government could employ only citizens, although one delegate wondered "why a law of this kind should apply to a Chinaman and not to a Finlander. From my personal knowledge the Chinaman is the more intelligent of the two.... Perhaps ... the Chinaman can't vote and the Finlander can. But that does not make it just and right."[145] Since the Chinese were barred from citizenship, they could not declare their intent to become citizens.

Delegates also looked to a government role in the prevention of labor-management conflict. Boards or courts of arbitration might peacefully resolve their differences. A railroad worker in Wyoming testified to the effectiveness of arbitration. Although agreements proposed by the arbiters were not mandatory, and no powers of enforcement were granted to them, provisions for arbitration were placed in constitutions in Wyoming, Idaho, Colorado, and Utah. Delegates sought to prevent the worst instances of conflict—and these were very soon to be upon them—by prohibiting the import of private armed forces into the state, except at the request of the government. In the Montana convention, J. K. Toole proposed that "no armed person or persons shall be brought into this state from any other state to preserve the peace, except upon the application of the legislature, or of the Executive when the legislature cannot be convened."[146] The targets of this provision, and others like it in Wyoming and Idaho, were mercenary forces assembled by employers. In support of Toole's proposal, William Field argued: "In Pennsylvania and other Eastern states in the past ... armed bodies of men have been imported ... for the purpose of intimidating and coercing honest laboring men....

[Congress investigated this and discovered that] in one valley alone . . . there were 712 armed men under corporations . . . to preserve the peace, and . . . the workingmen of those districts . . . were in a state which I would term chattel slavery."[147] Peter Breen explained, "The resolution . . . is offered particularly against those vast armed bodies of men, known as the Pinkerton detectives." In Washington Territory the constitutional convention "had the same matter before it, only they had an illustration of it last winter when there were armed forces of Pinkerton detectives brought into their coal mines. . . . We see examples of it all over the country."[148] Despite the territory's experience, Washington did not adopt the section. In Wyoming it was local experience that supported the proposal. Alexander Sutherland explained that the target of the resolution was

> the Pinkerton men, who we all know came into the territory a few years ago to suppress a strike. They stood around day after day not trying to put down an insurrection, but trying to start one. . . . I heard one of them say "I just wish they would start up something, I would like to turn loose on them." Some of these men were convicts who had been pardoned not ten days from the Lincoln penitentiary . . . that was the kind of men that were sent here; we stood it . . . and I want to see a law passed to stop it. We called for it in the legislature, but the bill was pocketed and pigeon holed until it was almost smothered and murdered.[149]

Wyoming too outlawed hired militias. Despite the good intentions of the delegates, and the provisions they wrote, no agency of government prevented private armed forces from intervening in Coeur D'Alene, Butte, Cripple Creek, and Ludlow in the years to come.

There were as well declarations of principle. Wyoming's Bill of Rights included a promise that "the rights of labor shall have just protection through laws calculated to secure to the laborer proper rewards for his service and to promote the industrial welfare of the state."[150] Utah's constitution included the same promise.[151] In Idaho the commissioner of immigration, labor, and statistics was required to collect information not only about labor's compensation and hours of work, but also "upon . . . its relation to capital, . . . and the means of promoting their material, social, intellectual and moral prosperity."[152] The general statements of state government's obligations swept away arguments about "class legislation" and the proper scope of police powers. By their inclusion of "shall," statements of principle were declarations of a proactive role for the states in the protection of labor. In that way they became the basis for court rulings approving state laws limiting hours of labor and, later, setting minimum wages.[153] It was legislation passed under these provisions that made the "pragmatic jurisprudence" of the western states possible, because the state's role as "paternalistic guardian of industrial workers" was "assigned in its constitution."[154] Eventually, the same pragmatic jurisprudence persuaded the Supreme Court to abandon Jacksonian restrictions on laws for the protection of labor.

Aware of their territories' lack of financial and political resources, and desirous of population, prosperity, and social peace, delegates to western constitutional conventions wrote law and designed institutions to "secure property" while also protecting the public against "oppression from its use." In their deliberations, the reader can trace the importance of the changing national political and legal environment. The rulings in the Granger cases, the increased activism of farmers, and the organization of labor were present in debates and constitutions. The distinctive history of the West, its dependence on outsiders for resources, and its political and geographic distance from the resources the region needed informed writing constitutions with many provisions for attempting to manage the fragile economies of their states. Distinctive too were the rights newly written in the West, positive rights meant for government to intervene between the many and the few.

Provisions for the protection of labor, like other provisions reported here, were drafted in the service of managing the periphery. There were instances of legislation in the constitutions. For example, there were sections limiting the workday of public employees and miners, and others limiting the labor of women and children. Detailed provisions in constitutions, unlike ordinary legislation, were safe from state courts, safe from legislative corruption, and safe from changes in party control, this last more likely in the competitive party politics of the western states. Equally often, delegates recognized that the dilemmas of the Gilded Age could not be resolved by legislation but were ongoing and required more government. More often than legislation, then, delegates created agencies, or confirmed the authority of existing agencies and governments, to resolve conflicts among residents or between residents and outside interests. The conventions wrote laws for rights to water and, more important, rules or principles for resolving disputes about competing claims to water, and delegated implementation to courts, counties, and new bureaucracies. Striving to be damned neither by the presence nor by the absence of railroads, delegates trod gingerly toward regulation, finally asserting that all corporations existed by the grace of government and so were its creatures, and insisted on the authority of state governments to regulate railroads. Anticipating conflicts between labor and employers, delegates outlawed mercenary militias. Too, delegates created bureaus to monitor working conditions below ground and to keep track of wages and hours. When the delegates' work was completed, they had designed more government—agencies, bureaus, courts, and commissions—to manage the periphery.

In the political economy of the western states toward the end of the nineteenth century, we see the peripheral politics and economics of uneven development. If older states were marching in step with New Jersey to accommodate corporate capital,[155] the West was toward the back of the line, where every step brought resistance, dissent, and argument. Nevertheless, the narrative of the western states is not simply the same story told at a later date, nor is the narrative an entirely negative or defensive one. The creation of institutions for management of the periphery and the greater accommodation of labor in western constitutions were evidence of collaboration between some political leaders and labor, of a shared recognition of contemporary dilemmas. At the conventions, when eight-hour provisions were proposed, not one delegate argued that eight-hour laws would deprive workers of the liberty to negotiate their work contracts individually; the use of the states' police powers to protect labor was controversial as a matter of economic stakes, but not controversial in law.

In the last quarter of the nineteenth century, the constitutional conventions of the western states expanded the purview of state government, creating new law and institutions. As Wiley Tinnin explained to the California convention, "We are embarking on a new era. We stand upon the shores of an unknown and unexplored sea."[156] State governments were both constrained and empowered. To manage the periphery, delegates at western constitutional conventions not only forged anchors but also began to tailor sails — bureaus of labor, mine commissioners, water masters, land trustees, and principles of labor law — that their small ships of state might navigate the wide seas of the Gilded Age.

4. Progressive Settlements

Arizona and New Mexico were the last two states of the first forty-eight to join the Union. Each territory held a constitutional convention in the closing months of 1910, working as progressive debate gained prominence in national politics, and each was granted statehood in 1912, the year progressive politicians were overwhelmingly endorsed in national elections. Three progressive issues were at the center of convention deliberations: direct democracy, protections for labor, and the regulation of corporations. The two conventions and their constitutions differed markedly in their response to these issues, by accommodation of or hostility to democratizing reform, altering the law of master and servant or allowing it to stand, and attempting to regulate corporations. In national politics the same issues tracked divisions among Republicans, Progressive Republicans, and Democrats. The centrality of these issues in convention deliberations marks the constitutions they wrote as political settlements, their debates as political argument, and their resolutions as political compromises. The results could hardly have been more different. Arizona adopted the country's most radical constitution (save Oklahoma, 1907), well to the left of Theodore Roosevelt and Woodrow Wilson. New Mexico adopted a very conservative constitution, considerably to the right of President Howard Taft.

The deliberations and constitutions in Arizona and New Mexico were political in another way. From 1872 until the election of President Franklin Delano Roosevelt in 1932, the western states, unlike states in other regions, exhibited competitive party politics.[1] Arizona and New Mexico were exceptions. In Arizona the Democrats had considerably more support in the electorate, and in New Mexico Republicans were more likely to reap majorities. The core constituents of Arizona Democrats were workers, overwhelmingly miners.[2] Their counterparts among New Mexico Republicans were Mexican Americans, most often subsistence farmers.[3] Although each party enjoyed an advantage, neither was entirely secure. The first governor elected in the state of New Mexico, for example, was a Democrat. And even in the heyday of the Democrats' support in the state of Arizona, Republican candidates sometimes won gubernatorial elections. For both Republicans in New Mexico and Democrats in Arizona, one goal of constitutional deliberations was to more firmly bind their core constituents to their party. In Arizona this meant meeting key demands of organized labor. Some of labor's demands were at the center of progressive politics, for example, democratizing reform. Others were for the benefit of workers in particular, for example, limiting hours of work, protecting child workers, and changing the law of master and servant. That list meant pushing Democrats further along the path of support for labor. In New Mexico the goal of bolstering party support moved Republicans to reinforce the rights of Mexican Americans by abolishing literacy tests and English-language requirements for voting or holding office, forbidding segregation in public schools, and requiring teachers in public schools to be bilingual. That list, although strongly supported by old-line Republicans, required the New Mexico party to abandon positions it had long held. In these ways, as well as others, Progressive Era constitutions, like the Gilded Age constitutions, were documents marked by their territories and region, products of their time, and followed from long-standing and far-flung conversations about constitutional provisions that began with the federal and first thirteen state constitutions, and on questions of master and servant, far older conversations.

The first section in this chapter introduces the territories of Arizona and New Mexico. The next three sections describe, in turn, deliberations about democratizing reform, the law of master and servant, and regulating corporations. A discussion comparing the constitutions and public policies of Arizona, New Mexico, and other western states to early twentieth-century constitutions in other states suggests western states were especially committed to democratizing reform and remained in the lead on labor legislation.

Territories and Conventions

Every founding constitutional convention took place in a territory with its own demography, politics, and economy. The extreme constitutions of New Mexico and Arizona can be traced to their distinctive politics and societies. In Arizona, as in Montana, Colorado, Nevada, Idaho, and Utah, the largest industry was mining. These territories and states were home to well-disciplined and vocal labor organizations. From 1890 onward, working miners in Arizona were a strong presence in the electorate. As Populists appeared in the West, they sought and received labor support in the mining states and territories. Later labor favored Socialists and Democrats. Certainly in 1910 mine workers were articulate, had an agenda, were organized, and voted.[4] George Hunt, later president of the constitutional convention and seven-term governor of Arizona, served in the Arizona territorial legislature from 1893 to 1909. There Hunt introduced several populist measures and bills favoring labor that were defeated, although they appeared in the 1910 constitution (for example, initiative, referendum, prohibition of blacklisting, and the eight-hour day).[5]

As these outcomes suggest, in Arizona the constitutional convention provided an important opportunity for organized workers to secure their goals. Labor was alert to this. Once Congress passed an enabling act, workers were quick to form the Labor Party, and the Democrats were quick to woo them.[6] Democrats were successful both because they agreed to support Labor's program at the convention and because among territorial politicians there were Democrats who had long been advocates for labor. Their alliance helped Democrats win a lopsided majority of delegates to the constitutional convention: forty-one Democrats were elected, and eleven Republicans. At the convention, the most prominent speakers among the Democrats were Thomas Feeney, Andrew Parsons, Michael Cunniff, and E. E. Ellinwood. Feeney was a veteran of the Spanish-American War, worked as a machinist in the Copper Queen mine, and was active in the labor movement. In the convention he was a very effective speaker about issues important to labor, explaining the dynamics of workers' situations on the job and in negotiation with employers, and both an adept tactician and strategic in argument and debate (exemplified by his opposition to child labor, discussed later). Andrew Parsons was a lawyer and eventually a county assessor; Parsons added his biting two cents to debate at critical moments. Michael Cunniff was a graduate of Harvard who briefly taught there and at the University of Wisconsin; he was the editor of *World's Work* for six years. In Arizona Cunniff partnered with his brother investing in and managing mines. At the convention he served on the committee on style; he wrote and rewrote many provisions. Cunniff often spoke in support of workers' demands and progressive policies; colleagues seemed to defer to his judgment. Ellinwood, counsel to the Copper Queen mine and Phelps-Dodge interests more generally, was the only conservative Democrat in this group. On some occasions his conservative preferences determined his vote. For example, he did not sign the constitution because he objected to the provision for recall of judges. On the other hand, there were times when Ellinwood's support or his proposal for wording or rewording a provision was key to getting it to pass. For example, Ellinwood drafted the provision creating personal liability for stockholders and suggested wording that facilitated expanding the scope of the corporation commission beyond public service corporations (both instances described later). The most vocal Republicans were Edmund Wells, Samuel Kingan, and Wilfred Webb. Wells was a lawyer, cattleman, and banker. He served in a succession of public positions from county attorney to associate justice of the Arizona Supreme Court. Kingan received his LLB from the University of Michigan and practiced law in Tucson. A strong opponent of direct democracy, Kingan refused to sign the constitution. Webb, a prosperous rancher and a leader among conservatives at the convention, "voted a firm ideological line" and refused to sign the completed constitution. Later, Webb worked against the election of George Hunt to the governor's office.[7]

New Mexico was part of a conquered region, a populous Mexican settlement whose residents and their descendants endowed the territory with more than half its citizenry into the twentieth century. Their politics, culture, and religion endured well beyond de facto US government. For example, the alcalde remained an important local official for decades after New Mexico became a US territory. Late in the nineteenth century, to the extent there was a public school system in New Mexico, it was Roman Catholic,[8] and in 1910 the territory was 90 percent Catholic.[9] That said, despite promises in the treaty that ended the war, in New Mexico, as in California and Texas, many Mexican landowners lost their land to Anglos, who, with their lawyers, dominated the courts. In the same years New Mexico was governed by the strongest and oldest governing coalition in the western states, a bipartisan leadership alliance known as the

Santa Fe Ring. Relations between the Ring and New Mexican society were tense. For example, when advocates of statehood held a constitutional convention in 1889, the Ring "bulldozed" the proceedings and included a provision barring anyone who could not read or speak English from voting or serving on juries, despite the fact that party leaders estimated two-thirds of Republicans were Mexican American. The proposed constitution was defeated by a popular vote of 16,180 to 7,493.[10]

Twenty years later the Republican advantage in New Mexico rested on the loyalty of Mexican American voters. This was a rational arrangement for each side. Republicans needed a popular base; Mexican Americans needed protection from Anglos hostile to them and to their religion. Desirous of Mexican support, Republicans offered the franchise, representation, opposition to school segregation, and political protections to Mexican Americans in the provisions of the 1910 constitution. Early returns marked Republican success: seventy-one Republican delegates were elected to New Mexico's constitutional convention, joined by twenty-eight Democrats and a lone Socialist. As debates were reported in the press, the most important Republican delegates were Thomas Catron and Holm Olaf Bursum. Catron was likely the most powerful man in New Mexico. He owned more land than any other person in the United States, was the autocratic leader of New Mexico's Republican Party, and was the leader of the Santa Fe Ring as well. In 1912, Catron was elected to the US Senate. Bursum, an active Republican, was a "very prominent cattle and sheep rancher . . . owning many thousands of acres." He also had substantial investments in mining. The first office Bursum held was sheriff of Socorro County; toward the end of his career he served on the Republican National Committee from 1920 to 1924.[11] Among Democrats Harvey Fergusson and Harry Daugherty were the most prominent spokesmen at the convention. Fergusson was the recognized leader of New Mexico Democrats, served one term as the territory's nonvoting delegate in Congress (defeating Catron in the election), was "a devout follower" of William Jennings Bryan, and became an ardent progressive. In the convention his devotion to progressive causes was not matched by skill in winning allies; he won no victories in debate or policy. Daugherty argued for direct democracy in the convention, to no effect.[12]

In 1989, Paul Kleppner published "Politics without Parties: The Western States from 1890–1984."[13] Kleppner argued that "weak partisans and independents," indifferent or hostile to parties, and uncertain or fickle in their partisan choices, were responsible for the region's varying election returns. Subsequent authors have followed his lead. In an examination of Populism in Idaho, Montana, and Colorado, Jessica Trounstine and I critiqued Kleppner and showed that in those states voters were consistent partisans. Moreover, in mining states governors played critical roles in industrial disputes. Consistently, Democratic governors were more sympathetic to labor, while Republicans favored employers.[14] Similarly, partisanship was important to politicians and to voters in Arizona and New Mexico.

In these years the press too was partisan. For the *Arizona Republican*, partisanship was not simply instrumental; it was a matter of principle: "Parties are formed with set principles and ideas, and it is the duty of every good citizen to ally himself with one or the other."[15] The *Santa Fe New Mexican* and *Arizona Republican* expressed stand-pat (conservative) Republican orthodoxy. The *Albuquerque Morning Journal* was also a Republican newspaper, sometimes crediting progressive Republicans in New Mexico for influencing convention proceedings, at other times berating them. The *Arizona Gazette* was consistently Democratic. Newspaper responses to the election of delegates to the constitutional conventions display the rhetoric of the partisan press. New Mexico elected delegates first. The day of the election the *Albuquerque Morning Journal* warned voters, "A Vote for a Freak Constitution Is a Vote against Statehood," and afterward reported that the Republican majority "exceeds most optimistic predictions of party managers."[16] For the *Journal* election results foretold the future: first, the Republican majority would deliver a safe and sane constitution to New Mexicans; second, "The republican party will govern the new state." The *Santa Fe New Mexican* too announced the Republican triumph and its consequence: "Clean Sweep by Republicans, Final Returns Verify Magnificence of Victory Won on Tuesday, SAFE AND SANE CONSTITUTION."[17] On the day of the election, the *Albuquerque Morning Journal* explained partisan differences this way: "Voters must bear in mind today, on one side are the republican candidates pledged to support the principles of a republican form of government in the constitution, to stand for a people's government through representation.... On the other hand are candidates openly on record in favor of revolutionary experiments, in favor of reversion to an un-American form of government."[18] By contrast, the *Arizona Gazette* was not positive, reporting, "New Mexico May Be in the Hands of Merciless Interests." This was no accident, for railroads and corporations had worked vigorously for Republican victory.[19]

In Arizona the *Arizona Republican* reminded readers every day from September 1 until the election of delegates on September 12 that, given Taft's adamant opposition to direct democracy, adoption of initiative, referendum, and recall would imperil statehood. It will have surprised no one, then, that the election of a strong majority of Democrats to the convention was announced with this headline: "Arizona Accepts Risk of Losing Statehood." Early on it seemed the impending "calamitous event" was beyond "the worst fears of republicans and the highest expectations of the democrats," yet the calamity surely happened.[20] The *Republican*'s editors argued, "If the democrats carry out their campaign promises, Statehood will be surely lost."[21] Similarly, the *Santa Fe New Mexican* reported that the election's result ensured the adoption of direct democracy and its inevitable consequence, that "Arizona May Stay Out."[22] In Arizona it was the *Gazette* that rejoiced, "Direct Legislation Wins All over New State of Arizona.... City of Phoenix Throws Off Choking Clutch of Machine from Throat and Votes for Manhood."[23] The *Albuquerque Morning Journal* celebrated with them with the headline "O'whelming Democratic Victory in Arizona."[24]

In Arizona and New Mexico alike, "the overshadowing issue" in the election of delegates "was whether direct legislation in the form of initiative, referendum, and recall should be written into the constitution."[25] In the event, Arizona was staunch in its support of democratizing reform, while New Mexico opposed it. Like Oregon, Arizona adopted the initiative, referendum, and recall; New Mexico provided only for the referendum. A second democratizing issue was how easy or difficult it was to amend the constitution. In Arizona the process was straightforward, much like placing an initiative on the ballot, while New Mexico's constitution created high barriers to popular efforts at amendment. Additional democratizing reforms were the creation of more elected (rather than appointed) officials, primary elections, and a preference primary for the election of federal senators. The Arizona Constitution included all of these; the New Mexico Constitution added a few positions to statewide candidacy, and also the referendum, but otherwise did not accept democratizing reforms.

A second set of issues concerned the law of master and servant, the collective name for a group of legal doctrines about relations between employers and employees, particularly the question of who bore responsibility for injury at work. The fellow servant rule, acceptance of risk, and contributory negligence were key supports for employers. In the United States, the fellow servant doctrine was first clarified in 1842 by a Massachusetts judge, who held that the master bore no responsibility for an employee's injury if it occurred as a result of an error by a coworker, even in the presence of management neglect.[26] The doctrine of acceptance of risk was the claim that, as the worker accepted employment, he or she understood the dangers of the job and was accepting the risk of that employment. Contributory negligence was the argument that the worker was at fault, and so responsible for his or her injuries. These principles shielded most employers against liability for even their most egregious neglect. The ironclad contract did away with the need for argument, since the employee agreed at the outset not to seek compensation from the employer for any injury sustained on the job. These rules were bolstered by laws setting limits of time and/or amount of funds awarded to injured workers. The very low probability of receiving compensation for injury under these rules encouraged the passage of laws to hold stockholders or managers personally liable for claims awarded to employees, providing another route to compensation for injured employees and their lawyers.

The differences between the Gilded Age and the first decade of the twentieth century were important. When Colorado, California, Montana, Idaho, Wyoming, and Utah wrote their constitutions (1876–1894), delegates saw intense conflicts between capital and labor just beyond the horizon. By 1910 those conflicts loomed large in the shared history of the West. The response in Arizona was a series of provisions protective of workers, disabling the common law defenses of employers, and creating greater employer liability. New Mexico provided only minimal protections for workers, leaving the law of master and servant intact, although the constitution did provide for greater employer liability. The revision or abrogation of these rules was on labor's agenda in every state; change was mostly incremental.

A third divide was the regulation of corporations. As an economic periphery of the United States, the West remained as dependent on and fearful of large corporations as it had been in the Gilded Age. By 1900 nationwide hostility to trusts, the experience of many disappointed hopes, and the lessons of earlier naïveté suggested the necessity of corporate regulation. Federal commissions and laws established the legitimacy of government regulation of industry. The constitutions of Arizona and New Mexico both included provisions to protect their future state governments from the naive and costly support of corporations and expressed the hope that new states might modify corporate behavior. Delegates at the Arizona convention expressed considerably more hostility to limited liability corporations, although even in Arizona, proposals that were punitive of errant corporations were not successful.

In session at the conventions, neither majority was content to rest on delegate votes alone to secure its goals. Majorities in each convention enabled the convention president to name committees with fellow partisans in the chair and in the majority. In New Mexico Republicans were committed to secrecy for convention deliberations. The convention did not hire a stenographer, nor were arrangements made to publish a collective account newspapers might have provided, as happened in Colorado. Moreover, conservative Republican papers — the *Santa Fe New Mexican* and the *Arizona Republican* — reported the New Mexico convention in broad strokes rather than reporting much of convention debate. The progressive *Arizona Gazette* and the *Albuquerque Morning Journal* provided more coverage.

In both conventions the majority reached critical decisions meeting in partisan caucus. In New Mexico Republicans appointed the Committee on Committees, which was, Dorothy Cline explained, "in effect [a] Little Convention since it selected committee members, screened proposals, controlled policies, [and] ran the caucus ... binding the Republicans to the majority vote."[27] Committees wrote tentative provisions that were sent to the Republican caucus for approval, assuring majority votes when the proposals were presented to the convention. Republicans precluded roll call votes in the New Mexican convention by requiring thirty votes to call them, one vote more than the number of Democrats and the Socialist combined. Republicans also sponsored a resolution "barring the introduction of any proposal previously considered or rejected by the Committee of the Whole" and another closing the convention to new proposals after October 22.[28]

In both conventions the minority party objected to majority rule. The *Santa Fe New Mexican* reported that in Arizona "Democrats, by resorting to caucus methods, have declared against making the convention a deliberative body and propose to conduct the whole proceedings on narrow partisan lines, which leaves the Republican minority in the role of spectators in the convention."[29] That description was something of an exaggeration; on many issues neither Democrats nor Republicans in Arizona were unanimous. Similarly, in New Mexico there were progressives among the Republicans who worked against the most conservative resolutions put forward by their stand-pat colleagues. In Arizona the result was that many votes were required to create majorities on some issues — the percentage of voters required to successfully place an initiative on the ballot, the exact wording of prohibiting blacklists, and the determination of contributory negligence are three examples. And in New Mexico, disagreement meant deliberations in the Republican caucus were not an efficient result of stand-pat unity but instead the consequence of strenuous argument. Democrats in New Mexico protested the "gag rules" imposed on the convention, which severely limited debates. More important to making sense of the proceedings, the commitment of New Mexico Republicans to secrecy was sufficient to achieve it. The published proceedings of the convention report only issues brought to the floor, and nothing of conversation and debate. One result is that even attempts at comprehensive accounts of state constitutions either omit New Mexico or provide noticeably less coverage of its convention.[30] I was dismissive of those omissions until I tried to follow the New Mexico meeting. Although I did not forsake New Mexico's convention, and the narrative provided here traces convention deliberations more fully than other accounts, it is nevertheless without the back-and-forth debate or the content, tone, and flavor of deliberations presented in my discussion of Arizona's convention and in my accounts of nineteenth-century conventions.

Democratizing Reform

Direct democracy was first advocated in the United States by the People's Party and was a prominent issue in the states from its adoption by North Dakota in 1898 until the end of World War I. Between 1898 and 1918, nineteen states adopted the initiative, a few more adopted the referendum, and several fewer adopted the recall. Ten of the states adopting the recall were in the West, the "peculiar geography" of direct democracy long noted by historians and political scientists.[31] Of the eleven western states, only New Mexico failed to adopt the initiative. Even in New Mexico, however, direct democracy was the reigning issue in campaigns for delegates to the constitutional convention in 1910.

At the Arizona constitutional convention delegates were well aware of the strong sentiment in favor of direct democracy among their constituents. Broad popular support for democratizing reform was evident in the delegates' pledges: thirty-nine were committed to the initiative and referendum, thirty-three to the direct primary, and thirty to recall.[32] "The Initiative, Referendum, and the Right of Recall" was the very first plank in the platform of the Labor Party earlier in the year. The convention had only been meeting a week when it received a letter from "the labor unions of the Globe district" proposing five measures; there too the very first was "The Initiative and Referendum and the Recall, as embodied in the constitution of Oregon."[33]

Oregon was iconic for western supporters of direct democracy. In New Mexico, Locomotive Engineers endorsed direct democracy by demanding initiative, referendum, and recall "as applied in the state of Oregon."[34] For opponents of direct democracy as well, Oregon's experience was exemplary, in their case, of the havoc wreaked by initiative and recall. Taking three examples from the press, the *Santa Fe New Mexican* noted that "Oregon awakes to folly" as a result of the initiative, reported the "mischief" of the recall in Washington, and editorialized against the "graft" in the initiative and referendum in Colorado.[35] On December 5 the *Arizona Republic* reported "the failure of the people to get what they thought they were getting" by voting in support of an initiative in Oregon. Similarly, the editorial continued, "It appears that the people of South Dakota now complain that results at the polls did not express their real sentiments.... And were it not for the present unthinking hue and cry for direct democracy no one would expect anything else" to result from replacing representative government with popular legislation.[36]

On October 28 the committee on legislation at Arizona's convention introduced a proposition creating initiative and referendum. Supporters of direct democracy had several precedents on which to draw and explained that the article drafted by the committee was "largely a copy of the Colorado law" enacted in 1909, the authors of which "had the advantage of the Oregon law," as well as the laws of South Dakota, Oklahoma, Montana and proposals in Maine and Missouri, and so had "perfected the matter about as well as it can be perfected."[37] If accumulated wisdom were to be found anywhere, this was surely the instance. There were frequent objections to detailed provisions, derided as placing "legislation" in state constitutions, and these objections were raised about the initiative. Mulford Winsor was quick to respond. Defending the inclusion of detail in the proposed article, he argued, "If there is any place where we should go into detail in this constitution it is in the matter of the initiative and referendum.... The people have expressed their wish that a check be placed upon the abuses by the legislature ... and this is the very reason for the agitation for the initiative and referendum ... (Applause)."[38]

Samuel Kingan and later Edmund Wells presented arguments against initiative and referendum in great and learned detail. Whether from conviction or prudence, in debate even the most determined opponents of initiative and referendum in Arizona did not argue that the practices of direct democracy were wrongheaded. They argued instead that placing direct democracy in the constitution was a strategic error that might cost Arizona statehood. This was so for three reasons. First, direct democracy violated the injunction that states adopt a "republican form of government." Second, direct democracy provisions might provoke President Taft to reject the constitution. Kingan began his remarks with that very point: "I am opposed to this proposal, for the reason that it is of doubtful validity under the enabling act and the constitution of the United States, and will delay if not defeat, statehood."[39] The US Constitution created and the enabling act enjoined the territory to create a "republican form of government." "A republic is a government by representation," Kingan argued, while a "democracy is government by the people acting directly."[40]

Third, direct democracy was corrosive of existing institutions. The initiative and referendum called on the electorate to enact laws, thereby destroying the legislative branch. And because the proposed article denied the governor power to veto laws passed by initiative, it destroyed the executive branch as well. Another delegate supplemented Kingan's remarks by explaining that a case from Oregon, then on appeal to the US Supreme Court, posed the question directly: Were the initiative and referendum constitutional? The possibility that the Supreme Court might declare them unconstitutional cautioned delegates to leave the initiative and referendum out of Arizona's constitution, even though it had "been demonstrated that the people of this territory favor them to the extent of demanding their embodiment in the constitution."[41] For all of these reasons, including initiative and referendum in the Arizona Constitution might cost the territory statehood.

Delegates recognized that, with few exceptions, Democrats supported direct democracy and Republicans opposed it. Democratic delegates outnumbered Republican delegates four to one at Arizona's convention, so the outcome of their debates was never in doubt. Provisions were debated at great length nevertheless. Opponents of initiative and referendum were given little quarter. Parsons dismissed arguments in opposition to direct democracy. Although the minority insisted that representation was essential to republican government, the founders began the federal constitution with "We the people." Arguments of the minority were met with ridicule: "The construction contended for by the gentlemen of the minority is repugnant to reason in this: they admit that the supreme power is vested in the people, but insist that they can only assert this power through representatives or agents. Thus we are presented with the unique legal proposition, viz. that an agent has more power than a principal who has supreme power."[42] For their part, contemporary Republicans were hardly recognizable as members of that once great party. "For forty odd years," Lamar Cobb explained,

> the Republican party continued their lease of government control, largely though the use of that magic name, Lincoln. The great emancipator was quoted as the best, the highest, and the undisputed authority on all political subjects. That was before the Republican Party had constructed, to the present towering height, its Babel tower of trusts.... [Now] the doctrines which he

taught are ... socialistic. What was Lincoln's definition of a Republican form of government?—"a government of, for, and by the people."[43]

Cunniff, chair of the committee on legislation, declared it was too late to entertain the arguments of the opposition, as these had been discussed at length: "The only reply that we of the majority, in accordance with our instructions, have to make, lies [in the provisions] there on the secretary's table." The roll was called. There were thirty-six ayes and six nays for initiative and referendum.[44]

A proposal for including recall in the constitution in Arizona raised several of the issues well rehearsed in the discussion of initiative and referendum, as well as some new ones. Several delegates objected to the recall of judges. E. E. Ellinwood pointed out, correctly but without effect, that the Founders' intent was to shield the judiciary from the vagaries of public opinion. Others warned—also correctly—that including recall in the constitution would cause President Taft to reject it.[45] Parsons argued at great length that there was ample evidence that making judges subject to recall was the will of the people in Arizona, by inference part of the mandate with which delegates were elected. Wood insisted that making judges subject to the recall was "brought about by the overt acts of the Arizona judiciary" demonstrating their indifference to the will of the people.[46] Article VIII was approved by a vote of thirty-five to eleven.

The *Arizona Gazette* was exuberant, headlining its coverage "Recall in All Its Glory Becomes Part of Law. Constitutional Convention Votes to Extend Provision Even to Judicial Offices. Progressive State Assured.... Arizona People Assured of Control of Officials."[47] If the *Arizona Republic* despaired after the election of delegates, it was apoplectic after the passage of direct democracy provisions, especially the recall. The *Republic* editorialized, "If it is true, as currently believed, that 'the recall' in its most vicious form is to be made part of the constitution, it is not worth while to give any further serious thought to the question of statehood."[48] Late in November the convention adopted additional democratizing reforms; provisions for amendments to the constitution;[49] and primary elections "for the nomination of candidates for all elective State, county and city offices, including candidates for United States Senator, and for representatives in Congress."[50]

In New Mexico few concessions were made to the call for more democracy. Thomas Catron's assessment of the initiative, referendum, and recall represents conservative Republican sentiment well: "They are heresies of and constitute the first movement in the direction of anarchy in this government of ours."[51] Republicans at the Santa Fe convention opposed direct democracy, and in this as for many issues they took their role as the majority seriously. The *Albuquerque Morning Journal* reported, "The majority members of the convention are a unit in the conviction that as the republicans are to be held responsible for the constitution the representatives of that party should write the instrument. There is not, however, the slightest disposition in any quarter that anything of a party nature should be injected into the instrument."[52] As for several issues, "the fate of direct democracy was settled at a caucus of the Republican members"; before those reports were published, the decisions reported in them had been made.[53] The *New Mexican* confidently predicted on September 8, two days after the election of delegates, that New Mexico would have a safe and sane Constitution, without initiative or recall, although the constitution would provide for the referendum; the outcome was just as the newspaper reported it was going to be.[54] Two weeks later the *New Mexican* explained the referendum proposed by the committee on legislation required 25 percent of the qualified voters in every judicial district to suspend a law.[55] The final form of the referendum was not yet decided. Five days later the *Albuquerque Morning Journal* reported progress in caucus negotiations:

> The initiative will not appear in the constitution in any form, neither will it be submitted to the people as a separate provision. The initiative is dead.
> All of these things were settled at a caucus of the republican members which was in session all of this afternoon. The settlement came only after a prolonged struggle, during nearly all of which the old guard was on the defensive. It is the result of a compromise.... The progressives agree to abandon their fight for the initiative in consideration of having their own way in all other matters for which they are contending.[56]

The resulting provision was "materially different" from the initial proposal, deleting a requirement that 25 percent of qualified electors in each of the counties in the state sign a petition for the measure to be on the ballot, and in its place required three-quarters of the counties to be sufficient. And at the election, the requirement was that the referendum win the approval of a majority of the votes cast, if the number was at least 40 percent of the vote cast in the prior general election. Both changes were credited to the progressives in the caucus.[57]

Another agreement, symbolic (because the outcome was determined) but time-consuming, was that supporters of the minority report, which included initiative and referendum, were granted hours of floor debate to make their case for direct democracy. As the convention moved to the Committee of the Whole, the majority report was read. Albert Fall, later elected to the US Senate, spoke in favor of it. Several Democrats spoke, Fergusson at great length, and conservative Republicans did too. The *New Mexican* derided the performance of Democrats and reported (without content) the remarks of Holm Bursum and Albert Fall to have been "brilliant." The *New Mexican* declared, "Initiative Is Buried."[58] At the defeat of initiative and recall the *Gazette* reported, "New Mexico Turns It Down. Sister Territory Prefers Grip of Corporations to Rule of the People."[59] Delegates could legitimately claim some achievements for popular rule; both the corporation commission and judges, even of the supreme court, were to be elected rather than appointed.

Writing about the Arizona convention, Mark Leshy claimed, "Every time the question was raised, delegates opted for more democracy, not less."[60] His argument is supported by the passage of direct democracy, a preference primary for federal senators, and other democratizing reforms. But it is not entirely correct. Some at the convention supported an educational or literacy qualification for voting. On this issue the opposition was vehement, articulate, and principled. Delegates objected, "We have men here [in Santa Cruz County] that are fifty or sixty years old, that have paid taxes and helped keep our county together before the new generation came . . . it is a matter of justice and not of policy. They have a right to vote."[61] And threatened: "Our Spanish American vote is about one-third of the total vote of [Yuma] county, and I tell you, gentlemen of the convention if this educational qualification is put into the constitution at the insistence of the Democrats in this body, when we go before the people in the ratification election you may expect a solid Spanish American vote against the constitution."[62] Proposals for literacy or educational qualifications for voters were defeated. The press recognized this as a cynical, merely symbolic accommodation. The constitution was neither the first nor the last word on the issue. The territorial legislature had earlier passed a literacy requirement, which, not rescinded at the convention, remained on the books. Arizona was one of the very last states to give up the literacy test, repealing it in 1972, seven years after the federal Voting Rights Act passed.

New Mexico's settlement was quite different. Neither initiative, nor recall, nor primaries for general elections, nor preference primaries for US senator were adopted. There was a referendum, although the barriers were so high that no referenda were put on the ballot. The constitution might be amended, but these provisions too were very restrictive. Indeed, the provision for amendment was so restrictive that Taft himself insisted the barriers to amendment be eased; Congress passed the Smith-Flood legislation to accomplish this.[63] On the other hand, Section 3 of the article on the franchise promised, "The right of any citizen of the state to vote, hold office, or sit upon juries, shall never be restricted, abridged or impaired on account of religion, race, language or color, or inability to speak, read or write the English or Spanish languages ... and the provisions of this section ... shall never be amended."[64] These provisions were unique among state constitutions in the United States and, according to Dorothy Cline, "made a deep imprint on the politics of New Mexico far into the future." Although nowhere credited in the press (including the Democratic press), party leaders among the Democrats "agreed it was essential to guarantee the civil, religious, and political rights" of New Mexico's Spanish-surnamed population.[65] The *Santa Fe New Mexican*'s headline celebrated, "Use of English Not Qualification for Office; Suffrage and Jury Duty Open to Spanish Speaking Citizens."[66]

The Republican press in both territories made much of Democrats' failure to support, and efforts to interfere with, voting by Mexican Americans. It was front-page news in the *Santa Fe New Mexican* that Arizona's convention passed an educational qualification for voting (later defeated); the report ran under the headline "Democrats Disfranchise Spanish Americans."[67] In addition, although Arizona allowed segregation of public schools should a school district choose it,[68] the New Mexico Constitution insisted that "children of Spanish descent ... shall never be denied the right . . . of admission . . . in the public schools . . . and they shall never be classed in separate schools, but shall forever enjoy perfect equality with other children in all public schools," and that teachers be "proficient" in both English and Spanish.[69] At the New Mexico convention, Spanish-surnamed delegates testified, with great feeling, about the importance of these provisions. Nepulmuncio Segura reported that in San Miguel County, where Democrats were in power, Mexicans were "kept out of school or placed in separated schools; how they are ordered out of barber shops and the doors are closed to them at political meetings . . . [they] would disfranchise him with a law formulated by Texans and Oklahomans." J. J. Aragon, from Eddy County, testified to the same troubles in public schools.[70]

The guarantees in New Mexico's constitution bound Mexicans to New Mexico's Republican Party for many years to come.

Master and Servant

By the time Arizona and New Mexico were drafting their constitutions, workers in western states had been battling the law of master and servant for more than a generation. Changes in the law of master and servant were most important to workers and, as managers recognized their own stakes in labor law, met stiff resistance. Labor aimed to abrogate or weaken the doctrines of assumption of risk, fellow servant, and contributory negligence and to bar ironclad contracts. Even when debate was simply conversational, it was important that representatives of labor justify their agenda by educating fellow delegates about their workplaces, the practices of employers and courts, the practical obstacles to bargaining between employer and employee, and how in practice the law of master and servant denied employees compensation for injury even when the employer was manifestly at fault. Supporters of protective legislation also took care to inform delegates about the steps other states had already taken to remedy these problems, not only other western states but also states with much longer experience with the travails of industrial workers.

The ability of labor spokesmen to present their experiences to other delegates was critical to their success in convention deliberation. In

Arizona, Thomas Feeney acquitted himself well and had the support of several colleagues. Although labor was advantaged by the delegates elected to the convention, and majorities of delegates usually supported one item or another on labor's agenda, every item brought to the Committee of the Whole was met with resistance. Votes were sometimes very close, and the presence of articulate allies and supporters was key to the passage of protections for labor. At the New Mexico convention, there were neither representatives nor allies of labor comparable to those in Arizona.

In Arizona there was considerable resistance to the prohibition of child labor. It was proposed that children be kept out of the workforce, especially morally or physically dangerous jobs. Some supporters of the provision raised Oklahoma's constitutional language as ideal. Other supporters balked at the Oklahoma loophole—that children could work if their parents gave permission—arguing that it was the most frail of protections. Opponents judged the proposal too sweeping. Mit Simms asked, "Does it mean to say that a child after he leaves school in the spring cannot go to a factory and work? That a boy of 14 cannot go into the mills of Phoenix or any other place and work. . . . It seems to me a little unfair, and I think we ought to encourage the boy rather than discourage him."[71] B. B. Moeur worried about "the child [who] had to make its own living. . . . It seems to me if you pass this bill you prohibit his getting employment and make him an object of poverty."[72] "I do not want to make any of them paupers," protested Feeney, "and that is just why I want the child labor law. We are making too many paupers by lack of these laws."[73] A fourth delegate agreed that although "the meaning and intent of this measure is good, it will result in more harm than good as presented." What of boys who delivered newspapers after school? "This would deprive those boys of a chance of helping themselves."[74] Feeney was having none of it:

> It seems strange, you are all in favor of the child labor law, but someone's butter factory or printing establishment or something else wants to hire a child not 15 years old. I am willing to let my boy . . . go to the age of 15 without being employed. I want him to run loose out in the fields and have a good time. . . . I think we are all agreed that we want a child labor law, and let us go to it.[75]

Feeney brought the conversation back to the dangers at hand. "In every state throughout the east, and the entire nation, there is agitation against child labor, and as has been well said, there has been more destructive than constructive criticism in this convention, and while there are few large manufacturing plants in this territory now, they may increase and we of the labor party want this."[76]

Others made the local case for legislation protective of children. Bolan described his practical experience: "Take for instance, around the hoisting works in a mine, they employ children under the age of fifteen years, where it is dangerous. As children they do not know the danger and consequently cannot use the precautions that persons over 16 years of age would use. I have also seen them working underground.... There is nothing we could do that would be of more good to the children." Ingraham cautioned against the damage to children, just as would occur if a saddle were put on a valuable colt: "I say if we work children, you will never work them as grown men." Meanwhile, "The cotton mills of the south and New England work children at 10 and 15 years, and they are grinding the children into profit so they may become diamonds or automobiles for the factory owners."[77] Connelly summarized:

> What we want is to get a law passed that will protect all children up to 15 years of age. You can talk about factories and railroads, but you leave out other things. I have known girls under 15 years of age working in "hash houses," working 14 hours a day. These are the kids we want to take care of.... And I have seen young girls working in the smelter. We want to take care of these children whether in a factory, mine or anywhere.[78]

Winsor proposed striking the original proposition and in its place voting on the substitute: "It shall not be lawful in the State of Arizona to employ any child under the age of 15 years in any hazardous or unwholesome capacity, and the legislature shall enact suitable laws to enforce the provisions thereof."[79] This article passed by a vote of twenty-two to twenty.[80]

Common law doctrines of assumption of risk and contributory negligence were defended; the blacklist too had defenders. When employer liability was being discussed, there was protest that it was legislation and did not belong in the constitution. Feeney explained that trusting the legislature would not work: "For twenty-five years labor has been knocking at the doors of the legislature for an employers' liability act, and has not gotten it."[81] The constitution as passed provided protection of "the safety of employees.... The Legislature shall enact an Employer's Liability law, by the terms of which any employer ... shall be liable for the death or injury ... of any employee in [the employer's service] in all cases in which ... death or injury ... shall not have been caused by the negligence of the employee."[82] Questions of negligence or assumption of risk were to be matters of fact, to be determined by a jury. The legislature was also enjoined to enact a workmen's compensation law. In the event, legislators and administrators in Arizona worked through the 1920s to create a system of workmen's compensation and employer liability.[83]

Would-be defenders of the fellow servant doctrine seemed resigned to its abrogation. In deliberations about the law of master and servant, Michael Cunniff was the chief and very able spokesman in defense of disabling the powerful weapons of employers. Provisions about assumption of risk and contributory negligence were parts of the constitution outlining employer liability. When the section was brought to the floor, Ellinwood immediately objected, arguing that the text had been dramatically changed, and delegates had not had enough time to consider it. He was joined by A. C. Baker, who argued, "The whole proposition is contradictory and absurd.... It absolutely cuts out contributory negligence. There is no such thing if we passed this, and no such thing as assumption of risk." Cunniff was quick in defense, insisting that "this copy has been revised to no greater extent than numerous others that have been presented," and went on to state the real difference between himself and critics of the provisions. "I am not so frightened," he said, "as the gentlemen who have just spoken in regard to cutting out these common defenses that have existed for some little time. This does not necessarily mean that every time a man is injured the employer will be mulcted a large sum of money. It is merely to insure the using of every possible safety appliance ... and to make the employers hold life less cheaply."[84] Cunniff continued by reminding his colleagues that after the federal Common Carriers Liability Law was enacted, President Roosevelt argued that "intrastate commerce will be left to ... the several states.... Almost all civilized nations have enacted legislation embodying principles of this kind, and removing from the employee all the burden of the assumption of risk." In sum, Cunniff claimed, "there is nothing novel in this proposition," and "this is more important for the protection of industrial workers than anything else that will appear in this constitution."[85] After further discussion the convention agreed the section should follow Oklahoma's constitution, providing that assumption of risk and contributory negligence should be questions of fact, to be decided by a jury.[86] Cunniff proposed another section, providing that actions to recover damages would never be abrogated, nor would limits ever be imposed on the amount recovered. This too passed.[87] Labor was denied rights to strike, boycott, or organize unions. Despite these disagreements, provisions for the protection of labor, and revisions of the common law doctrines of master and servant, cemented labor's allegiance to the Democrats.

New Mexico's constitution did not have an article on labor. There were, however, provisions for the protection of labor scattered across the constitution. Imprisonment for debt was abolished in the Bill of Rights.[88] The article on mines and mining required the legislature to appoint an inspector of mines and to legislate standards ensuring the safety of mine workers. In addition, the article prohibited children younger than sixteen from being employed in underground work. The constitution also prohibited ironclad contracts and provided for employer liability. The discussion of the corporation commission also occasioned a discussion of the law of master and servant. The minority report included a proposal that the law of master and servant "be abrogated as to every employee of every transportation company or common carrier" in New Mexico. Holm Bursum, like many an elected politician, claimed that his preferences had been endorsed by his success at the polls. Bursum dismissed the proposal, claiming that "the people of New Mexico did not care to assume the burden of managing the affairs of the railroads, of interfering with their internal affairs in matters pending between the railroads and their employees. The people are not anxious to invest this commission with the powers of an arbitration board." The proposal failed.[89]

Corporations

The promise and disappointments of railroads illustrate well the dilemmas corporations posed for western communities. Before the Civil War, territories, states, and communities were anxious to provide assistance to prospective railroad builders, imagining that they and the railroads would share a prosperous or disappointing future; subsequent experience demonstrated beyond debate that railroads might thrive while their hosts faltered. Nevertheless, because the territories were distant from markets and suppliers, western communities were dependent on railroads for prosperity and growth. By 1910 the problems railroads brought to their communities were well known. Farmers had their own grievances against railroads, voiced loudly by the People's Party. Railroads posed public dangers in the construction of grade crossings. Railroads were the common enemy in Wyoming, Virginia, and Mississippi, where they were the target of restrictions strongly supported by both labor and more affluent citizens. Railroads corrupted legislatures, not least by issuing legislators free passes; politicians aligned themselves with popular resentment by declining the railroad passes they were offered. When George Hunt was elected governor of Arizona, he refused the passes offered to him. In New Mexico too there was strong opposition to free railroad passes, and the convention resolved that there should be prison sentences for legislators who accepted them.[90] These disappointments resulted in efforts to regulate corporate behavior and to hold corporate managers, stockholders, and trustees liable for injuries to workers and communities as well as for corporate debt. Federal regulation of railroads set a precedent for the states. Both constitutions reviewed here ban all kinds of material assistance to corporations by any level of government. In Virginia, South Carolina, and earlier Mississippi, it was railroads that were the target for constitutional restraint on use of the fellow servant doctrine; in Wyoming it was railroads that were the target of modifying common law defenses for employers and for provisions forbidding limits on the amount that might be awarded to workers or their survivors for injuries.[91]

Arizona and New Mexico created corporation commissions.[92] In New Mexico the *Albuquerque Morning Journal* reported that the committee charged with writing the article did so "with painstaking care" over the course of six weeks, a devotion that "had its reward" when the convention adopted its majority report without amendment. The commission was to have three elected members and responsibility for chartering and registering corporations as previously performed by territorial secretary. The commission had broad powers over public service corporations and common carriers. It was to set the rates and charges of all railroad, express, telephone, and other transmission companies, and to ensure that railways supplied the state with sufficient cars, rails, crossings, and depots; the commission could also hold hearings, inspect corporate records and books, and subpoena evidence and individuals. Appeals of commission decisions, and enforcement of them, were delegated to the state supreme court. A minority report, signed by three of the four Democratic members of the committee, proposed instead that appeals be brought to the state legislature. Insisting that the supreme court was a better venue, Albert Fall countered that "the demand of the public had been to do away with the crying evil of corporate influence in the legislature, and this the committee had done"; rather than petitioning and lobbying the legislature, corporations "would be forced to go to the commission, and from the commission to the highest court in the state."[93]

Two weeks later, Arizona delegates began to create a corporation commission. Among the first issues debated was the liability of stockholders. It was limited liability that made corporations attractive to investors and immoral in the eyes of their opponents. It was proposed that shareholders be liable for the par value of their stock, including amounts not yet paid to purchase it. The immediate objection was that the provision would especially hurt small corporations. E. E. Ellinwood defended the provision, pointing out that he was hardly an innovator but instead had taken it from the constitution of Oregon, and that it had not driven out small corporations from that state, or from Michigan, where there was a similar provision. James E. Crutchfield further defended the provision, arguing that

> the ease with which professional gamblers induce the people to take stock in a proposition where they stand a chance of making ten to one, and are not subject to any claim, is the string by which most promoters get hold of people; and if you make the stockholders personally liable for their part in the expense, all kinds of joint-stock companies will become an investment rather than merely gambling concerns, and the more solid development of this country will result.[94]

The proposal failed by a vote of thirty-three to ten.

Delegates proceeded to consider more general proposals for the commission. A central difference of opinion was immediately apparent; some delegates thought government had little if any business regulating corporations, and tried to restrict the province of the commission. Others thought corporate regulation absolutely necessary for healthy economic growth in Arizona, and tried to broaden the commission's scope and powers. Over the course of three discussions and many close votes, it became clear that although there was likely a majority in favor of regulation, exactly what to do and how to do it were difficult puzzles, and a solution favored by a majority was going to require more specific debate and careful design. E. E. Ellinwood quickly proposed that the purview of the corporation commission be limited to "public service" corporations, which would have removed most corporations from its supervision. Another delegate countered that "it should be the sense of all [members of this convention] that there should be some supervision of all corporations in general. . . . The purpose of this is to place reasonable restrictions upon all corporations in the state."[95] Cunniff too spoke in favor of a more expansive provision; he praised the state of Texas, "the only one that controls corporations, and in almost every other state I know the corporations control the state. . . . We need to have supervision over banks, and supervision over insurance companies. . . . There is nothing more valuable than the establishment of machinery to do these things."[96]

A. R. Lynch was immovable in opposition, insisting that "the business of a private corporation is not a matter of public concern. . . . There is not a member on this floor but has some little private business concern in which he is interested and which he is working on for his own advancement. As the public, you have nothing to do with those things; it is none of your business."[97] Jacob Weinberger foresaw a grim outcome. "If you give this power," he argued, "you are giving dangerous power to any set of people or officers."[98] C. M. Roberts thought opponents of regulating corporations were just plain wrong. "It seems to me," he said, "that God Almighty did not create any corporations, and they have no power the state did not grant them . . . [hence] the state has the right to exercise jurisdiction over the powers it has given [them]."[99] His colleagues were not persuaded, and the restriction of the corporation commission's jurisdiction to public service corporations remained. The *Arizona Gazette* applauded the work of the convention, headlining its report "People Relieved from Extortion of Railroads" and "Splendid Bit of Work."[100]

Debate about the corporation commission was not finished. A week later the commission was again the subject of consideration by the Committee of the Whole. Several delegates wanted to increase the scope of the commission beyond public service corporations; various proposals to accomplish that were defeated. Eventually a change was adopted that broadened the commission's scope. The new phrasing was "Any corporation whose stock shall be offered for sale to the public." This wording, proposed by E. E. Ellinwood, expanded the scope of the commission and did away with any threat to closed corporations, a worry that underlay opposition in earlier debate (recall Lynch, claiming "not a member on this floor but has a little private concern . . ."). Inclusion of the rewritten provision passed by a vote of twenty-five to twenty-two.[101]

The two corporation commissions had similar powers—to regulate and set rates of public service corporations, to require annual reports from them, and to examine their books. The purview of the New Mexico commission was restricted to public service corporations, while the Arizona commission might inquire into the activities of any corporation that sold stock to the public. In both states railroads were the particular target and were prohibited from discrimination of many sorts, including discrimination in setting charges for long and short hauls. Arizona did create greater liability for corporate stockholders in banks and insurance companies, requiring that stockholders "be held individually responsible, equally and ratably, and not one for another, for all contracts, debts, and engagements of such corporation of association, to the extent of the amount of the stock therein, at the par value thereof, in addition to the amount invested in such share or stock."[102]

There is no published comparative research on the powers or effectiveness of state corporation commissions, nor even a list of which states had such agencies or gave those powers to their state legislatures.[103] Similarly, some states created commissions for industrial relations in an effort to manage disagreements between employers and employees. Provisions for state corporation commissions are good indicators of the balance of popular sentiment about corporate organizations, and industrial commissions a measure of public concern about relations between labor and capital, but I suspect that for corporation commissions—as for protections for labor—state governments were simply not powerful enough, or possibly not courageous enough, to be effective. Along these lines, western states, like other states, were experimenting to discover what was and was not possible. Testifying before President Wilson's Industrial Commission in 1914, Senator Edward Costigan of Colorado lamented at length that state's failure to implement or enforce regulations for corporate behavior or the settlement of industrial disputes. Costigan's concluding remarks show that he judged these efforts were beyond the capacity of state governments, and his colleagues seem to have agreed with him. Rather than cast their hopes with state governments, the commission's twelve recommendations proposed new obligations for the federal government.[104]

I began this chapter with the observation that state constitutional debates in the decades following 1900 centered on political issues, and that as a result, the constitutions represented political settlements—compromises, or one-sided victories, or even consensus—among the delegates. The constitutions included agreements about direct democracy, protections for labor, modifications of the law of master and servant, and corporate regulation by state government. Passing provisions required majority support from delegates. More broadly, because the decisions of constitutional conventions involved enormous stakes, and because the public both was very attentive to convention deliberations and was going to vote on the constitutions, settlements included, at least implicitly, some agreement between politicians and their prospective constituents. Agreements sometimes were and sometimes were not shared by leaders of the two parties. Politicians' commitments were meant to ensure voter loyalty, in hopes of consistently winning, for their own party, more than half of the votes cast. In some states political settlements were sturdy and provided guides to the decade or more ahead; this was true for Arizona and New Mexico.[105] Elsewhere agreement was fleeting; Oklahoma provides the example.

Arizona's political settlement as expressed in the constitution was, after Oklahoma's, the most radical in the country. For "more democracy" the settlement included initiative, referendum, recall including judges, primary elections, and a preference primary for federal senators. Not entirely enamored of more democracy, Arizona maintained a literacy test. The constitution granted labor demands to abrogate the fellow servant doctrine for every employee, rethink assumption of risk and contributory negligence, allow compensation for injury without limits of value or time, and create workmen's compensation. Workers did not receive relief from injunctions, the right to organize unions, or the right to strike. The constitution also created a corporation commission with authority over a broad range of organizations. These arrangements supported a continuing Democratic advantage in Arizona politics. George W. P. Hunt, president of the convention, was elected the first governor of the new state and served six additional two-year terms as governor; his final victory was in 1930. It did turn out to be the case, as critics warned, that inclusion of recall in the constitution caused President Taft to refuse to sign it, and recall was deleted. The first legislature of the state of Arizona enacted the recall, including judges, on March 21, 1912, and went on to pass many other progressive laws.[106]

The political settlement in New Mexico was conservative. In one arena the constitution was liberal and egalitarian, providing key protections to Spanish-speaking voters and prospective officials, as well as to their children. These protections followed from the continuing presence of old-line Republicans who, consistent with the party's stance dating from the Civil War, fought school segregation and insisted on constitutional protection for Mexican voters. Taken together, these provisions secured the Mexican vote for the Republicans. The alliance recommended itself to both parties—Republicans in need of votes and Mexican Americans in need of political protection and support. Beyond protections for Spanish-speaking voters, "more democracy" in New Mexico was confined to increasing the number of elected officials and a provision for referenda. Several important measures for the protection of labor were scattered across the constitution. These arrangements assured a continuing Republican advantage in state politics until the election of FDR. Taft opposed the New Mexico Constitution, finding that provisions for amendment posed too high a barrier. At his insistence, the process for amending the constitution was eased to facilitate constitutional change.

In addition to Arizona and New Mexico, twelve states held constitutional conventions between 1900 and 1920, and six of them resulted in the adoption of new constitutions or amendments to existing constitutions.[107] For the most part, choices made by convention delegates elsewhere lay in the policy space between the constitutions of Arizona and New Mexico. Some made progress toward more democracy. Enacting direct democracy was impossible in the very malapportioned legislatures of Ohio and Massachusetts; supporters of more democracy campaigned for constitutional conventions, where direct democracy passed. Michigan adopted initiative and referendum. In Ohio and Nebraska, constitutional conventions placed proposed amendments on the ballot, forty propositions in Ohio and forty-one in Nebraska. Toward more democracy, Nebraska voters approved fully enfranchising women, allowing soldiers stationed in the state to vote, and providing for greater ease of amending the constitution (Nebraska adopted initiative and referendum earlier). For economic management, voters approved empowering the legislature to set minimum wages and conditions for the employment of women and children, restrictions on public utilities, and the creation of an industrial commission to administer laws about labor disputes and profiteering.[108] In Ohio voters passed some democratizing reforms, direct primaries, initiative, and referendum but declined to grant women the vote or to delete the word "white" from qualifications for voting. For the protection of workers, voters approved prohibiting limits on wrongful death awards, abolishing prison contract labor, and instituting workmen's compensation, an eight-hour day for public sector workers, and mechanics liens, but they declined to limit contempt proceedings and injunctions in labor disputes.[109] Connecticut added protections for women and child workers.

To Arizona's left, Oklahoma's founding constitutional convention (1906–1907) produced a most provocative constitution. In Oklahoma as in Arizona, the Democrats enjoyed an ample majority at the constitutional convention. Oklahoma's constitution included more provisions to protect labor and farmers and required more of corporations than constitutions elsewhere. These provisions were owed both to very articulate spokesmen for labor and farmers at the convention, and to the appearance of a disciplined Farmers Union (successor to the Farmers' Alliance) and well-organized workers in the territory.[110] Oklahoma delegates wrote provisions for direct democracy in cities as well as the state. There was also a literacy test for voters. For labor the constitution abrogated the fellow servant doctrine for employees of railroads, abrogated ironclad contracts, required that contributory negligence and assumption of risk be matters of fact to be decided by a jury, created an eight-hour day for public sector workers, forbade the employment of children under fifteen in hazardous occupations, and forbade as well the employment of boys younger than sixteen or females of any age underground in mines. The constitution created both an elected commissioner of labor and a commissioner of mines, oil, and gas. The constitution specified in addition that the state be divided into mining districts, each of which would have its own mine inspector. For farmers the constitution provided for a generous homestead exemption and a board of agriculture, of which all five members were required to be working farmers.

Charles Beard saw in Oklahoma "the spirit of fierce opposition to monopolies and that jealousy of large business enterprises which have filled the statute books of western states with drastic measures, [and] appear in almost every article of the Oklahoma Constitution." In addition to creating a corporation commission, "the powers of which leave nothing to be added,"[111] the Oklahoma Constitution required every corporation to submit any differences it had with its employees to a board of arbitration. For all the Sturm und Drang following the adoption of the Oklahoma constitution, and there was plenty of it, the political settlement it represented had little staying power. The dominant coalition at the convention was largely opportunistic, an ad hoc aggregation without a sufficiently strong foundation either among politicians or in the populace to survive. Worse, economic decline destroyed the Farmers' Union, and more successful agricultural interests stymied labor's agenda in the state legislature. The result was that after a resounding victory in 1907, in 1908 Democrats could barely deliver the state to Bryan.[112]

Since not all responses to the issues of the Progressive Era were placed in constitutions, a better comparative account can be found by asking more broadly, in the first two decades of the twentieth century, what decisions did states make about direct democracy, the law of master and servant and protections for labor, and the regulation of corporations? Were there differences among the regions? Chapter 3 showed that the western state constitutions of the Gilded Age were distinctive both for their provisions for the protection of labor and for their embrace of broad positive injunctions to the state governments they created. Were the western states equally distinctive in the Progressive Era?

There is no question that the western states were more likely to embrace direct democracy and other democratizing reforms than states in other regions. There is considerable research on the "peculiar geography" of direct democracy, so named by Nathan Persily. Of nineteen states that adopted the initiative between 1898 and 1918, ten were in the West. Persily connected the adoption of direct democracy in the West to the proximity of their founding conventions, on the one hand, and to the corruption of their state legislatures and diffusion from neighbors, on the other.[113] Persily did not say, although he might have, that a key element of the founding conventions is that they were more representative, more attentive to the public, and of better character than the territorial legislatures that preceded them. Of the nineteen states that adopted the initiative, four did so at constitutional conventions, adding Ohio and Massachusetts to Arizona and Oklahoma. For Ohio and Massachusetts, malapportionment made enacting direct democracy in the legislature impossible; only constitutional conventions provided an arena in which proponents of direct democracy might succeed.[114]

Thad Kousser and I investigated adoption of the initiative. We began with the question, why would politicians delegate the power to write legislation to voters? On the basis of historically grounded intuitions, we developed a model that accurately predicted the adoption of the initiative or its absence in forty-three of the forty-eight states. We argued that when politicians were confident that they and a majority of voters were of the same mind, and politicians were frustrated in their efforts to deliver policies to constituents who shared their views, politicians would strongly support adoption of the initiative. Politicians' frustration often followed from malapportionment, which disabled their efforts in state legislatures. Politicians might lack confidence where electorates were diverse or where states were very closely divided between the political parties; these doubts dissuaded them from supporting the initiative. We observed diffusion among the western states.[115]

In western discussions about the initiative, Oregon's adoption of direct democracy was iconic because, supporters explained, it was another western state. The research I conducted with Kousser showed that Oregon exemplified the main causes of the adoption of the initiative across the states. Oregon's legislature was corrupt and unresponsive, its distance from the public increased by malapportionment. Agitation for direct democracy began as early as 1891, on the part of the Knights of Labor, Portland Federated Trades, the Grange, and the Farmers' Alliance. This coalition was short of a majority; progress required expanding it to include prominent lawyers, businessmen, and bankers, as well as women's clubs and newspaper editors. The enlarged coalition succeeded in electing representatives to the state legislature, which offered the public constitutional amendments to create direct democracy in 1902. Voters endorsed the amendments by wide majorities. Oliver West was elected governor in 1911, and his experience justified progressives' faith that they and the public were of one mind. West did not agree much with the legislature; he vetoed sixty-three bills it passed. Moreover, the legislature did not pass bills he proposed. Using the initiative and the referendum, Oregon voters passed women's suffrage, Prohibition, workmen's compensation, an eight-hour workday for public sector workers, and strict employer liability, justifying West's confidence that he and a majority of Oregon voters were in agreement on these issues.[116]

Initiative, referendum, and recall were what Theodore Roosevelt had in mind when he insisted that the solution to problems of democracy was more democracy; more democracy was also found in other innovations. More democracy was provided by the enfranchisement of women, primary elections, and popular election (or preference primaries) for federal senators. The western territories and states enfranchised women early; Wyoming Territory was the very first, in 1869. Ten of the eleven western states enfranchised women before the passage of the Nineteenth Amendment; New Mexico alone failed to do so. Outside of the West, only New York, Michigan, South Dakota, Oklahoma, and Kansas fully enfranchised women before the Nineteenth Amendment was signed.[117] The West was also at the forefront of the direct election of senators. Oregon pioneered by creating a preference primary and then by requiring candidates for the state legislature to pledge to support the candidate with the most votes in the preference primary.[118]

In the same years there were also strong advocates of less democracy, supporting voter registration, the poll tax, and literacy tests. Proponents of less democracy were most successful in the states of the Confederacy but were certainly not confined to the South. In the first two decades of the twentieth century, literacy tests were in place in nine southern states, four New England states, and four states in the West; the standout region was the Midwest, where not one state had a literacy test.[119] Similarly, eleven states imposed poll taxes, nine in the South, Nevada, and New Hampshire, and none in the Midwest.[120]

For the protection of workers, as for direct democracy, constitutions were not the only venue for writing law; states passed legislation modifying the doctrines of master-servant relations. To compare the progress of US regions in protecting labor would require a tally of laws passed in each state in those twenty years, a project well beyond what can be presented here. I can, however, offer a few observations. Protecting labor and employer liability were naturally related. An example is the right of action against employers for injury causing death. Fatal injuries were not covered in the common law, as it was long contended that there was "no mode of estimating compensation for the death of a man."[121] By 1914 nearly every state had passed legislation mandating employers' obligations to survivors of workers who suffered fatal injuries on the job. Some states created industrial commissions to arbitrate or advise when there were conflicts between workers and employers. Efforts to protect labor sometimes also revealed continued resistance to the idea of limited liability for investors. For example, stockholders of all corporations were held liable for wages to employees in five states.[122] We do know that all was not resolved in the first twentieth-century generation; each element in the law of master and servant remained an area of struggle for years to come. In the first twentieth-century generation, the western states passed more laws for the protection of labor and, as they had in the Gilded Age, offered more provisions to protect workers, in their state constitutions.

5. Creating the Western States

From the meetings of small, alternately timorous and defiant communities on the far frontier, through the long meetings and longer agendas of the Gilded Age, to the political debates and decided opinions at the midpoint of the Progressive Era, the constitutional conventions reported here trace the development of the western territories. Delegates had many achievements to their credit. They wrote documents that satisfied a majority of the voting public, as well as the demands and restrictions in federal enabling acts. Their creations were long-lived: nine of the eleven founding constitutions reviewed here remain in place, if much amended.[1] Delegates created state identities from territorial ones. They designed the institutions of government and devised new governing institutions. They added to the collective repertoire of constitutional rights. They wrote law where little existed for rights to water and priorities in its distribution, and for the protection of labor. They chipped away at the law of master and servant.

The proceedings of the conventions and the constitutions demonstrate the seriousness of purpose of the delegates, their attention to public sentiment, the importance of occupational representation, the reflection of territorial party balance, and the uninterrupted presence of national concerns. Especially in the Gilded Age, debates and constitutions provided for the empowerment of state government, the elaboration of state institutions, and the expansion of rights of individuals and government's obligations to them. The two twentieth-century conventions in Arizona and New Mexico show the conventions as sites of partisan agendas and political settlements. Delegates to the Arizona and New Mexico conventions also debated progressive issues of more democracy, protections for labor, and the regulation of corporations. In every convention a few delegates—respected for their accomplishments, gifted with a greater ability to persuade, or otherwise powerful—exercised extraordinary influence over deliberations. In this chapter I review the claims and arguments of *Democratic Beginnings*, what the proceedings reveal about the conventions as deliberative bodies, show how convention debates trace the development of the West, and briefly look ahead at western states on the eve of World War I.

Conventions

Delegates to the founding conventions of the western states had an understanding of their purpose and task quite different from the nation's founders. The nation's founders began from presuppositions about men in general (that they were not angels) and rulers in particular (that they ever sought to expand their power), and designed "a machine that would go of itself" to operate unchanged far into the future.[2] Delegates to the western state conventions did not aspire to create constitutions that would never change. Rather, they felt duty-bound to adopt innovations of proven utility and contemporary views of fairness, and they expected their successors to do the same. As a "select committee of the people" offering a document for the approval of their fellow citizens, their work was a practice of democratic republicanism.

Delegates were industrious and pragmatic, and their conversations were usually civil.[3] In these lengthy and relatively small meetings, it was important to delegates to have the respect and understanding of their colleagues. Although not reported by me here, delegates frequently interrupted conversations or roll call polls to explain the reasons for their votes. Some claimed they had become persuaded of the virtue of policies hitherto dismissed, or maintained their views and elaborated on the principles at stake, or distanced themselves from acting from self-interest or subservience to some large interest (a railroad or water company, for example). Delegates were elected, and they most often included representation of a territory's occupations and its partisan balance. This meant that, more than state or territorial legislatures, constitutional conventions provided opportunities for conversation across social divisions. This was critical for conversations about labor. In the matter of out-of-state militias, at several conventions laborers were supported by the memories of more privileged delegates. In Wyoming, Alexander Sutherland recalled "Pinkerton men [who] ... stood around day after day not trying to put down an insurrection, but trying to start one."[4] The relatively small number of delegates, and weeks or months of meetings, meant delegates came to know each other's preferences, special interests, and foibles. As delegates worked six to nine hours a day, sometimes six days a week, often at a substantial distance from their families and livelihoods, they made significant, and sometimes extraordinary, commitments of time and resources. The views of delegates who brought their experience and knowledge of governance, or of the government in Washington, were especially valued. Former territorial governors were found among the delegates; although they had once been demonized as incompetent carpetbaggers, their views weighed heavily at the conventions.

More than state or territorial legislators, delegates were attentive and responsive to popular sentiment because of their close reflection of the occupations and partisanship of their constituents, and also because the adoption of the constitutions they wrote rested on approval by popular vote. Moreover, the public was much more attentive to the conventions than it was to territorial or state legislatures. There were precedents for popular rejection of proposed constitutions. Sometimes constitutions were rejected because a majority of the population was not persuaded that statehood was in their interest and so preferred territorial status. On other occasions, too many constituents were alienated by one or another article or section in the proposed document. Debates reported in the proceedings or minutes show over and over again delegates reminding their colleagues of possible popular defeat. Some claimed that their promises to those who elected them determined their votes on policies or provisions. Others threatened that the proposal at hand, if adopted, would ensure defeat of the constitution by their constituents. Rejected constitutions in the region and the nation argued that these were not idle considerations; the result was that claims about constituents' preferences reliably drew the attention of delegates.

Finally, convention debates reveal that delegates were ever part of national conversations. Westerners were not residents of island communities; rather, by birth, identity, and participation in Madison's extended commercial republic and Mr. Lincoln's War, they were, across immense distances, Americans. They conversed, corresponded, and organized with their fellows—politicians, merchants, farmers, workers, reformers, Democrats, Populists, and Republicans—and, considering earlier contributions to constitutional debate, delegates who wrote constitutions in other times and places in the United States.

Delegates did not start from nothing. Strategies, tactics, and precedents were created in practice, in courts, and in territorial legislatures. The initial forays of the territories form the subtext, and sometimes provided the actual text, of convention deliberations. The text of the constitutions was merely the tip of an iceberg of common law, legislative compromise, judicial decision, and extragovernmental practice. Delegates argued, presented evidence, relied on broadly recognized national values, or called on the low but solid ground of self-interest to move a majority of their colleagues to consensus. For all of scholars' attention to the competition of interests, occupations, regions within territories, or alignments and divisions among delegates, few scholars have examined which arguments turned the tide, or which changed votes, turning minority into majority. And frustrated as scholars may be about secret negotiations or committee proceedings unknown to us, it remains the case that much of the action that mattered was on the floor, and we can read and follow it.

The proceedings of constitutional conventions show the paths of deliberative processes. The importance of David Alan Johnson's tracking of votes in Nevada lies in carefully following those dynamics. Johnson followed debates on taxes by focusing on the arguments of Charles DeLong and his allies, who persuaded fellow delegates of the practical meaning of the centrality of mining to Nevada's economy. Here too is the importance of talented individuals in moving conversations forward. In Oregon, George Williams calmed the fears of Matthew Deady and others about the presence of corporations in the future of the state. Deady was a powerful figure in his own right, so even if his had been the only misgivings (they were not, although certainly they were the most strongly felt), they would have required a response. In Arizona the intelligence and assertiveness of Thomas Feeney brought a majority of delegates to support various provisions for the protection of labor, especially his emphatic and heartfelt arguments against the employment of children. Feeney, a machinist at the Copper Queen mine, was articulate and straightforward in explaining the utility of protections for labor. Whenever the conversation drifted away from protection, Feeney brought the conversation back to that central concern. Of course it helped that Feeney had articulate allies. He was joined in advocating severe restrictions on child labor by Patrick Connelly, a railroad engineer, and John Bolan, a miner at Bisbee, among others. Michael Cunniff, the convention's Harvard-educated authority, supplemented their case.[5] By contrast, at the New Mexico convention the self-defeating oratory of Harvey Fergusson—who accused his political opponents of being tools of the railroads when he too worked as counsel to railroads—weakened the case for progressive measures, as did the rambling, ineffective speech of his ally Harry Daugherty.[6]

The outcomes of constitutional conventions followed from a range of dynamics. For example, despite delegates' sensitivity to popular sentiment, popular majorities did not always get what they wanted. Decisions about rights to and property in water illustrate this well. In every territory, the supremacy of first in claim, first in right as the criterion for property in water was a triumph for the mining industry and, accompanied as it most often was by the abandonment of riparian rights, a defeat for farmers. In Colorado's civil and optimistic deliberations, there was agreement about priorities for the use of water and, since no set of rules could settle all disputes, delegation of decisions to the lower courts. Their relatively successful implementation of this scheme, as described in chapter 3, led other states to adapt Colorado's provisions to their own circumstances. Idaho's neat division into mining and farming areas promoted an agreement that included regional autonomy within the territory. In more autocratic Wyoming, the big guys (cattle ranchers) often did get what they wanted, in this instance a single state authority to resolve disputes about water. In contrast to the civil and cooperative discussion of protections for labor in Wyoming, discussion of water issues left small farmers bullied out of successfully defending their interests.

Decisions about railroads showed striking uniformity across the nation. As first described by George Miller, areas without railroads were often very deferential to railroad demands. Territories with more railroad track, service, and experience were likely to be hostile to them.[7] At California's 1878 convention, for example, one delegate recalled that in

1860 "the people were willing to give [the railroads] all they asked, and all [the railroads] did was take all the people gave them."[8] A striking exception is Nevada, which, although very much in need of railroads, denied Leland Stanford's request for assistance building the Central Pacific. Evidence from the experience of other territories, suspicion of Stanford, and confidence in the drawing power of the Comstock Lode brought about their decision. Too, railroads, rarely funded by local investors, were perfect targets for territory-wide hostility. Along those lines, Mississippi's constitution of 1868 abrogated the fellow servant doctrine for railroad employees, as Virginia, Oklahoma, and other states did later.

Borrowing provisions from other states was common practice in writing state constitutions. At the western conventions the experiences of other states were raised to inform collective decisions. The information provided might reasonably be described as morality tales — sensible choices rewarded and foolish ones punished. The punishments for foolish choices were harsh. In Nevada delegates were told of "impatient Minnesota," which suffered great debt by lending to railroads; of Oregon and Missouri, which "lagged behind sister states" because of ill-considered constitutional provisions about corporations; and of Massachusetts, where many "were degraded into the condition of mere servants of machinery." In Arizona delegates were asked to consider that in New England and the South, the cotton mills "were grinding the children into profit so they may become diamonds or automobiles for others." Sensible choices were rewarded. Georgia was "the empire of the South" because of its laws enabling the formation of corporations, and Texas, "the only [state] that controls corporations," enjoyed great prosperity. These assertions were not challenged and seem to have affected deliberations.

The proceedings show that delegates paid particular attention to other western constitutions. Colorado delegates borrowed from Illinois and Missouri, thought of as western states in 1876. Conventions that followed often borrowed from Colorado, not only because it was a western state but also out of recognition of Colorado's success at recruiting settlers and its sustained prosperity. For issues of more democracy, delegates turned to Oregon, a pioneer among western states in adopting initiative, referendum, and recall, even though the initiative was first adopted in South Dakota. And the contrary case, California's rejection of New York State's policies on banks, was on the grounds of the new state's differences in population and circumstance. Delegates were also attentive to federal legislation, presidential opinions, and federal court rulings. The creation of the Interstate Commerce Commission in 1887, *Munn v. Illinois,* and Theodore Roosevelt's encouragement of state activities all influenced constitutional debates. Confirming government's authority to regulate corporate behavior, these national policies supported advocates of state regulation of corporations and legislation for worker safety. And, of course, borrowing was a way to partake of accumulated wisdom. This was manifestly the case in Arizona, where supporters of direct democracy explained that the article drafted by the committee was "largely a copy of the Colorado law" enacted in 1909, the authors of which "had the advantage of the Oregon law," as well as the laws of South Dakota, Oklahoma, and Montana and proposals in Maine and Missouri, and so had "perfected the matter about as well as it can be perfected."[9]

Scholars have frequently remarked on the presence of so-called legislation in constitutions. In debate a provision that was too detailed or that was resisted as otherwise inappropriate was often dismissed as legislation. The objection often raised that a proposal was legislation, and hence an inappropriate addition to constitutional text, was frequently shorthand for substantive opposition. Legislation was in constitutions because constitutions were the most secure place for measures to which delegates were committed. Constitutional provisions were safe from state supreme courts. They were safe from legislative meddling, indifference, or corruption. Worries about state supreme courts and legislators were not fanciful. If a measure was supported by one party and not the other, placement in the constitutions made provisions safe from changes in party majority in the state legislature, always possible in states with competitive party systems, and possible too even in lopsided New Mexico and Arizona. For all of these reasons, it was imperative to seize the time, when at a convention the time was right.

The rules of convention deliberations also mattered. This is best exemplified by New Mexico, whose convention adopted a rule that allowed each subject to be discussed only once. Its importance may be measured by comparison to Arizona. No doubt was ever expressed, in either party's press or by delegates from either party, that Arizona's convention would adopt direct democracy. Yet, as in so many policy decisions, the devil rested in the details. The detail that mattered most was the proportion of voters required to place an initiative on the ballot and to pass it. John Leshy reported that on this issue the difference of a few percentage points marked a person as conservative or liberal.[10] To reach consensus on those specifics, delegates held three discussions, each on a different day, and took several roll call votes. On the last vote, a few delegates changed from "no" to "yes," allowing the provisions to pass, a strong example of deliberation at a constitutional convention. Had the Arizona convention operated by New Mexico rules, direct democracy may well have been defeated. As victors write history, so those in the ascendant write rules. Of course at the Arizona convention the Democrats wrote the rules. Similarly, Vladimir Kogan and Michael Binder have argued that rules were key to decisions at California's second constitutional convention, and that the rules were written by the Nonpartisans, the party with the largest delegation.[11] California in 1878, Arizona, and New Mexico serve as reminders that parties mattered at constitutional conventions.

Two Histories and a Western Path

I have shown in this extended essay that the conventions engaged the central national controversies of their time and traced the arc of western development from California's convention in 1849 to writing the constitutions of Arizona and New Mexico in 1910. Conversations at the conventions led to agreements that enabled writing constitutional provisions, and to understandings common to early twentieth-century politics in the West. Territorial geography, economy, and politics were at the center of deliberations and the provisions written into the constitutions. The constitutions and law that followed reflect the imprint of investors and industrialists, workers, farmers, populist activists, and their allies in each territory, represented at the constitutional conventions.

The first three conventions were steeped in antebellum principles and values. There was agreement in the West and elsewhere about chartering corporations, Jacksonian evenhandedness in public policy, and who should vote; the particulars of each convention's deliberations and decisions were shaped by territorial concerns, parties, and personalities. In the first generation, national conversations are evidenced by the prominence of antebellum principles and values: concern about the puzzling limited liability corporation, worries about the value of money, and struggles between North and South. At the same time, distance from the settled states and the nation's capital, and the apparent indifference of the federal government, meant the territories were on their own in managing these changes. Territorial narratives appear in conversations about territorial or state identity—California's population was "peculiarly a laboring people," while Oregon's effort was to maintain its pristine rural community. Nevada delegates simultaneously accepted the territory's industrial economy, resented corporations' successful resistance to taxes despite their costly demands on territorial government, were confident in prosperity based on the Comstock Lode, and persisted nevertheless in thinking of their territory as "little sage-brush Nevada."[12] These images reveal the importance of territory—people, geography, and economy—to delegates' deliberations.

Both national and territorial narratives appear in delegates' conversations about limited liability corporations and banks. Like their rules for voting, western responses to corporations aligned with the rules written by their contemporaries in other regions. Corporations in all three territories, as in most states, were to be created by general laws rather than by special legislation as gifts to favored constituents.[13] Corporations and banks raised issues at the heart of antebellum tenets about the critical role of character and virtue in a democratic republic. The corporation shielded its owners from responsibility for their mistakes, encouraging them to take unreasonable risks, enabling them to operate, without fear of the consequences, in bad faith with their employees and their home communities. The freedom of stockholders and managers to engage in unprincipled behavior looked especially wanting when compared with the standards to which ordinary citizens were held for paying their debts, or taking responsibility for their actions. Banks were worse. Not productive of anything, bankers were little short of gamblers, disrupting markets with currency of uncertain value. More, banks brought with them "the cunningest of men."

Beyond specific malfeasance, the appearance of corporations posed threats to society, and delegates were thoughtful about those costs. They were, after all, writing founding documents for new political communities. The morality tales I reviewed earlier in this chapter were part of debates about how to accommodate corporations in their constitutions and their territories. Even at this early date, all three assemblies recognized that investors in their economies were likely to be outsiders, some from nearby California, others from the eastern states. In California, William Gwin put their mission dramatically and succinctly: "We are a new people, creating from chaos a government; left free as air to select what is good, from all republican forms of government. Our country is like a blank sheet of paper, upon which we are required to write a system of fundamental laws."[14] Rodman Price added another purpose: "The people expect this convention will interpose its power as a shield to protect the commercial and laboring classes from the frauds and abuses" of bank activities.[15] California delegates were forced to reconcile themselves to the presence of banks, and Oregon's delegates to the presence of corporations. They did this by different means. California delegates wrote into their constitution individual stockholder liability for the obligations of corporations, and double liability for bank stock, thereby making owners responsible for their errors. Oregon delegates were persuaded to think of corporations as associations of fellow citizens, pooling their resources to support economic development, and so obviating the need to depend on outside investors and ensuring their concern for the welfare of workers and their community. Nevada's situation was different. Here corporations were not abstract; rather, the territory's mining industry, the reigning force in its economy, consisted of corporations with large and diverse workforces. Because their relations were for the most part amicable, the delegates had only to recognize that community prosperity was tied to mining, and then to reconcile themselves to not imposing taxes on the mines. This, with some difficulty, they did.

In the last quarter of the nineteenth century the growth of industry, "trusts," holding companies, and corporations with national reach, clashes between labor and management, continued large-scale immigration, the dominance of the gold standard and the argument for free silver, the organization of the Farmers' Alliance and the near national victory of the People's Party in 1896 headlined national politics. In the same years, six of the remaining eight western states joined the Union, and a seventh, California, wrote its second constitution. As discussed at length in chapter 3, delegates spent sustained energy attempting to manage their relations with outside investors, hoping to reap the rewards and avoid the pitfalls of economic growth. To achieve that goal, delegates expanded the authority and reach of state governments and authorized the creation of new agencies and officials in the states.

When delegates assembled, some things remained the same. In every delegation there were men who viewed corporations as immoral in principle for the same reasons people had decades earlier. Thinking about corporations also became more complex. Some delegates insisted that, since corporations were the creations of states (which granted them corporate status and privileges), state governments were entitled to regulate their behavior. This claim is present in Wyoming's constitution, Article X, Section 2: "All powers and franchises of corporations are derived from the people and are granted by their agent, the government ... and the right and duty of the State to control and regulate them ... is hereby declared." Eminent domain was claimed in several constitutions to include the state's lawful ability to regulate, or even shut down, corporations. Similarly, it was argued that "the police power of the state is supreme over all corporations as well as individuals." [16]

Countervailing this bravado was the experience that corporations, especially large corporations and those with holdings in several states, in practice existed independent of state governments and were a force in their own right. The behavior of irrigation companies demonstrated this. In Montana, for example, although legislation granted county commissioners the authority to set prices for water, it had "been practically abrogated" as companies went directly to the farmers demanding "contracts at exorbitant prices."[17] Railroads, meanwhile, were both absolutely necessary and not to be trusted; experience demonstrated that investing in their construction was foolish. At California's second convention, we read of the bitterness railroads left behind. As men had willingly "turned [their] pockets wrong side out" to assist railroads, all the railroads "did was take all the people gave them." Railroads also posed dangers to their workers and to their communities; once established, they were hardly fair in setting rates and providing services. Finally, corporations raised complex dilemmas, as James Hale commented in California's discussion of water companies: "There are two distinct phases of this question.... One is the security of the rights of those parties who make these appropriations [of water], and the other to secure the public against oppression from their use."[18] Aye, there was the rub, not only for irrigation and water companies but also for railroads, mines, manufacturers, and banks.

Delegates also developed a more practical understanding of corporations and labor. The western states established their leadership by including protections for labor at their Gilded Age constitutional conventions. From Colorado's placement of a ban on ironclad contracts in its 1876 constitution to Arizona's constitutional declaration that "the law of master and servant is forever abrogated in the state of Arizona," constitutional conversation about protections for labor engaged a single cast of dramatis personae. Each of them appeared in Wyoming. There was the proponent who rested his advocacy of the proposal on his experience as a worker; this delegate argued for the necessity of the proposal by explaining what happened in the mine or at the smelter. There were allies of workers, ready to vote in support of proposals, sometimes providing more learned and articulate defenses of protections for labor. There was the opponent who, paralleling proponents, rested his opposition on his experience as an employer. Another might oppose measures as unenforceable, an objection most frequently leveled against the blacklist. There was an opponent who saw in the proposal a rending of the entire fabric of the law of master and servant. And there was a respondent who explained that the proposition was more limited, hence not so radical. There were opponents who insisted on the prerogatives of employers. There were opponents of protections who thought it best to rely on beneficent market forces, and there were defenders of protections for labor who were infuriated by territorial and state courts. There were speakers who were patient and calm, others who were intemperate, delegates who were respectful, and those who were demeaning or sarcastic. Although some statements seem, to the contemporary reader, better reasoned and effective, while other arguments seem implausible or spurious, readers—absent a sufficient number of roll call votes, all too often the case—cannot determine whose disquisitions changed minds and whose did not. Many delegates asked for time to explain their votes, both those who had been consistent and those who had changed their thinking midstream, or wanted to explain how they weighed the pluses and minuses of proposals on the floor. Few final tallies failed to follow comfortably from the partisan balance of the conventions.

There was widespread agreement on mine inspection and construction requirements to protect miners; even New Mexico endorsed these measures. There were still delegates who objected to protections for labor as class legislation; Clagett of Idaho, for example, would not support giving employees first claim on the assets of bankrupt corporations because he thought the government "should not have pets of any kind." In deliberations, however, the damage to young people of being in the labor force, the threat their immature judgment posed to other workers, the shadow cast over their lives by working when young, and other arguments persuaded delegates to limit children's choices and their hours. For questions of acceptance of risk, contributory negligence, and the fellow servant doctrine, conversation was necessary to get to majority consensus. Even so, only Arizona abrogated the fellow servant doctrine.

The delegates at the New Mexico and Arizona constitutional conventions in 1910 were writing amid progressive activism both nationwide and close at hand. Across the states, workers' and farmers' organizations were active on their own behalf, and progressives campaigned for a long list of reforms (among them, civil service, votes for women, popular election of senators, primary elections, direct democracy, and limiting the hours of work, especially for women and children). In Arizona and New Mexico too, residents were attentive to progressive reform. In 1910, as at earlier conventions, the characteristics of each territory shaped the resolution of their generation's issues. In the event, as shown in chapter 4, the two territories marched in parallel formation. Republicans in New Mexico were anxious to secure the allegiance of Mexican voters, as Democrats in Arizona worked to win the fealty of labor. In substance New Mexico and Arizona were far apart, Arizona committed to democratizing reform and protection of workers, and New Mexico opposed to government meddling in relations between workers and employers and resistant to democratizing reform. New Mexico's exception to its conservatism was its Republican commitment to Spanish-speaking voters, including constitutional provisions forbidding the use of speaking or reading English as a qualification for voting, and banning school segregation. Newspapers broadcast these protections as in sharp contrast to Democratic policies in territories and states. For its part, Arizona kept its literacy test to qualify for voting and allowed segregation as a local option for schools.

From a national perspective, Arizona was far to the left in progressive politics, and New Mexico firmly on the right. One shortcoming of following the West by looking at constitutional conventions is that at any moment only a selection of states were writing their constitutions. To provide a broader picture of the West, the next section briefly reviews regional progress in labor law and more democracy. The review shows that even compared with other western states, Arizona went further in both protections for labor and popular democracy. For the most part, however, the western states joined Arizona in protecting workers, and pursuing more democracy, more than states in other regions.

Sequelae

Within a few years after Arizona and New Mexico became states, the western states were, as they had been in the Gilded Age, in the lead in providing protections to labor and, as they were to be for some time, prominent in the pursuit of more democracy. Many labor protections were adopted at constitutional conventions. This was the case not, I think, because the conventions were more responsive to popular pressures than were state legislatures. In this instance the key characteristics were the assembly of delegates with diverse occupations and backgrounds, meeting for weeks of deliberation, in which it was possible to have conversations across great distances in social standing, education, experience, and politics. In that setting delegates were able to persuade one another to change their views. The western states, more than states in other regions, also embraced more democracy. They did this by adopting direct democracy, fully enfranchising women, arranging for the de facto popular election of federal senators, and, in almost every state, dismantling barriers to voting (poll taxes, literacy tests, English language requirements).

Master and Servant

I have argued in several places in this book that constitutional conventions were especially suited to popular input and achieving consensus on difficult subjects, and that one result is that they were more productive of protections for labor than territorial legislatures. That said, in the years following the conventions, many states passed laws protecting the safety of workers and making it more likely that they might receive compensation for injuries suffered on the job. I think this was in part because the conventions raised the public profile of labor and increased politicians' awareness of their presence in the electorate. Whether or not that is so, the adoption of protective measures in some states made it more likely that other states would follow suit. In addition, although the constitutional convention was a venue in which labor was effective, conventions also had costs. The constitutional convention was difficult, risky, and expensive; as a result, it was a last resort for changing law. For all of these reasons, in many states, laws for the protection of labor, and enacting democratizing reform, were accomplished by the initiative or the state legislature. Alternately, a politician might see an opportunity that by supporting a particular reform, more voters would support him and perhaps his party. Each of these paths served to bring protections for labor to pass.

In some states, normal politics showed the presence of both labor and allies of labor. By 1896 seven states had weakened the fellow servant doctrine or reduced its availability to employers; six states had restricted or abrogated the fellow servant doctrine for railroads.[19] By the same year, only ten states or territories were without a bureau of labor,[20] and in an effort to improve worker safety, twenty-five states had enacted regulations for the construction of mines.[21] A dozen states had abrogated ironclad contracts (five in the West; another two had done so for railroad employees). Three states had banned the use of private militias, all three as they wrote their constitutions.

Arizona was at the forefront of states dismantling the law of master and servant. The Arizona Constitution abrogated the fellow servant doctrine in every place of employment and declared assumption of risk and contributory negligence to be matters of fact to be determined by juries. The constitution granted labor demands to abrogate the fellow servant doctrine for every employee, rethink assumption of risk and negligence, allow compensation for injury without limits of value or time, and create a system of workmen's compensation (workers did not receive relief from injunctions, the right to organize, or the right to strike).

Colorado was the first state to abrogate contracts where, as a provision for employment, the prospective employee was required to renounce any right to action for injury, and the rest of the western states, as well as a majority of states in other regions, followed. Protecting labor and employer liability were naturally related. Among western states the fellow servant doctrine was abrogated in Arizona, Colorado, and Utah, and abrogated for railroads in Montana. In Nevada the fellow servant doctrine was only available as a defense for employers without fault in provision of equipment and other measures for the safety of workers (for example, underground supports in mines). Contributory negligence was, in most states, made a matter of fact to be determined by a jury and more, not a bar to recovery of damages from the employer (juries decided how much the employee and how much the employer were at fault). In almost every state, assumption of risk could only be used as a defense by the employer if it could be shown that the employer was faultless in the provision of equipment and other measures for the safety of workers.

In southern states rules were uneven. For example, the fellow servant doctrine was intact in Kentucky and Georgia ("the master is not liable to one servant, for injuries arising from the negligence ... of other servants"), while in North Carolina employers were liable for damages even where a fellow servant was at fault. In Louisiana the fellow servant doctrine was not an available employers' defense, although it might be used to decrease damages. Virginia, Oklahoma, and Mississippi abrogated the fellow servant doctrine for railroads. Similarly, in northeastern states the law varied, most commonly providing assumption of risk as a defense only for employers entirely without fault, and requiring the employer to prove contributory negligence. In Massachusetts the fellow servant doctrine stood unaltered; in Maine it was abrogated for railroads.

More Democracy

Theodore Roosevelt famously claimed that the cure for the problems of democracy was more democracy. By "more democracy" Roosevelt meant in particular direct democracy—initiative, referendum, and recall. Scholars have long recognized the welcome reception given direct democracy in the West. There is no question that the western states were more likely to embrace direct democracy and other democratizing reforms than were states in other regions. There is considerable research on the "peculiar geography" of direct democracy, so named by Nathan Persily. Of nineteen states that adopted the initiative between 1898 and 1918, nine were in the west (Wyoming and New Mexico were the exceptions).[22] Five states enacted the initiative at constitutional conventions, two in the Southwest (Arizona and Oklahoma) and three in the Northeast (Ohio, Michigan, and Massachusetts). In those three states, malapportionment made enacting direct democracy in the legislature impossible; only the constitutional convention provided an arena in which proponents of direct democracy might succeed. In 1898, South Dakota was the first state to adopt the initiative, quickly followed by Oregon, which adopted the initiative, referendum, and recall. Supporting Persily's claim about diffusion (and consistent with constitutional borrowing from states in the same region), for western states Oregon's law became something of a mantra. Proponents of direct democracy almost always demanded, as did the Labor Party in Arizona, "Initiative, Referendum, and Recall, as embodied in the Constitution of Oregon."[23]

Nebraska pioneered the popular election of US senators in 1875. In 1901, Oregon arranged de facto popular election of senators with a system of asking candidates for the state legislature to pledge that, were they elected, they would vote for the candidate who received the most votes in a preference primary. In the first election at which this system was in place, the state legislature ignored the popular choice. Later, Democrats and Republicans in both houses sent Democrat George Chamberlain, the popular choice, to the Senate. George Haynes, writing in 1906, thought "these elaborate arrangements are but a complicated method of bringing moral pressure to bear" upon the state legislatures and found them ineffective. Nevertheless, Haynes saw "growing determination on the part of the people of the western states that, in electing senators, their state legislatures ... shall presume to exercise no independence of choice, but shall merely register the people's expressed will."[24]

Contemporary commentators were unanimous in reporting the energy and commitment of residents of the western states to deprive their state legislators of the power to select federal senators. The movement to direct election of senators reveals not only populist sentiment but also hostility, resentment, and contempt for state legislatures. State legislatures were held in contempt for corruption and, in the matter of electing senators, for being incompetent, often deadlocked, leaving states without representation in the Senate.[25] Todd Zywicki has argued that the western states were especially eager for the popular election of senators because the region's representation suffered from the rapid turnover of its senators. This was especially costly when important Senate positions were awarded on the basis of seniority. Envious of the southern states, whose senators enjoyed very long tenures, western leaders hoped that voters would be more sympathetic to incumbents than state legislators were, which did turn out to be the case.[26] Frederic Austin Ogg reported that "by 1912 senators were popularly nominated in twenty-nine of the forty-eight states; and in the majority of cases popular election was, in law or fact, equivalent to election."[27] Even more state legislatures passed resolutions urging Congress to pass an amendment that would enable voters in the states to elect their senators. Ogg counted all states with primary elections for senator. A more restricted count, including only those with a system like Oregon's, counted a dozen states in 1912, seven of them in the West.[28]

Women were enfranchised earlier in the West than in other regions. The vote was one of several policies designed to attract women westward, in an effort to balance the region's overwhelming proportion of male residents. Three territories—Wyoming in 1869, Utah in 1870, and Washington in 1883—adopted woman suffrage and endorsed that decision when they became states by placing woman suffrage in their constitutions. None of the other western states did so, and not for want of trying by supporters of woman suffrage. Henry Blackwell, traveling to campaign for woman suffrage, spoke in North Dakota and Washington and at the Montana constitutional convention.[29] The territorial supreme court in Washington rescinded woman suffrage, and the territorial legislature enfranchised women again in 1888, only to have the territorial supreme court again rescind it. In 1910 the state of Washington again enfranchised women, this time without challenge. Colorado (1893) and Idaho (1896) too enfranchised women before 1900. The remaining western states, save

New Mexico, joined them — Arizona in 1910, California in 1911, Oregon in 1912, and the last, Montana and Nevada, in 1914. By that year fifteen states had fully enfranchised women, and ten of them were in the West. They were joined by five other states, (Kentucky, Michigan, New York, Oklahoma, South Dakota) and the territory of Alaska.[30] This hardly means enfranchising women was always easy in the West, even absent interference from supreme courts; Oregon held three unsuccessful referenda on woman suffrage before one passed.[31] Taken together, the enactment of democratizing reforms shows that the western states embraced more democracy, insistent on popular choices of candidates and policy. They did so with reservations: Arizona and California maintained literacy tests; Nevada held on to the poll tax.

Of the former Confederate states in 1900, as politicians enacted disfranchising legislation across the South, Dewey Grantham wrote that "their concept of democracy ... was 'Herrenvolk democracy' — a democratic society for whites only."[32] Grantham might well have added that democracy in the South was not even for all whites; many white men were disfranchised by the same laws that kept African Americans from voting. Southern states were not alone in making those choices. The western embrace of more democracy was hardly universal. Arizona and California maintained literacy tests; Nevada held on to the poll tax. Not only did Arizona, California, and Nevada enact laws restricting voting, but they and other western states also disfranchised all those ineligible for citizenship — Chinese, Native Americans, and African Americans. Northern states too held fast to restrictions on voting; only in the Midwest was every state without a poll tax or literacy test.

Constitutions and Conventions

Constitutional conventions were special events. They provide a portrait of communities at the time they met. I have explained here how territorial history created precedents for constitutions' content and how argument and deliberation at the conventions led to their provisions. The conventions and constitutions trace the path of the western states from the last antebellum decade to the midpoint of the Progressive Era.

I have argued here that constitutional conventions had institutional characteristics that summoned men of greater social stature and better character than served in territorial or state legislatures. Election, the sustained attention of the public, and the electoral verdict on their labors also made them more responsive to public sentiment. I have presented delegates who were not citizens of island communities but were ever part of a national conversation, a tremendous achievement for an allegedly weak state. Delegates saw themselves engaged in the practice of democratic republican government, and as the beneficiaries of the experience of US history. And so they tried to assemble the best provisions, and the most modern understandings of equity and progress, for the constitutions they wrote. Accumulated wisdom was often insufficient. Delegates were confronted over and over again by issues for which they and their fellow citizens had no experience, and law and politics provided no precedent. Worse, the federal government was distant and indifferent, offering no assistance as territorial, and later state, societies worked to meet these challenges. For these issues they were standing "on the shores of an unknown and unexplored sea." Across sixty years, delegates were thoughtful, industrious, creative, and pragmatic in their efforts to respond to the changing environments of their time. Their legacy was an array of laws, rights, institutions, and principles, many still in the constitutions they wrote.

Notes

1. Upon the Shores of an Unknown Sea

1. I read only a portion of the proceedings of the constitutional conventions of Utah and Washington; those states receive little attention in the text.
2. Michael Kammen, *A Machine That Would Go of Itself: The Constitution in American Culture* (New York: Knopf, 1986).
3. John J. Dinan, *The American State Constitutional Tradition* (Lawrence: University Press of Kansas, 2006), 4, 63.
4. Smith was a farmer and an important Democrat. Equally important for his role at the convention and his support for the Indiana Bill of Rights, Smith was an exponent of classic republican virtues. In a eulogy for a colleague, Smith praised the man's "self sacrifice, patriotism, and an unflinching and unwavering devotion to the cause of republicanism and the best interests of the State and the people." Paul A. Johnson, *Founding the Far West: California, Oregon, and Nevada, 1840–1890* (Berkeley: University of California Press, 1992), 159. Smith's last political act was casting one of Oregon's Electoral College votes for the Breckinridge-Lane ticket in 1860. Charles H. Carey, *General History of Oregon through Early Statehood* (Portland, OR: Binfords & Mort, 1971 [1922]), 774.
5. Charles H. Carey, ed., *The Oregon Constitution and Proceedings and Debates of the Constitutional Convention of 1857* (Salem, OR: State Printing Department, 1926), 102 (hereafter cited as Carey, *Oregon Constitution*).
6. *Proceedings of the Constitutional Convention Held in Denver, December 20, 1875 to Frame a Constitution for the State of Colorado* (Denver, CO: Smith-Brooks Press, 1907), 723 (hereafter cited as *Proceedings . . . Colorado*).
7. Albert Ellis, *A History of the Constitutional Convention of the State of Oklahoma* (Muskogee, OK: Economy Printing, 1923), 60–64.
8. Carey, *Oregon Constitution*, 248.
9. J. Ross Browne, *Report of the Debates of the Convention of California, on the Formation of the State Constitution, in September and October, 1849* (Washington, DC: Jon T. Towers, 1850), 115 (hereafter cited as *Report . . . California*).
10. This remark was in reference to the size of juries in criminal cases. Andrew J. Marsh, *Official Report of the Debates and Proceedings in the Constitutional Convention of the State of Nevada: Assembled at Carson City, July 4, 1864, to Form a Constitution and State Government* (San Francisco: Eastman, 1866), 55.

11. Beverly Paulik Rosenow, ed., *Journal of the Washington State Constitutional Convention, 1889* (Buffalo, NY: William S. Hein, 1999), v.

12. Tinnin offered the examples of Egypt, India, and Italy: "We have no precedent to provide us, for [those countries] know nothing of human rights, and live a life of bondage and poverty." *Debates and Proceedings of the Constitutional Convention of the State of California, Convened at the City of Sacramento, Saturday, September 28, 1878* (Sacramento, CA: State Printing Office, 1880), 2:1019–1020.

13. *Proceedings . . . Colorado*, 211.

14. *Report . . . California*, 113.

15. For readers who have not themselves read the minutes of these conventions, being persuaded by arguments about debates and delegates is necessarily something of an act of faith. This book is no exception.

16. Elbert Herman Meyer, "The Constitution of Colorado," *Iowa Journal of History and Politics* 2 (1904): 256–274, 256.

17. Richard Franklin Bensel, *Sectionalism and American Political Development, 1880–1980* (Madison: University of Wisconsin Press, 1984).

18. *Proceedings . . . Colorado*, 723.

19. A detailed literature review may be found in my "Managing the Periphery in the Gilded Age: Writing Constitutions for the Western States," *Studies in American Political Development* 22 (Spring 2008): 32–52, 33–37.

20. There were some accommodations of farmers; see the discussion of water law in chapter 3, especially Colorado and Idaho.

21. Henry Bromwell, "The Constitutional Convention," in *The History of the State of Colorado*, ed. Frank Hall (Chicago: Blakely Printing, 1890), 288–321.

22. For Colorado, see the account of successive votes in David Wayne Hensel, "A History of the Colorado Constitution in the Nineteenth Century" (PhD diss., University of Colorado, 1957), 23–71; Carey, *Oregon Constitution*, 5–24; T. A. Larson, *History of Wyoming* (Lincoln: University of Nebraska Press, 1990), 236–241.

23. Christian G. Fritz, "The American Constitutional Tradition Revisited: Preliminary Observations on State Constitution-Making in the Nineteenth-Century West," *Rutgers Law Journal* 25, no. 4 (1994): 97; *Idaho Weekly Statesman*, August 3, 1889, 2.

24. John D. Hicks, *Constitutions of the Northwest States* (Buffalo, NY: John S. Hein, 1990 [1924]), 27.

25. John D. Leshy, "The Making of the Arizona Constitution," *Arizona State Law Journal* 20, no. 1 (1988): 44. Bryce also thought that writing a constitution was "specially interesting to thoughtful and public-spirited citizens" and the convention free of the pressure ("influence") and patronage of state legislatures.

26. E. R. A. Seligman, "The Taxation of Corporations," pts. 1 and 2, *Political Science Quarterly* 5 (1890): 269–308; 5 (1890): 438–467.

27. New Mexico, Wyoming, and California had important mining districts.

28. *Progressive Men of the State of Montana* (Chicago: A. W. Bowen, 1902), 62; Robert Wayne Smith, *The Coeur d'Alene Mining War of 1892* (Corvallis: Oregon State University Press, 1961), 86.

29. Bromwell authored, with Agipeto Vigil, a long and spirited minority report arguing for woman suffrage. *Proceedings . . . Colorado*, 266–271.

30. Marsha L. Baum and Christian G. Fritz, "American Constitution-Making: The Neglected State Constitutional Sources," *Hastings Constitutional Law Quarterly* 27 (2000): 199–223, 199.

31. Fritz, "Constitutional Tradition," 945–998, 982.

32. In 1899 the Colorado Supreme Court declared an eight-hour law unconstitutional, and the Washington court twice overturned initiatives that enfranchised women. James Edward Wright, *The Politics of Populism: Dissent in Colorado* (New Haven, CT: Yale University Press, 1974), 233–234; Gale Fege, "How Washington Women Won the Right to Vote," *HeraldNet*, October 4, 2010.

33. G. Alan Tarr, *Understanding State Constitutions* (Princeton, NJ: Princeton University Press, 1998), 7.

34. George A. Glynn, ed., *The Convention Manual for the Sixth New York State Constitutional Convention, 1894* (Albany, NY: Argus, 1894), pt. 2, vol. 2, 236–242 (hereafter cited as Glynn, *Convention Manual*).

35. Kermit Hall, "Mostly Anchor and Little Sail: The Evolution of American State Constitutions," in *Toward a Usable Past, Liberty under State Constitutions*, ed. Paul Finkelman and Stephen E. Gottlieb (Athens: University of Georgia Press, 1991), 388–417, 406.

36. Hicks, *Northwest States*, 31.

37. Carl Brent Swisher, *Motivation and Political Technique in the California Constitutional Convention 1878–79* (Claremont, CA: Pomona College, 1990 [1930]), 75.

38. Glynn, *Convention Manual*, 764; *Official Report of the Proceedings and Debates of the Convention Assembled at Salt Lake City of the Fourth Day of March, 1895 to Adopt a Constitution for the State of Utah* (Salt Lake City, UT: Star Printing, 1898), 1878.

39. Burt Neuborne, "State Constitutions and the Evolution of Positive Rights," *Rutgers Law Journal* 20, no. 4 (1989): 881–901, 893.

40. Ibid., 897–898.

41. Ibid., 897.

42. Judith S. Kaye, "The Common Law and State Constitutional Law as Full Partners in the Protection of Individual Rights," *Rutgers Law Journal* 23 (1992): 727–752.

43. Emily Zackin, *Looking for Rights in All the Wrong Places: Why State Constitutions Contain Positive Rights.* (Princeton, NJ: Princeton University Press, 2013), 36. Moreover, Zackin's account of labor activism in support of labor rights

contravenes the long-held understanding that organized labor in the United States was entirely focused on rewarding friends and punishing enemies. Zackin's work is a productive departure from the resolute textualism common to scholars of state constitutions.

44. Although sometimes the beliefs attributed to one era are present decades later. Johnson observed this in California: although their values remained constant, it was the changing world that created crises for Californians thirty years after their founding constitution was written. And in 2000, belief in the moral economy, and rejection of the sanctity of contract, provoked some in the international community to declare that justice required that, for some developing countries, the crushing burden of debt be eliminated rather than repaid. See, for example, Alessandra Stanley, "Pope's Labor Rally Joins Mass and Rock Concert," *New York Times*, May 2, 2000; and Editorial, "Expending Debt Relief," *New York Times*, October 1, 2000.

45. Tarr, *Understanding*, 131.

46. Paul Herron is tracing the trajectory of southern state constitutions from the secession conventions through the disfranchising conventions at the end of the nineteenth century. See, for example, "The State Conventions of Congressional Reconstruction and the Centralization of American Constitutional Authority" paper presented at the annual meeting of the Midwest Political Science Association, Chicago, Illinois, April 11, 2013). The complete account appears in his dissertation, "State Constitutional Development in the American South, 1960–1902" (Brandeis University, 2014).

47. This is the argument of Immanuel Wallerstein, *The Modern World-System I: Capitalist Agriculture and the Origins of the European World Economy in the Sixteenth Century* (Berkeley: University of California Press, 2011). Like Andre Gunder Frank before him, Wallerstein rejected the mainstream economic understanding of trade, the theory of comparative advantage, which claimed that trade worked to the benefit of all nations, and mainstream social science theories of development, which postulated steps of development rather like the development of individuals from childhood to adulthood. Andre Gunder Frank, "The Development of Underdevelopment," *Monthly Review*, September 1966, 17–31. Frank contended that "historical research demonstrates that contemporary underdevelopment is in large part the historical product of past and continuing economic and other relations between the satellite underdevelopment and the now developed metropolitan countries.... These relations are an essential part of the structure and development of the capitalist system on a world scale as a whole" (18).

2. FRONTIER FOUNDINGS

1. Eric Biber, "The Price of Admission: Causes, Effects, and Patterns of Conditions Imposed on States Entering the Union," *American Journal of Legal History*

46 (2004): 119–208. Provisions might include anything from stipulations about who was to be enfranchised to the date on which the first election after admission was to be held.

2. David Alan Johnson, *Founding the Far West: California, Oregon, and Nevada, 1840–1890* (Berkeley: University of California Press, 1992), 101.

3. [New York] *Workingman's Advocate,* May 8, 1830.

4. John Joseph Wallis, "Constitutions, Corporations, and Corruption: American States and Constitutional Change, 1842 to 1852," *Journal of Economic History* 65 (2005): 211–246, 214.

5. Charles H. Carey, ed., *The Oregon Constitution and Proceedings and Debates of the Constitutional Convention of 1857* (Salem, OR: State Printing Department, 1926), 255 (hereafter cited as Carey, *Oregon Constitution*).

6. William H. Hale, *Useful Knowledge for the Producers of Wealth, Being an Inquiry into the Nature of Trade, the Currency, the Protective and Internal Improvement Systems, and into the Origin and Effect of Banking and Paper Money* (New York: George H. Evans, 1833), 15.

7. Amy Bridges, *A City in the Republic: Ante-bellum New York and the Origins of Machine Politics* (New York: Cambridge University Press, 1984), especially chapter 2, which offers a discussion of antebellum values.

8. Wallis, "Constitutions," 220; see chapter 3, below, for the subsequent appearance of similar statements.

9. Imprisonment for debt largely disappeared in the East by the early 1830s in response to agitation by the Workingmen's Parties.

10. J. Ross Browne, *Report of the Debates of the Convention of California, on the Formation of the State Constitution, in September and October, 1849* (Washington, DC: Jon T. Towers, 1850), 125 (hereafter cited as *Report . . . California*). On Botts, see Woodrow James Hansen, *The Search for Authority in California* (Oakland, CA: Biobooks, 1960), 103–104; and Johnson, *Founding*. Johnson reports that Botts later supported the Breckinridge-Lane ticket. Johnson, *Founding,* 267.

11. Rodman Wilson Paul, *Mining Frontiers of the Far West 1848–1880* (New York: Holt, Rinehart, and Winston, 1963), 2. Paul presented Turner's arguments.

12. Johnson, *Founding,* 73–74. After President Buchanan removed Brigham Young as governor of the territory of Utah, Young called his more distant followers to return to Salt Lake City.

13. The early relations "between Aboriginal Americans and Europeans which belong to history may be briefly given. . . . The savages were in the way; the miners and settlers were arrogant and impatient; there were no missionaries or others present with even the poor pretense of soul saving or civilizing. It was one of the last human hunts of civilization, and the basest and most brutal of them all." Hubert Howe Bancroft, *History of California* (Baltimore: Regional Publishing, 1964), 474.

14. Shirley Ann Wilson Moore, "'We Feel the Want of Protection': The

Politics of Law and Race in California, 1848–1878," *California History* 81 (2003): 96–125, 99.

15. David Montejano, *Anglos and Mexicans in the Making of Texas, 1836–1986* (Austin: University of Texas Press, 1987); the discussion is in the appendix, "On Interpreting Southwestern History," 309–322, 311.

16. Richard Melzer, "New Mexico on the Eve of Statehood," *Southern New Mexico Historical Review* 19 (2012): 1–39, 27.

17. Lewis and Clark's exploratory journey took place in 1804–1806. Pomeroy compares migration to closer points with migration to the Far West. Between 1840 and 1850, total population growth in the Oregon, California, and Utah was 117,271, while population growth in Iowa (the least populous midwestern state) was 149,102. Earl Pomeroy, *The Pacific Slope: A History of California, Oregon, Washington, Idaho, Utah, and Nevada* (Lincoln: University of Nebraska Press 1991), 15, 32–33.

18. Johnson, *Founding*, 107.

19. Pomeroy, *Pacific Slope*, 40–41.

20. *Report . . . California*, 114. Rodman Price migrated to California from New York; he was a Bear Flag insurgent, and so another delegate already committed to founding California as a state. Johnson, *Founding*, 106.

21. Pomeroy, *Pacific Slope*, 48. And so there was another group of citizens recognized by Price, "those engaged in commercial pursuits, who are characterized by the greatest enterprise." *Report . . . California*, 114.

22. Pomeroy, *Pacific Slope*, 68–69. Pomeroy continues, "Government developed in the hands of influential men who knew what it was about and in the framework of relations with the main part of the nation east of the Mississippi River."

23. Quoted in Pomeroy, *Pacific Slope*, 124–125.

24. One early observer said Native Americans "had learned the vices of the white man but none of the virtues." To potential missionaries this was an invitation, yet their efforts faced demons unknown to them. Europeans brought old country diseases with them; the indigenous people they sought to save had no immunity to these. So, Blackfeet children were brought to attend Methodist schools, with the result that more than half of them passed away. No more tutored in germ theory than their potential saviors (Louis Pasteur's initial breakthroughs in germ theory occurred in the 1860s), the Blackfeet responded with violence. The best-known and largest Methodist settlement was attacked, all of the men killed, and all of the women and children taken captive. Their release was purchased years later. Charles J. Carey, *General History of Oregon through Early Statehood* (Portland, OR: Binfords & Mort, 1971 [1922]), 312–314.

25. Ibid., 281, 312.

26. Ibid., 478.

27. Johnson identified thirty-one of the sixty delegates as farmers and noted that eight who were counted as lawyers were also farmers. Johnson, *Founding*, 243.

28. Pomeroy, *Pacific Slope*, 73.

29. Carey, *General History of Oregon*, 478.

30. Johnson, *Founding*, 58.

31. Pomeroy, *Pacific Slope*, 73.

32. Johnson, *Founding*, 283. That said, Oregon was home to strong support of slavery and the Confederacy; some leaders considered joining a Pacific pact of territories to form a separate republic. Others, as late as 1868, tried to withdraw Oregon's support of the Fourteenth Amendment.

33. Browne is quoted in Russell R. Elliott, *History of Nevada* (Lincoln: University of Nebraska Press 1987), 145.

34. Browne in ibid., 146.

35. Johnson, *Founding*, 95.

36. These advances built on early agricultural and ranching initiatives by Mormon settlers. Elliott, *Nevada*, 118–121.

37. Paul, *Mining*, 68–69.

38. Ibid., 69.

39. Gilman M. Ostrander, *Nevada, the Great Rotten Borough* (New York: Knopf, 1966), 4.

40. Pomeroy, *Pacific Slope*, 51. The same developments fueled the growth of iron foundries and the manufacture of mining equipment in San Francisco. Paul, *Mining*, 50–51.

41. *Territorial Enterprise* [Virginia City, Nevada], October 15, 1862.

42. *Report . . . California*, 18. Semple was a strong opponent of California's military government and, earlier, participated in the Bear Flag Revolt. Johnson, *Founding*, 40.

43. Charles H. Carey, ed. *The Oregon Constitution and Proceedings and Debates of the Constitutional Convention of 1857* (Salem, OR: State Printing Department, 1926) (hereafter, *Oregon Constitution*), 74, 72.

44. Andrew J. Marsh, *Official Report of the Debates and Proceedings in the Constitutional Convention of the State of Nevada: Assembled at Carson City, July 4, 1864, to Form a Constitution and State Government* (San Francisco: Eastman, 1866), 416 (hereafter cited as *Official Report . . . Nevada*). Johnson, a former governor of California (and father of Hiram Johnson), served as president of the convention. Elliott, *Nevada*, 85–86.

45. In California's Bill of Rights, for example, the first eight came from New York, and the last eight from Iowa. *Report . . . California*, 31.

46. Botts's early life and respect for the North from Hansen, *Search for Authority in California*, 103; see also 103–104; *Report . . . California*, 64. Botts was committed "to a commercial republic consisting of market-minded farmers

and dynamic city systems, made coherent by the fostering arm of government." Johnson, *Founding*, 115. Johnson also reports that Botts later supported the Breckinridge-Lane ticket. Ibid., 267.

47. *Official Report . . . Nevada*, 55.

48. Johnson, *Founding*, 117; Gwin's statement, *Report . . . California*, 116.

49. Carey, *Oregon Constitution*, 102.

50. David Johnson provides a full discussion of California boundary debates. In addition to the slavery question, the more extensive proposed boundary would have made Californios a smaller portion of the state population (which Californios sensibly opposed) and included many Mormons. Another objection was that the larger territory included US citizens not represented at the convention. For the proposed territory, see the map in Johnson, *Founding*, 132; *Report . . . California*, 175.

51. *Report . . . California*, 189.

52. Johnson, *Founding*, 88. Nevadans wrote, "The paramount allegiance of every citizen is due to the Federal Government." *Official Report . . . Nevada*, 52. For conventions in the Reconstruction South, see Paul Herron, "The State Conventions of Congressional Reconstruction and the Centralization of American Constitutional Authority" (paper presented at the annual meeting of the Midwest Political Science Association, Chicago, Illinois, April 11, 2013).

53. *Official Report . . . Nevada*, 832.

54. In 1869, a generation after California's convention, a decade after Oregon's, and five years after Nevadans wrote their constitution, the territory of Wyoming granted women the vote.

55. *Report . . . California*, 63.

56. Ibid., 65. Johnson reports that Gilbert, who emigrated from New York, "had been at the center of San Francisco's political insurgency since 1848." Johnson, *Founding*, 106.

57. Jose Antonio de la Guerra y Noriega, recorded in Browne's *Report* as Mr. Noriego [sic]; his remarks are at *Report . . . California*, 63.

58. Ibid., 71. This was not, to some, the best imaginable answer. Wozencraft said he "supposed the majority of the members on this floor were not willing to deprive the descendants of Indians of the elective franchise. Many of the most distinguished officers of the Mexican Government are Indians by descent. At the same time, if 'full-blooded Indians who held property' were allowed to vote," it would be difficult to implement enfranchising only some Native Americans. Hence he was "in favor of the amendment to exclude all Indians." Ibid., 69.

59. Ibid., 49.

60. Carey, *Oregon Constitution*, 361. In California that possibility was raised well before the discussion of voting. Seven days after the convention's first meeting, as the Bill of Rights was being considered, it was suggested to include

provisions to "prevent free persons of color from immigrating and settling in the state, and to effectively prevent" slave owners from bringing slaves to California, only to free them. *Report . . . California*, 49.

61. Carey, *Oregon Constitution*, 362.

62. *Official Report . . . Nevada*, 786.

63. The question and answer are in Carey, *Oregon Constitution*, 318; the propositions and their outcomes are pages 429–430.

64. *Report . . . California*, 139; Dimmick, *Alta* editor, in Johnson, *Founding* 106. Dimmick was dismayed by the thought of African Americans in California on account of their "indolence and deficiency in force of character." Johnson, *Founding*, 129.

65. Watkins continued, "he was born upon our soil he speaks our language he has been taught our religion, and his destiny and ours are eternally linked. Fate never forged bolts stronger than those which connect his future with ours; and, for weal or woe, we are in the same boat, and must finish the voyage together. Sir, to me the duty of the American statesman is a plain one, and that is to ameliorate . . . and to see that tyranny forges no more chains." Carey, *Oregon Constitution*, 385.

66. This is the claim of Alexander Keyssar, not agreed to by all scholars. Alexander Keyssar, *The Right to Vote: The Contested History of Democracy in the United States* (New York: Basic Books, 2000), 55, table 9, 351–355.

67. *Official Report . . . Nevada*, art. II, sec. 1, 832.

68. Ibid., 104.

69. Ibid., 81.

70. It was also true, however, that states might reap great rewards from corporations chartered by special legislation. John Wallis reported, "As long as legislatures granted charters individually, states faced a constant conflict over how many charters they should issue and they had to continuously balance the possibility of creating . . . private rents by limiting charters against the benefits of wider public access to corporate forms and lines of business. A way to avoid [that] conflict was a general incorporation act." Wallis, "Constitutions," 215. States were still required, of course, to raise revenue.

71. Johnson, *Founding*, 7. Johnson also saw the "idealization of self-seeking within a market society," that government existed "to encourage and protect the 'release of private energy,'" that "laissez-faire [was] a central conviction among them," and that "the widest range of freedom that could be afforded the individual and pursuit of self-interest was indistinguishable from the public good" (ibid., 7). My presentation of California delegates' views, with their reservations about market society, the presence of "the cunningest of men," and their imposition of liability on stockholders, stands in stark contrast to Johnson's portrait.

72. Provisions about corporations are found in art. IV, secs. 31–36, Legislative Department, *Report . . . California*, appendix vi.

73. Earl, *Report . . . California*, 65; art. IV, secs. 31, 34, and 35, *Report . . . California*, appendix, vi.

74. Ibid., 328.

75. Ibid., 125.

76. Ibid., 113.

77. Ibid., 118.

78. Ibid., 125.

79. *Official Report . . . Nevada*, 164. Article VIII, sec. 6, Municipal and Other Corporations, read, "No bank notes or other paper currency shall ever be permitted to circulate as money in this State, . . . except the Federal currency, and the notes of banks authorized under the laws of Congress." Ibid., 844.

80. *Report . . . California*, 117. More important, the mint would provide redeemable paper currency. On the mint, see Ralph W. Marquis and Frank P. Smith, "Double Liability for Bank Stock," *American Economic Review* 27 (1937): 490–502, 494.

81. *Report . . . California*, 136.

82. After 1910, thirty-two states adopted enhanced liability for stockholders, meant to provide insurance for depositors. Double liability provisions were intended for the protection of "noteholders," that is, holders of bank-issued currency. Note holders were "the chief creditors of rural banks . . . and in cases of insolvency the holders of the circulating media issued by the banks bore the greatest losses." Although deposits were increasing in urban banks, "it was not until the middle of the nineteenth century that depositors as a class became numerous or important enough to demand or warrant protection. As a result, most of the state laws imposed double liability only on the stockholders of banks which issued bills or notes as circulation." The establishment of the Federal Deposit Insurance Corporation in 1933 provided protection for deposits; soon thereafter, double liability disappeared. Marquis and Smith, "Double Liability," 495, 497.

83. Art. XI, secs. 1, 2, and 6, *Oregon . . . Constitution*, 423–424.

84. Carey, *Oregon Constitution*, 255.

85. Ibid., 26.

86. Ibid., 255.

87. Ibid., 230.

88. Ibid., 258.

89. Johnson, *Founding*, 152.

90. Carey, *Oregon Constitution*, 249.

91. Johnson, *Founding*, 148; Carey, *Oregon Constitution*, 252, 255. Here Williams was describing the Willamette Woolen Mill. Davis Schuman, "The Creation of the Oregon Constitution," *Oregon Law Review* 74 (1995): 611–641, 638. Williams chaired the firm's board of directors. Johnson, *Founding*, 147 (chair); *Oregon . . . Constitution*, 234 (bona fides).

92. Art. IV, secs. 6 and 9, Carey, *Oregon Constitution*, 424; *Report . . . California*, art. XI, sec. 9, appendix, xi.

93. *Official Report . . . Nevada*, 388–390. Thomas Fitch Jr. was a newspaperman and a prized orator who campaigned for the young Republican Party. He was rewarded with an appointment as cashier for the new mint in San Francisco. Uninterested, Fitch returned to his work for the party; in June 1863 he moved to Nevada. Johnson, *Founding*, 203–204.

94. For DeLong, Johnson, *Founding*, 208; remarks, *Official Report . . . Nevada*, 391.

95. The classic statement of this observation is George H. Miller, *Railroads and the Granger Laws* (Madison: University of Wisconsin Press, 1971), 42–58.

96. *Official Report . . . Nevada*, 168–169.

97. Ibid., 177.

98. Quoted in Johnson, *Founding*, 79. More likely than not, the "foreign" interest was in San Francisco.

99. Counties, towns, and cities were allowed to support railroads. Art. VIII, secs. 9 and 10, *Official Report . . . Nevada*, 844.

100. Ibid., 392.

101. Ibid., 340.

102. Ibid., 341.

103. Ibid., 356. Lockwood was a mechanic with thinly disguised hostility to magnates; he stated that "capital is sensitive not to principles of patriotism, . . . but to the principles of loss and gain." Johnson, *Founding*, 224; *Official Report . . . Nevada*, 356.

104. *Official Report . . . Nevada*, 229.

105. See Robin Einhorn, *American Taxation, American Slavery* (Chicago: University of Chicago Press, 2006). Einhorn argues that the origin of the equal taxation clauses is found in the deliberation of southern states after the war for independence. Slave owners insisted on the injunction that "every species of property" be taxed equally to avoid high taxes on their slaves.

106. *Official Report . . . Nevada*, 224. Later, Fitch made the same argument: "We have to submit this Constitution to the people; a people whose passions may be aroused very easily on the subject of taxing the mines." Ibid., 226.

107. Ibid., 520.

108. Ibid., 225. Johnson spoke for himself: "Unless all property that has a cash value in the market is subjected to taxation, unless we have a government founded on those immutable principles of justice, equity and right, I, for one, want far distant the day when we shall adopt a State Constitution." Ibid., 319.

109. Ibid., 226.

110. Ibid., 362. Estimates were made for the constitutional convention of 1863 (of which the proposed constitution was voted down) and reported to the convention by Johnson, a delegate at both conventions.

111. See, for example, the conversation among delegates after Johnson's report. Ibid., 363–364.

112. Ibid., 223.

113. Ibid., 224. Another possibility was taxing bullion taken from the mines. Earl proposed this. The proposal had the advantage that government would determine the takings and the taxes. "The legislature could frame an act by which we could tax that bullion for State purposes," once assessed in "a government assay office." *Ibid.*, 364. The convention did not pass the proposal. Later bullion taxes were attempted and were a source of controversy for many years. See Lynn E. Williamson, "The Bullion Tax Controversy," *Nevada Historical Society Quarterly* 15, no. 4 (1972): 3–21; Elliott, *Nevada*, 153–157.

114. *Official Report . . . Nevada*, 351. Brosnan, along with Johnson, was the delegate who most often reminded the convention of its elevated purpose. He was later a justice of the Nevada Supreme Court. Elliott, *Nevada*, 79.

115. *Official Report . . . Nevada*, 368. He continued, "When business is good in the mines, business is good with the agriculturalists; and just as the mines pay and flourish, just in that proportion the whole country will prosper, and just in that proportion we will be ale to carry on our State Government," suggesting that taxing the mines might well not be necessary. Ibid., 369.

116. Ibid., 329 (Johnson speaking). Lockwood, too, presented this argument: "Who is it that wants a greater number of judges? Why the mining interest. Who is it that wants a remodeling of our form of government? It is the mining interest." Ibid., 356.

117. Quoted in Johnson, *Founding*, 225–226.

118. *Official Report . . . Nevada*, 369.

119. Ibid., 431.

3. Managing the Periphery

1. In this chapter I rely on the proceedings of the conventions and on George A. Glynn, ed., *Convention Manual for the Sixth New York State Constitutional Convention, 1894* (Albany, NY: Argus, 1894), pt. 2, vols. 1 and 2 (hereafter cited as Glynn, *Convention Manual*) for the texts of constitutions written before it was printed. For all their hundreds of pages, the journals are incomplete. For example, there are no notes or journals from committee meetings, where one imagines there were many tough arguments, allowing provisions to be drafted before being discussed at the convention. And they are an insufficient source for explanation. Secondary sources and additional primary sources give greater depth to constitutional debates and their resolution. Newspaper coverage, which was all explicitly partisan, is a source for party positions on various issues, not always clear in convention debate. Too, newspaper coverage discusses which

interests lobbied for, or were likely to benefit or suffer from, possible constitutional provisions. For this chapter I read convention coverage in the *Denver Daily Tribune,* the *Rocky Mountain News,* scrapbooks of delegates to the Colorado convention, the *Cheyenne Weekly Leader,* the *Helena Daily Herald,* and the *Idaho Weekly Statesman.* Their coverage suggests that the papers were reluctant to criticize convention proceedings, possibly for the same boosterish reasons that led the press to present idealized descriptions of the delegates. Delegates' post hoc discussions of the conventions can provide more frank appraisals of the proceedings (although sometimes self-congratulation inhibits full disclosure), as well as discussions of pressures from lobbyists and constituents not provided in the proceedings.

2. G. Alan Tarr observed, without elaboration, that in the late nineteenth century authors "incorporated into their constitutions detailed legislation to regulate railroads and other corporations" and "created institutions designed to monitor and, where necessary, curb illicit practices and abuses" even as they "acknowledged... that the prosperity of their states was... linked to the success of large 'foreign' corporations." G. Alan Tarr, *Understanding State Constitutions* (Princeton, NJ: Princeton University Press, 1998), 115–116. Andrew P. Morriss is the exception. Morriss has offered an account of Wyoming's adoption of a centralized system for the allocation of water, "Lessons from the Development of Western Water Law for Emerging Water Markets: Common Law vs. Central Planning," *Oregon Law Review* 80 (2001): 861–946.

3. J. Ross Browne, *Report of the Debates of the Convention of California, on the Formation of the State Constitution, in September and October, 1849* (Washington, DC: John T. Towers, 1850), appendix, iii–iv (hereafter cited as *Report... California*); *Proceedings and Debates of the Constitutional Convention of Idaho 1889,* vols. 1 and 2 (Caldwell, ID: Caxton Printers, 1912), 2:2049–2052 (hereafter cited as *Proceedings... Idaho*); *Proceedings of the Constitutional Convention Held in Denver, December 20, 1875 to Frame a Constitution for the State of Colorado* (Denver, CO: Smith-Brooks Press, 1907), 663–667 (hereafter cited as *Proceedings ... Colorado*); *Journal of the Constitutional Convention, State of Wyoming* (Cheyenne, WY: Daily Sun, Book and Job Printing, 1893), Constitution 5–9 (hereafter cited as *Journal... Wyoming*). Freedom of religion: Idaho sec. 4, *Proceedings... Idaho,* 2:2049–2050; Colorado sec. 4, *Proceedings... Colorado,* 664. Rights of the accused: *Proceedings... Idaho,* 2:2050; Colorado sec. 16, *Proceedings... Colorado,* 665; Wyoming sec. 10, *Journal... Wyoming,* Constitution, 6. Treatment of prisoners: Wyoming secs. 15 and 16, *Journal... Wyoming,* Constitution, 7. Right to education: Wyoming sec. 23, Constitution, 8. Broad guarantees: Wyoming Rights of labor, sec. 22, Constitution, 8. Equality: sec. 3, Constitution, 6 ("rights and privileges of citizens shall be without distinction of race, color, sex, or any circumstance whatsoever...").

4. G. Alan Tarr and Robert F. Williams, "Foreword: Western State Constitutions

in the American Constitutional Tradition," *New Mexico Law Review* 28 (1998): 191–196, 192. Also of interest on the importance of state bills of rights is Rachel A. Van Cleave, "Constitutions in Conflict: The Doctrine of Independent State Grounds and the Voter Initiative in California," *Hastings Constitutional Law Quarterly* 21 (1994): 95–137.

5. In 1878 lead, copper, and zinc were discovered in Coeur d'Alene. Robert Wayne Smith, *The Coeur d'Alene Mining War of 1892: A Case Study of an Industrial Dispute* (Corvallis: University of Oregon Press, 1961), 2. For Montana, see Michael P. Malone, Richard B. Roeder, and William L. Lang, *Montana: A History of Two Centuries* (Seattle: University of Washington Press, 1991), 50.

6. Rodman Wilson Paul, *Mining Frontiers of the Far West* (New York: Holt, Rinehart, and Winston, 1963; repr., Albuquerque: University of New Mexico Press, 2001), 145.

7. Ibid., 124. The consultation at Swansea was insufficient, and Hill hired Richard Pearce. Pearce studied at the Royal School of Mines in London and the mining academy at Frieberg, each home to the most advanced geologists and mining engineers in Europe. Knowledge was substantially advanced after the founding of the US Geological Survey (USGS) in 1879. The leaders of the USGS were committed to providing practical knowledge to the American mining industry. USGS staff included Samuel Emmons, who had studied at the École des Mines in France as well as in Frieberg. Emmons wrote a report on silver mining and processing at Leadville that became "the miners' bible." The USGS, Emmons's report, and the success of more advanced smelters in Colorado persuaded mining industrialists that science and engineering were key to success in their enterprise. Ibid., 129–134.

8. Ibid., 147, 139.

9. Ibid., 148–149.

10. Smith, *Coeur d'Alene Mining War*, 3; Malone, Roeder, and Lange, *Montana*, 175.

11. The state's population of miners grew with the industry. "The 2200 stubborn miners [of Colorado Territory] in 1870 found their ranks swelled to 28,970 by 1880." In 1870, 1,216 of the 2,200 miners were US born; of immigrants, 80 percent were from England, Wales, and Ireland. In 1880, too, US-born miners were the majority (65 percent). Ten years later just under half of Colorado's miners were born in the United States, while the other half were immigrants. Colorado miners, and other workers as well, joined unions. In 1892 the state's Bureau of Labor Statistics announced that, with 15,789 men in 206 unions, Colorado's population included a larger proportion of organized workers than any other state. Paul, *Mining Frontiers*, 127–128.

12. Smith, *Couer d'Alene Mining War*, 3

13. Merrill G. Burlingame and K. Ross Toole, *A History of Montana* (New York: Lewis Historical Publishing, 1957), 2:342–347.

14. David B. Griffiths, *Populism in the Western United States 1890–1900* (Lewiston, NY: Edwin Mellen Press, 1992), 1:274.

15. The Emma Mine was on a strike identified in 1868. The mine was promoted with sample ores and a "laudatory scientific report," which greatly exaggerated the value of the unmined ore. Investors from San Francisco to London invested a million dollars in the Emma Mine, despite rumors that all was not as claimed. The promotion of the mine was so successful that it increased willingness to invest in other mines in Utah. The collapse of the mine in 1873 revealed it to be "one of the really notable swindles of Anglo-American history." As well publicized as the initial strike, the collapse and the swindle dissuaded potential investors from funding Utah mines. Paul, *Mining Frontiers*, 152–153.

16. That management-labor relations deteriorated once owners were outsiders, see Griffiths, *Populism*, 1:275. The definitive source on events in Coeur d'Alene is Smith, *Coeur d'Alene Mining War*.

17. T. A. Larson, *History of Wyoming* (Lincoln: University of Nebraska Press, 1990), 167; Burlingame and Toole, *History of Montana*, 315–316. The decline followed close upon the very harsh winter of 1885–1886: "In the spring of 1886 . . . cattlemen . . . found the carcasses of up to 85 per cent or more of their herd in the ravines or piled up along the drift fences." The next winter was no better; in the spring of 1887, dead cattle "were piled in the coulees," and the *Rocky Mountain Husbandman* declared, "Range husbandry is over, is ruined, destroyed." Ernest Staples Osgood, *The Day of the Cattleman* (Chicago: University of Chicago Press, 1929), 218, 221–222.

18. W. Turrentine Jackson, "The Wyoming Stock Growers' Association: Political Power in Wyoming Territory, 1873–1890," *Mississippi Valley Historical Review* 33 (1947): 572–594.

19. In Montana for organizing roundups, legal arrangements were tried first, and when they failed, the roundups were managed by the Stockgrowers Organization. The organization too had difficulty restraining ranchers from independent action. Osgood, *Day of the Cattleman*, 129–132.

20. Jackson, "Wyoming Stock Growers," 575.

21. Ibid., 573–574; Burlingame and Toole, *History of Montana*, 571. One symptom of the enmity between stock ranchers and farmers was that Populism in Wyoming and New Mexico took the form of fighting, literally as well as in politics, over land. Griffiths, *Populism*, 1:328–332; Robert W. Larson, *New Mexico Populism: A Study of Radical Protest in a Western Territory* (Boulder: Colorado Associated University Press, 1974), 7, 9–10. Wyoming, Montana, and Idaho were also home to large sheep ranches, as was New Mexico. Earl Pomeroy reported that

in the early 1880s sheep ranchers in Washington and Oregon "moved wholesale ... to Idaho and Montana" (*Pacific Slope,* 105).

22. Carl Brent Swisher, *Motivation and Political Technique in the California Constitutional Convention, 1878–9* (Claremont, CA: Pomona College, 1930), 8. Swisher notes, in addition, that in "Southern California the sheep industry was nearly destroyed." Swisher, *Motivation and Political Technique,* 8.

23. Robert G. Dunbar, "Agriculture," 281–310, in Burlingame and Toole, *History Montana,* 281–284.

24. Griffiths, *Populism,* 2:436.

25. Swisher, *Motivation and Political Technique,* 7–8.

26. James Edward Wright, *The Politics of Populism: Dissent in Colorado* (New Haven, CT: Yale University Press, 1974), 22.

27. Thomas A. Clinch, *Urban Populism and Free Silver in Montana* (Missoula: University of Montana Press, 1970), 66.

28. Amy Bridges and Jessica Trounstine [Hills], "Not in Kansas Anymore: Populists in Western States" (paper presented at the annual meetings of the Midwest Political Science Association, Chicago, Illinois, April 5, 2003). Labor and farmers alike used the opportunity presented by the Populists to increase the pressure on state politicians, with some success. In Colorado, Idaho, Montana, and Utah, the Populist Party was key to the passage of eight-hour legislation in the 1890s. And later, Populists were also critical to support for labor in state courts. These developments came about after the constitutional conventions had finished their work.

29. Donald Wayne Hensel, "A History of the Colorado Constitution in the Nineteenth Century" (PhD diss., University of Colorado, 1957), 97.

30. Dennis Colson, *Idaho's Constitution: The Tie That Binds* (Moscow: University of Idaho Press, 1991), 233–234.

31. Larson, *History of Wyoming,* 238.

32. Swisher, *Motivation and Political Technique,* 22–23 (election); 24 (delegates).

33. Bromwell authored, with Agipeto Vigil, a long and spirited minority report arguing for woman suffrage. *Proceedings ... Colorado,* 266–271.

34. Thomas Jondrie Vivian and D. G. Waldron, *Biographical Sketches of the Delegates to the Convention to Frame a New Constitution for the State of California, 1878. Together with a Succinct Review of the Facts Leading to the Formation of the Monterey Convention of 1849, a List of Its Members, and the Constitutional Act of 1878* (San Francisco: Francis and Valentine, 1878), 153–154.

35. Virginia Trenholm, ed., *Wyoming Blue Book,* vol. 1 (repr. of pt. 1, *Wyoming Historical Blue Book,* by Marie Erwin) (Cheyenne: Wyoming State Archives and Historical Department, 1974), 92–93; Larson, *History of Wyoming,* 255.

36. Toole saw direct democracy as a powerful aid in the fight against corruption. "It is the sure weapon," he argued, "with which to put to flight the briber

and the lobbyist, and drive them, like Hagar, to the wilderness." Richard Brown Roeder, "Montana in the Early Years of the Progressive Period" (PhD diss., University of Pennsylvania, 1971), 177.

37. *Progressive Men of the State of Montana* (Chicago: A. W. Bowen, 1902), 62; Smith, *Coeur d'Alene Mining War*, 86.

38. Larson, *History of Wyoming*, 249.

39. In addition, women were eligible to run for office, and three were appointed justices of the peace almost immediately after the constitution was adopted. Larson, *History of Wyoming*, 78–84, 86 (justices of the peace). Wyoming was one of three territories to adopt woman suffrage; the other two were Washington and Utah. Although five western states adopted woman suffrage before 1900 (the other two were Colorado and Idaho), not one first enfranchised women at its constitutional convention. Every western state save New Mexico enfranchised women before the Nineteenth Amendment was passed. Gordon Morris Bakken found convention discussions of woman suffrage fascinating; his very extensive research is summarized in chapter 8 of *Rocky Mountain Constitution Making, 1850–1912* (Westport, CT: Greenwood Press, 1987).

40. Hensel, "Colorado Constitution," 404–405. See also Carl Abbott, Stephen J. Leonard, and David McComb, *Colorado: A History of the Centennial State* (Boulder: Colorado Associated University Press, 1982), 40.

41. *Proceedings . . . Idaho*, 2:1358.

42. *Proceedings and Debates of the Constitutional Convention Held in the City of Helena, Montana, July 4 to August 17, 1889* (Helena, MT: State Publishing Company, 1892), 500 (hereafter cited as *Proceedings . . . Montana*).

43. Wright, *Politics of Populism*, 31–40.

44. *Proceedings . . . Montana*, 497.

45. Clinch, *Urban Populism*, 14.

46. Griffiths *Populism*, 2:441–442.

47. Donald Pisani has shown that the claim that riparian rights were the exclusive water rights practice in the East is incorrect. Prior appropriation had precedents in eastern states. Donald J. Pisani, *Water, Land, and Law in the West: The Limits of Public Policy, 1850–1920* (Lawrence: University Press of Kansas, 1996). Nevertheless, it was the argument presented at these conventions, by Senator William M. Stewart, for example, speaking at Montana's convention. *Proceedings . . . Montana*, 806.

48. *Debates and Proceedings of the Constitutional Convention of the State of California, Convened at the City of Sacramento, Saturday, September 28, 1878* (Sacramento, CA: State Printing Office, 1880), 2:1021 (hereafter cited as *Debates and Proceedings . . . California*). Hale was a lawyer, elected on the Whig ticket to be a county judge; after four years he was elected to the state senate, thence to serve as reporter for the California Supreme Court. Hale also served as presidential elector

for California Republicans. "Though a pronounced Republican, Mr. Hale is not prejudiced, and is fully aware of how much more important the State's interests are than those of his party." Vivian and Waldron, *Biographical Sketches*, 117–118.

49. H. P. H. Bromwell, "The Constitutional Convention," in *History of Colorado*, ed. Frank Hall (Chicago: Blakely Printing, 1890), 2:288–321, 2:311.

50. *Denver Daily Tribune*, January 19, 1876, 4. Delegates to the convention refused to hire a stenographer but allowed the press access to their deliberations, which were published by the *Denver Daily Tribune* in 1907.

51. *Denver Daily Tribune*, February 19, 1876, 4.

52. *Denver Daily Tribune*, March 2, 1876, 4.

53. Bromwell, "Constitutional Convention," 313.

54. *Debates and Proceedings . . . California*, 2:1020.

55. Ibid., 2:1021. Herrington was a skilled carpenter and worked for years at related trades. At twenty-four he decided to pursue formal education, soon graduated from Asbury University (Indiana), and a few years later moved to California. There Herrington opened a furniture business and later read law; he practiced for many years, was appointed district attorney for Santa Clara County, and was elected to the state legislature in 1863. Herrington was a Democrat until 1861, thereafter a Republican, and was elected to the convention on the Workingmen's ticket. Vivian and Waldron, *Biographical Sketches*, 122.

56. *Debates and Proceedings . . . California*, 2:1021.

57. Ibid., 2:1021.

58. Ibid., 2:1025. Cross was educated at Northwestern University, worked as a lawyer in Illinois for about twenty years, and moved to California, where he continued to practice law. He was elected to the convention on the Workingmen's ticket. Vivian and Waldron, *Biographical Sketches*, 73.

59. *Debates and Proceedings . . . California*, 3:1373. Joseph Brown was a lawyer and was principal of a private academy in Missouri. Having moved to California, he became a county undersheriff five years later, served three terms in the state legislature as a Democrat, and was elected to the convention on the Democratic ticket. Vivian and Waldron, *Biographical Sketches*, 123.

60. *Debates and Proceedings . . . California*, 3:1373.

61. Ibid., 3:1373.

62. Ibid., 2:1021.

63. Swisher, *Motivation and Political Technique*, 14.

64. *Debates and Proceedings . . . California*, 2:1027.

65. Ibid., 3:1374.

66. Ibid., 3:1375.

67. *Proceedings . . . Idaho*, 3:1123.

68. Ibid., 2:1123.

69. Ibid., 2:1361.

70. Colson, *Idaho's Constitution*, 162–163.
71. *Proceedings . . . Montana*, 138–139.
72. *Journal . . . Wyoming*, 293. First appropriation rights were discussed more than once and were finally approved on September 21. Ibid., 537.
73. Ibid., 498–500.
74. Ibid., 500–501, 534–537.
75. Morriss, "Western Water Law," 905–937.
76. Jackson, "Wyoming Stock Growers," 571–594.
77. Morriss, "Western Water Law," 911.
78. Ibid., 866.
79. Ibid., 866.
80. *Proceedings . . . Montana*, 675.
81. *Debates and Proceedings . . . California*, 2:1021.
82. *Proceedings . . . Montana*, 472.
83. Ibid., 500.
84. *Helena Daily Herald*, August 2, 1889, 4.
85. *Proceedings . . . Colorado*, 728.
86. George H. Miller, *Railroads and the Granger Laws* (Madison: University of Wisconsin Press, 1971), 42–58.
87. This argument was offered in Miller's classic narrative (*Railroads*) and in Hensel's analysis of votes at the Colorado constitutional convention ("Colorado Constitution"; see below). Kanazawa and Noll found that at the Illinois convention "railroads had most success with delegates from areas without service, and less success with delegates from monopolized areas than from more competitive ones," while "party affiliation appears to have been unimportant." Mark T. Kanazawa and Roger G. Noll, "The Origins of State Railroad Regulation: The Illinois Constitution of 1870," in *The Regulated Economy: A Historical Approach to Political Economy*, ed. Claudia Goldin and Gary D. Libecap (Chicago: University of Chicago Press, 1994), 13–54, 46.
88. Hensel, "Colorado Constitution," 145.
89. *Denver Daily Tribune*, February 29, 1876, 4.
90. Bromwell, "Constitutional Convention," 305.
91. *Denver Daily Tribune*, February 28, 1876, 4.
92. *Debates and Proceedings . . . California*, 1:488.
93. Ibid., 1:488.
94. Ibid., 1:480.
95. Estee was a lawyer, from San Francisco, and had served in the state legislature, where he was chosen speaker of the assembly in 1874. Swisher, *Motivation and Political Technique*, 28.
96. *Debates and Proceedings . . . California*, 1:377, 382.
97. Ibid., 1:454.

98. Ibid., 1:600.
99. Ibid., 1:377.
100. Ibid., 3:1228.
101. Ibid., 3:1227.
102. Ibid., 3:1227. Dudley was a Republican lawyer, elected on the Nonpartisan ticket. Vivian and Waldron, *Biographical Sketches*, 160.
103. *Debates and Proceedings . . . California*, 3:1228.
104. S. E. Moffett, "The Railroad Commission of California: A Study in Irresponsible Government," *Annals of the American Academy of Political and Social Science* 6 (1895): 469–477, 477.
105. *Proceedings . . . Idaho*, 1:880; on Morgan, see *Idaho's Constitution*, 235, 180.
106. *Proceedings . . . Idaho*, 1:882. Clagett's political views shifted left in the following years. Still a Republican, Clagett was elected to the state legislature in 1892, ran unsuccessfully for governor as a Populist in 1894, and was elected to the state senate on the same ticket in 1896. Griffiths, *Populism*, 2:446–447.
107. *Proceedings . . . Idaho*, 1:885.
108. Ibid., 1:884–885.
109. Montana Constitution art. XV, sec. 6, *The Constitution of the State of Montana as Adopted by the Constitutional Convention Held at Helena, Montana, July 4, 1889 and Ending August 19, 1889* (Helena, MT: Independent Publishing, 1889), 50–51 (hereafter cited as *Constitution . . . Montana*); Wyoming Constitution art. X, sec. 2, *Journal . . . Wyoming*, Constitution, 39; Idaho Constitution art. XI, sec. 5, *Proceedings . . . Idaho*, 2:2075.
110. *Journal . . . Wyoming*, 581.
111. Hensel, "Colorado Constitution," 418, 152.
112. Art. XII, sec. 3, *Debates and Proceedings . . . California*, 1:383–388.
113. Utah Constitution art. XI, sec. 18, Francis Newton Thorpe, ed., *The Federal and State Constitutions, Colonial Charters, and Other Organic Laws of the States, Territories, and Colonies Now or Heretofore Forming the United States of America* (Washington, DC: Government Printing Office, 1909), 3724 (hereafter cited as Thorpe, *Federal and State Constitutions*).
114. Colorado Constitution art. XV, sec. 8, *Proceedings . . . Colorado*, 698; Idaho Constitution art. XI, sec. 8, *Proceedings . . . Idaho*, 2:1062; Montana Constitution art. XV, sec. 9, *Constitution . . . Montana*, 52; Utah Constitution art. XI, sec. 11, Thorpe, *Federal and State Constitutions*, 3724; Washington Constitution art. XII, sec. 10, Glynn, *Convention Manual*, pt. 2, vol. 2, 634. Wyoming's constitution declared the government's eminent domain prerogatives over corporations in general, and again over railroads. Art. X, secs. 4 and 9, *Journal . . . Wyoming*, Constitution, 50.
115. Wyoming Constitution art. X, sec. 2, *Journal . . . Wyoming*, Constitution, 50.
116. Emily Zackin, "To Change the Fundamental Law of the State: Protective Labor Provisions in U.S. Constitutions," *Studies in American Political Development* 24, no. 1 (2010): 1–23.

117. Howard Gillman, *The Constitution Besieged: The Rise and Demise of Lochner Era Police Powers Jurisprudence* (Durham, NC: Duke University Press 1993), 71.

118. Melvin I. Urovsky, "State Courts and Protective Legislation in the Progressive Era: A Reevaluation," *Journal of American History* 72 (1985): 63–91, 72.

119. William Forbath, *Law and the Shaping of the American Labor Movement* (Cambridge, MA: Harvard University Press, 1991), 41.

120. Gillman, *Constitution Besieged*, 18.

121. *Proceedings . . . Colorado*, 609.

122. *Journal . . . Wyoming*, 443. Anthony Campbell was admitted to the bar in Pennsylvania, moved to Cheyenne, and, a Democrat, was appointed US attorney for Wyoming in 1885 by President Cleveland; he served until 1990 and thereafter was attorney to Standard Oil and other large corporations. Trenholm, *Blue Book*, 542.

123. *Journal . . . Wyoming*, 447–448. Thomas Reed immigrated to the United States as an adult, enlisted in the Union army in 1867, and served until 1872. Thereafter, until his retirement in 1909, Reed worked for the Union Pacific Railroad. A Democrat, Reed was a member of the Cheyenne City Council and the House of the Wyoming legislature. Trenholm, *Blue Book*, 554.

124. *Journal . . . Wyoming*, 450. George Baxter, a Democrat, was a graduate of West Point and served in the cavalry for three years. In Wyoming he worked in banking and traded in cotton. Trenholm, *Blue Book*, 94.

125. *Journal . . . Wyoming*, 452. George Smith, a Republican, was admitted to the bar in Pennsylvania, served as a volunteer in a Pennsylvania regiment in the Civil War, and moved to Rawlins, Wyoming, in 1873. There he practiced law and served as county attorney. Trenholm, *Blue Book*, 553.

126. This claim contradicts many sources, which state that Montana and Wyoming also abrogated the fellow servant doctrine. The source cited for the claim is Hicks, who saw the provision as an effort to undermine fellow servant, which it failed to do. As related earlier, efforts to abrogate the fellow servant at the Wyoming convention met with effective resistance. Arizona was the first western state to declare in its constitution that "the fellow servant doctrine is forever abrogated in the state of Arizona." Section 193 of the Mississippi Constitution of 1890 lists several protections for railroad workers. Ironclad contracts are abrogated; the negligence of fellow servants did not, in every circumstance, protect the employer from liability, nor may employee knowledge of dangerous conditions serve as a defense for the employer. Glynn, *Convention Manual*, 1086.

127. *Journal . . . Wyoming*, 450. In Wyoming, cattle ranchers and farmers had their own reasons to resent railroads, which may have increased general support for this resolution. Louis Palmer, a Democrat, was a lawyer elected attorney general of Sweetwater County several times. Trenholm, *Blue Book*, 549.

128. The resolution to ban ironclad contracts passed unanimously (*Journal... Wyoming*, 454) and appears in the constitution in art. XIX, *Journal... Wyoming*, Constitution, 51; California art. 12, sec. 17, *Proceedings and Debates... California*, 3:1518; Montana Constitution art. 15, sec, 16, *Constitution... Montana*, 52; Utah art. XVI, sec. 5, Thorpe, *Federal and State Constitutions*, 3728; compensation in Wyoming, art. X, sec. 4, *Journal... Wyoming*, Constitution, 39; defeated in Idaho, *Proceedings... Idaho*, 2:1106–1107.

129. *Proceedings... Idaho*, 2:1373–1375.

130. *Proceedings... Montana*, 239–240.

131. Judson Ferguson, commissioner of the Bureau of Agriculture, Labor, and Industry in Montana, provides an example. Ferguson is discussed in chapter 2 of Roeder, "Montana in the Early Years" (see, e.g., pp. 27–34). See also Alexander Trachtenberg, *Laws for the Protection of Coal Miners in Pennsylvania, 1824–1915* (New York: International Publishers, 1942), 89.

132. *Journal... Wyoming*, 764.

133. *Proceedings... Idaho*, 2:1378.

134. Ibid., 2:1380.

135. Ibid., 2:1380.

136. *Journal... Wyoming*, 765.

137. Ibid., 765–766.

138. *Proceedings... Montana*, 202–209; *Proceedings... Idaho*, 2:1381–1385.

139. Harry N. Scheiber, "Race, Radicalism, and Reform: Historical Perspective on the 1879 California Constitution," *Hastings Constitutional Law Quarterly* 17 (Fall 1989): 35–80, 50.

140. California Constitution art. XIX, *Debates and Proceedings... California*, 3:1510.

141. *Debates and Proceedings... California*, 1:634

142. Connie Chiang, "Chinatown Will Cease to Exist: Race, Nature, and Fire at Monterey's Chinese Fishing Village, 1906" (paper presented at the annual meetings of the Western History Association, San Diego, California, 2001); Paul Crane and Alfred Larson, "The Chinese Massacre," pts. 1 and 2, *Annals of Wyoming* 12 (1940): 47–55; 12 (1940): 153–161; Roy T. Wortmann, "Denver's Anti-Chinese Riot, 1880," *Colorado Magazine* 42 (1965): 275–291.

143. *Proceedings... Montana*, 214–215.

144. *Proceedings... Idaho*, 2:1387–1389.

145. *Journal... Wyoming*, 405.

146. *Proceedings... Montana*, 130.

147. Ibid., 140. William T. Field was a labor delegate at the convention and in 1890 was a candidate for Congress on the Democratic ticket. Clinch, *Urban Populism*, 45–46.

148. *Proceedings... Montana*, 129–130.

149. *Journal... Wyoming*, 403. Alexander Sutherland, a Republican, was a

successful rancher and served in the House of the first state legislature of Wyoming. Trenholm, *Blue Book*, 550.

150. Wyoming art. I, sec. 22, *Journal . . . Wyoming*, Constitution, 8.

151. Utah Constitution art. XCI, sec. 1, Thorpe, *Federal and State Constitutions*, 3728.

152. Idaho Constitution art. XIII, sec. 1, *Proceedings . . . Idaho*, 2077–2078.

153. Declarations of government's obligations to labor also appear in a few contemporary constitutions from other regions. In Arkansas the General Assembly was asked "to require . . . means to be provided . . . to secure as far as possible the lives, health, and safety of persons employed in mining. And shall provide for enforcing such enactments by adequate pains and penalties" (Arkansas art. XIX, sec. 18, Glynn, *Convention Manual*, pt. 2, vol. 1, 147). Even more expansively, Mississippi's constitution of 1890 mandated the legislature to "provide for the protection of employes [sic] of all corporations . . . from interference with their social, civil, or political rights" by their employers (Mississippi art. VII, sec. 191, Glynn, *Convention Manual*, pt. 2, vol. 1, 1084).

154. Joseph F. Tripp, "Progressive Jurisprudence in the West: The Washington Supreme Court, Labor Law, and the Problem of Industrial Accidents," *Labor History* 24 (1983): 342–365, 344. See also R. Douglas Hurt, "Populist-Endorsed Judges and the Protection of Western Labor," *Journal of the West* 17, no. 1 (1978): 19–26.

155. Jonathan Chausovsky, "State Regulation of Corporations in the Late Nineteenth Century: A Critique of the New Jersey Thesis," *Studies in American Political Development* 21 (Spring 2007): 30–65. Chausovsky's central argument is that, rather than seeing New Jersey as a special case for its "untethering of the corporation from prior legislated restraints," we should recognize that "many states actively adjusted many elements of their corporation law in the decades after the Civil War, often in the direction of greater liberalization" (30–31). Chausovsky looks at thirty-five states over thirty-five years, ending in 1900, providing a very broad view of changes in laws affecting corporations. In 1900 there were forty-five states in the Union. Of the eleven-state west, Chausovsky's sample includes only California and Oregon, so his conclusions may not hold for the West.

156. *Debates and Proceedings . . . California*, 2:1020.

4. Progressive Settlements

1. Paul T. David, *Party Strength in the United States, 1872–1970* (Charlottesville: University Press of Virginia, 1972), 43, 50.

2. Tru Anthony McGinnis, "The Influence of Organized Labor on the Making of the Arizona Constitution" (MA thesis, University of Arizona, 1930), chap. 1.

3. Richard A. Melzer, "New Mexico on the Eve of Statehood, 1910–1912," *Southern New Mexico Historical Review* 19 (January 2012): 1–39.

4. McGinnis, "Organized Labor," chap. 1.

5. Hunt's defeated proposals included initiative and referendum, blocked by the governor, taxing sleeping car companies, creating a Board of Health and Vital Statistics, outlawing the blacklist, and banning *bolatas*, which were scrip that could be used only in company stores. His successful proposals included a compulsory school law and requiring licensing of physicians. A poll tax passed despite his opposition. And Hunt was the only member of the territorial legislature to decline the railroad pass offered to him, as it was to every member of the legislature. John S. Goff, *George W. Hunt and His Arizona* (Pasadena, CA: Socio Technical Publications, 1973), 19–22.

6. For negotiations between Hunt and the upstart Labor Party, see McGinnis, "Organized Labor," 30–34. McGinnis argues that labor never thought the Labor Party would nominate a slate to run for delegates to the convention, but organized the party to pressure Democrats to support its demands.

7. Except where noted otherwise, information on the delegates in Arizona is from Delegates to the Arizona Constitutional Convention, in John S. Goff, *The Records of the Arizona Constitutional Convention of 1910* (Phoenix: Supreme Court of Arizona, 1991), 1387–1398; 1390 (Feeney); 1395 (Parsons); 1389 (Cunniff); 1397 (Wells); 1392–1393 (Kingan); 1397 (Webb) (hereafter cited as Goff, *Arizona Constitutional Convention*); Gordon Morris Bakken, *Rocky Mountain Constitution Making, 1850–1912* (Westport, CT: Greenwood Press, 1987), 2, 22.

8. Howard Roberts Lamar, *The Far Southwest 1846–1912: A Territorial History* (Albuquerque: University of New Mexico Press, 2000), 156.

9. Melzer, "New Mexico," 23.

10. Lamar, *Far Southwest*, 163–165. Dorothy Cline attributed the defeat of the 1891 constitution to Mexican American voters. Dorothy I. Cline, *New Mexico's 1910 Constitution: A 19th Century Product* (Santa Fe: Lightning Tree, 1985). Larson thought Anglo discontents were more important; some Anglos feared "Mexication domination," plausible given their large presence in the population. Robert W. Larson, *New Mexico's Quest for Statehood, 1846–1912* (Albuquerque: University of New Mexico Press, 1968), 168.

11. Cline, *1910 Constitution*, 31–33 (Catron); 34–35 (Bursum). Bursum as large landholder and livestock rancher, election as sheriff: Finding Aid to Holm O. Bursum Mss, Center for Southwest Research, University of New Mexico, Albuquerque.

12. Calvin A. Roberts, "H. B. Fergusson, 1848–1915: New Mexico Spokesman for Political Reform," *New Mexico Historical Review* 57 (1982): 237–255.

13. Paul Kleppner, "Politics without Parties: The Western States 1900–1984," in *The Twentieth-Century West: Historical Interpretations*, ed. Gerald W. Nash and Richard Etulain (Albuquerque: University of New Mexico Press, 1989), 295–338.

14. Amy Bridges and Jessica Trounstine [Hills], "Not in Kansas Anymore:

Populists in Western States" (paper presented at the annual meetings of the Midwest Political Science Association, Chicago, Illinois, April 5, 2003).

15. *Arizona Republican,* May 7, 1891, quoted in Mark E. Pry, "Statehood Politics and Territorial Development: The Arizona Constitution of 1891," *Journal of Arizona History* 35 (1994): 397–426, 401.

16. *Albuquerque Morning Journal,* September 16, 1910, 1.

17. *Santa Fe New Mexican,* September 8, 1910, 1.

18. *Albuquerque Morning Journal,* September 6, 1910, 2.

19. *Arizona Gazette,* September 7, 1910, 1. "The railroads deadheaded trains from a number of towns to send out their men who were known to be friendly. . . . Money was used lavishly in the coal camps and among the natives. . . . Heavy Republican majorities polled wherever the Mexican population was heaviest." *Arizona Gazette,* September 8, 1910, 1.

20. *Arizona Republican,* September 13, 1910, 1; *Arizona Republican,* September 13, 1910, 2.

21. But they might not. "Indeed," the editors continued, "the *Republican* has certain knowledge that they do not intend to keep their promises." They might well take the proposed constitution to Washington, present it to Taft, be told he would not accept it, and return to Arizona claiming, "We kept our promise to you." The result would be that "the people . . . and the . . . laboring man . . . will find out they have been buncoed, as usual." *Arizona Republican,* September 13, 1910, 2.

22. *Santa Fe New Mexican,* September 13, 1910, 1. In the same article, the *New Mexican* also reported unsuccessful attempts by Arizona Democrats to keep people of color from voting.

23. *Arizona Gazette,* September 13, 1910, 1.

24. *Albuquerque Morning Journal,* September 13, 1910.

25. Larson, *New Mexico's Quest,* 273.

26. Morton Keller, *Affairs of State: Public Life in Late-Nineteenth Century America* (Cambridge, MA: Harvard University Press, 1977), 401.

27. Cline, *1910 Constitution,* 31–42.

28. Not reintroducing proposals: *Santa Fe New Mexican,* October 12, 1910, 10; also Cline, *1910 Constitution,* 45; no new proposals: *Santa Fe New Mexican,* October 14, 1910, 8; Cline, *1910 Constitution,* 45.

29. *Santa Fe New Mexican,* October 14, 1910, 8.

30. Gordon Morris Bakken, "The Arizona Constitutional Convention of 1910," *Arizona State Law Journal* 5, no. 1 (1978): 1–29; John Dinan, *The American State Constitutional Tradition* (Lawrence: University Press of Kansas, 2006). Dinan does not discuss New Mexico, Colorado, or Washington because their conventions did not hire stenographers, Table 1–2, 27.

31. Nathan A. Persily, "The Peculiar Geography of Direct Democracy: Why the

Initiative, Referendum, and Recall Developed in the American West," *Michigan Law and Public Policy Review* 2 (1997): 11–41.

32. John D. Leshy, "The Making of the Arizona Constitution," *Arizona State Law Journal* 20, no. 1 (1988): 32–33.

33. "Labor's Declaration of Independence," Labor Party of Arizona, 1910, George W. P. Hunt Papers, Arizona Room, Hayden Library, Arizona State University, Tempe (copy in author's possession); Goff, *Arizona Constitutional Convention*, 44.

34. *Albuquerque Morning Journal*, October 11, 1910, 4.

35. Washington: *Santa Fe New Mexican*, October 3, 1910, 4; Colorado: *Santa Fe New Mexican*, October 17, 1910, 4.

36. *Arizona Republican*, December 5, 1910, 2.

37. Goff, *Arizona Constitutional Convention*, 189–190.

38. Ibid., 193.

39. Ibid., 198.

40. Ibid., 198.

41. Ibid., 206.

42. Ibid., 747–748.

43. Ibid., 744.

44. End of debate on the initiative Cuniff and vote count see Goff, *Arizona Constitutional Convention*, 750–751.

45. Goff, *Arizona Constitutional Convention*, 805; Bakken, "Arizona Constitutional Convention," 3n7.

46. Goff, *Arizona Constitutional Convention*, 806–808.

47. *Arizona Gazette*, November 10, 1910, 1; see also "Recall Is Adopted by the Convention.... No Official Is Exempted," *Arizona Gazette*, December 1, 1910, 1; and "Storm Rages as Recall Passes for Last Time," *Arizona Gazette*, December 7, 1910, 1, 8. Taft was not the only politician in Washington who opposed recall. If Arizonans imagined Democrats in Congress would support them, the *Republic* recognized they were wrong. "It is a safe prophecy that not a single Democrat from the south can be found in either house ... who would approve the revolutionary proposal to make judges subject to 'the recall.'" *Arizona Gazette*, October 29, 1910, 2.

48. *Arizona Republican*, October 29, 1910, 2. US attorney general George Wickersham was in complete agreement with the editors of the *Arizona Republic*. As voters "do not and can not" pay sufficient attention to politics to understand them, "The propositions submitted to the electors under the scheme of the initiative and referendum are fixed and put before the voters without the advantage of the examination, discussion and debate which have been, throughout the whole history of English-speaking people, the crucible in which legislative projects have been tried out before enactment into law." And as only a small number of

signatures will be required to place propositions on the ballot, "under the guise of serving the people," proponents of direct democracy "are seeking to lay hands on the power of the people and to arrogate to themselves the popular tribunate." Delivered to the Yale University faculty of law and placed in the *Congressional Record*, 1911.

49. "Constitution Made Easy of Amendment Today," *Arizona Gazette*, November 26, 1910, 1.

50. "Direct Primary Is Cause of Discussion," *Arizona Gazette*, November 30, 1910, 1.

51. Larson, *New Mexico's Quest*, 281.

52. *Albuquerque Morning Journal*, October 27, 1910, 1.

53. *Albuquerque Morning Journal*, October 26, 1910. 1. These events also reported by Dorothy Cline in *1910 Constitution*, 41–48, esp. 41–42.

54. *Santa Fe New Mexican*, September 8, 1910, 1.

55. *Santa Fe New Mexican*, October 21, 1910, 1.

56. *Albuquerque Morning Journal*, October 16, 1910, 1.

57. The *Journal* often demeaned opponents of the old guard by calling them "so-called progressives." In this instance, the praise cited above was trimmed by this follow-up: "While the progressives might have forced the caucus to adopt the initiative as a republican measure [this claim is likely wrong, AB] they were so divided among themselves as to the kind of initiative they wanted that they despaired of ever reaching an agreement." *Albuquerque Morning Journal*, October 26, 1910, 1.

58. *Santa Fe New Mexican*, October 28, 1910, 1.

59. *Arizona Gazette*, October 18, 1910, 8.

60. Leshy, "Arizona Constitution," 62.

61. Goff, *Arizona Constitutional Convention*, 865.

62. Ibid., 872.

63. Lamar, *Far Southwest*, 434.

64. *Santa Fe New Mexican*, October 1, 1910, 1. A similar promise was repeated in art. XXI Compact with the United States, sec. 5. Here franchise rights were established without regard to race, color, or previous condition of servitude, but language was not mentioned.

65. Cline, *1910 Constitution*, 45–46.

66. *Santa Fe New Mexican*, October 20, 1910, 1.

67. *Santa Fe New Mexican*, November 2, 1910, 1.

68. Arizona also considered antimiscegenation provisions.

69. New Mexico Constitution, art. XII secs. 8 (teachers), 10 (equality of children); NBER/Maryland State Constitutions Project, New Mexico Constitution of January 1, 1911, http://www.stateconstitutions.umd.edu/Search/results.aspx?srch=1&state=percent27NMpercent27&CID=269&art=12&sec=8&amd=&key=&Yr=.

70. *Santa Fe New Mexican*, October 28, 1910, 5.

71. Goff, *Arizona Constitutional Convention*, 441.
72. Ibid., 441.
73. Ibid., 443.
74. Ibid., 441.
75. Ibid., 443.
76. Ibid., 441.
77. Ibid., 442.
78. Ibid., 444.
79. Ibid., 446.
80. Ibid., 447.
81. Ibid., 545.
82. Ibid., 1435.
83. Ellinwood—of all people—proposed, following the American Association for Labor Legislation, "legislation without regard to negligence, for the reason that neither scheme of employers' liability ... is economically sound, or ethically just." Goff, *Arizona Constitutional Convention*, 549.
84. Goff, *Arizona Constitutional Convention*, 881.
85. Ibid., 882.
86. Ibid., 883–884.
87. Ibid., 885.
88. New Mexico Constitution art. XVII, sec. 2.
89. *Santa Fe New Mexican*, November 12, 1910, 1.
90. *Albuquerque Morning Journal*, November 19, 1910, 1.
91. Virginia Constitution 1902 art. XII, sec. 162 (http://cofinder.richmond.ed/admin/docs/Virginia_192.pdf); South Carolina Constitution 1895 art. IX, sec. 15 (http://www.lcarolana.com/SC/Documents/SC/_Constitution_1895.-df); Mississippi Constitution 1890 art. VII, sec. 193 (http://www.mdhistorynow.mdah.state.ms.us/artiles/103/index.php?s=extra&id=270). In each case the article specified that the rights of railroad employees were to be the same as the rights of non-employees. Wyoming, *Journal ... Wyoming*, Constitution 48.
92. Oklahoma set the precedent in its 1906 constitution. That remarkably long document contained several provisions for monitoring corporations and protecting workers.
93. *Albuquerque Morning Journal*, November 13, 1910, 2.
94. Goff, *Arizona Constitutional Convention*, 611.
95. Ibid., 1390 (Ellinwood's occupation); 613 (the proposal).
96. Ibid., 614.
97. Lynch was a most conservative Democrat and a lawyer. Ibid., 1993; 614 (his remarks).
98. Ibid., 613.
99. Ibid., 614.

100. *Arizona Gazette*, November 24, 1910, 1.
101. Goff, *Arizona Constitutional Convention*, 972.
102. Ibid., 1429.
103. Research under way by Jonathan Chausovsky promises to shed light on these questions.
104. Colin B. Goodykoontz, ed., *Papers of Edward P. Costigan Relating to the Progressive Movement in Colorado 1902–1917* (Boulder: University of Colorado, 1941), 308–317, esp. 316–317.
105. That said, politics in the ensuing years did not simply proceed from whatever consensus existed at the conventions; many who objected unsuccessfully to one provision or another were, if weak at the convention, sometimes powerful in state society and politics. As explained in chapter 1, constitutions may create rules and institutions for the resolution of conflict, but they do not preclude and sometimes provoke conflict. More, disagreement may occur on the shop floor or in the streets, outside of regular political channels.
106. Sharon Faye Kearney, "Arizona Legislature 1912–1914: A Study of State Progressivism" (MA thesis, California State University, Fullerton, 1977), 41. For a broader scope, see David R. Berman, *Politics, Labor, and the War on Big Business: The Path of Reform in Arizona, 1890–1920* (Boulder: University Press of Colorado, 2012).
107. The twelve states were Alabama, Arkansas, Connecticut, Louisiana, Massachusetts, Michigan, Nebraska, New Hampshire, New York, Ohio, Oklahoma, and Virginia. In four states there was no change. Louisiana adopted an unsatisfactory constitution that differed little from its 1898 predecessor; proposals at the New York convention were strongly opposed by one interest or another, so no constitutional change resulted; the proposed constitution for Arkansas was rejected by the voters; the New Hampshire convention adjourned without making recommendations because the United States was engaged in World War I, and dissatisfaction with the state constitution seemed unimportant. Another two, Virginia and Alabama, focused on disfranchisement.
108. Addison E. Sheldon, "The Nebraska Constitutional Convention 1919–1920," *American Political Science Review* 15 (1921): 391–400, 394–395; A. B. Winter, "Constitutional Revision in Nebraska: A Brief History and Commentary," *Nebraska Law Review* 40 (1961): 480–595, 588–589.
109. John D. Buenker, *Urban Liberalism and Progressive Reform* (New York: Charles Scribner's Sons 1973); in Ohio, Constitutional Convention 149–150, direct democracy 140–141.
110. Keith L. Bryant, "Labor in Politics: The Oklahoma State Federation of Labor during the Age of Reform," *Labor History* 11, no. 3 (1970): 259–276; H. L. Meredith, "The 'Middle Way': The Farmers' Alliance in Indian Territory, 1889–1896," *Chronicles of Oklahoma* 42, no. 4 (1969): 377–387.

111. Charles Beard, "The Constitution of Oklahoma," *Political Science Quarterly* 24 (1909): 104, 105.

112. James R. Scales and Danney Goble, *Oklahoma Politics: A History* (Norman: University of Oklahoma Press, 1982), 41–44.

113. Persily, "Peculiar Geography."

114. In my own investigations, I found that in every western state that adopted the initiative, there were connections between labor activists and populist voters on one hand, and direct democracy on the other, in rhetoric, voting, leadership, or all three. There have also been quantitative inquiries about the national pattern of adoption of direct democracy. Shaun Bowler, Todd Donovan, and Caroline J. Tolbert, *Citizens as Legislators: Direct Democracy in the United States* (Columbus: Ohio State University Press, 1998); Shaun Bowler, Todd Donovan, and Eric D. Lawrence, "Choosing Direct Democracy: On the Creation of Initiative Institutions in the American States" (paper presented at the annual meeting of the American Political Science Association, Washington, DC, September 2005); Shaun Bowler and Todd Donovan, "Direct Democracy and Political Parties in America," *Party Politics* 12 (2006): 649–669. Donovan and colleagues found a strong relation between the adoption of direct democracy and votes for the People's Party and radical third parties. Later work by Donovan and colleagues, as well as work by Smith and Fridkin, called attention to party strength and party competition. This makes sense, since passage of direct democracy requires both popular support and the support of elected politicians. Daniel A. Smith and Dustin Fridkin, "Delegating Direct Democracy: Interparty Legislative Competition and the Adoption of the Initiative in the American States," *American Political Science Review* 102 (1999): 333–350.

115. Amy Bridges and Thaddeus Kousser, "Where Politicians Gave Power to the People: Adoption of the Citizen Initiative in the US States," *State Politics and Policy Quarterly* 11, no. 2 (2008): 167–197.

116. Ibid., 173. Evidence about agreement between Governor West and Oregon voters contradicts the account provided in Daniel A. Smith and Joseph Lubinsky, "Direct Democracy during the Progressive Era: A Crack in the Populist Veneer?," *Journal of Policy History* 14 (2002): 349–383.

117. Alexander Keyssar, *The Right to Vote: The Contested History of Democracy in the United States* (New York: Basic Books, 2000), table A20. Many states enfranchised women to vote in school elections; Texas and Arkansas enfranchised women to vote in primary elections, the only elections that mattered in those one-party states. Ibid., tables A17, A19.

118. For a summary of the campaign for, and enactment of the Oregon System see Amy Bridges and Thad Kousser, "Where Politicians Gave Power to the People," *State Politics and Policy Quarterly* 11 no. 2 (San Diego, CA: University of California): 167–197, 173.

119. Keyssar, *Right to Vote*, table A13.

120. Ibid., table A10.

121. Bureau of Labor Statistics, *Labor Laws of the United States, with Decisions of Courts Relating Thereto,* Bulletin No. 148, pts. 1 and 2 (Washington, DC: Government Printing Office, 1914).

122. The five states were Massachusetts, Minnesota, New Jersey, Pennsylvania, and Tennessee. Ibid., 79.

5. Creating the Western States

1. California wrote a new constitution in 1878, and Montana in 1972.

2. Michael Kammen, *A Machine That Would Go of Itself: The Constitution in American Culture* (New York: Vintage, 1986).

3. In these conversations the bullies—Bursum in New Mexico and Burritt in Wyoming—were outliers. Both men were successful at fending off provisions they found objectionable and securing their preferences in constitutional text.

4. *Journal of the Constitutional Convention, State of Wyoming* (Cheyenne, WY: Daily Sun, Book and Job Printing, 1893), 403.

5. John S. Goff, *The Records of the Arizona Constitutional Convention of 1910* (Phoenix: Supreme Court of Arizona, 1991), 1390 (Feeney); 1388 (Connelly); 1387 (Bolan); 1389 (Cunniff) (hereafter cited as Goff, *Arizona Constitutional Convention*).

6. Fergusson was not always ineffective. In 1896, running against a powerful Republican candidate, Fergusson triumphed. As the territory's delegate to the House, Fergusson won support for a bill giving the territory two sections of land for schools. Dorothy I. Cline, *New Mexico's 1910 Constitution: A 19th Century Product* (Santa Fe, NM: Lightning Tree, 1985), 38. Daugherty gave a long speech about a funeral for a child, the child meant to be the initiative. *Albuquerque Morning Journal*, October 29, 1910.

7. George H. Miller, *Railroads and the Granger Laws* (Madison: University of Wisconsin Press, 1971), 42–58.

8. *Debates and Proceedings of the Constitutional Convention of the State of California, Convened at the City of Sacramento, Saturday, September 18, 1878* (Sacramento, CA: State Printing Office, 1880), 1:488 (hereafter cited as *Debates and Proceedings . . . California*).

9. Goff, *Arizona Constitutional Convention*, 189–190.

10. John D. Leshy, "The Making of the Arizona Constitution," *Arizona State Law Journal* 20, no. 1 (1988): 44.

11. Vladimir Kogan and Michael Binder, "Parties without Brands? Evidence from California's 1878–79 Constitutional Convention," SSRN, November 3, 2014.

12. Andrew J. Marsh, *Official Report of the Debates and Proceedings in the Constitutional Convention of the State of Nevada: Assembled at Carson City, July*

4, 1864, to Form a Constitution and State Government (San Francisco: Eastman, 1866), 388–90.

13. For California and Oregon this was not enough. California added double liability for stockholders to its constitution; later, other states enacted double liability for stockholders of banks.

14. J. Ross Browne, *Report of the Debates of the Convention of California, on the Formation of the State Constitution, in September and October, 1849* (Washington, DC: John T. Towers, 1850), 116.

15. Ibid., 113.

16. Article X, Sec. 2, *Journal of the Constitutional Convention, State of Wyoming* (Cheyenne, WY: Daily Sun, Book and Job Printing, 1893), Constitution, 37.

17. *Proceedings and Debates of the Constitutional Convention Held in the City of Helena, Montana, July 4 to August 17, 1889* (Helena, MT: State Publishing Company, 1892), 292, 300.

18. *Debates and Proceedings . . . California*, 2:1021.

19. F. J. Stimson, *Handbook to the Labor Law of the United States* (New York: Scribner's, 1907), 164. Research for the book was conducted in 1896.

20. Ibid., 166.

21. Ibid., 148.

22. New Mexico adopted only the referendum; Wyoming did not adopt direct democracy until 1968.

23. "Labor's Declaration of Independence," Labor Party of Arizona, 1910, George W. P. Hunt Papers, Arizona Room, Hayden Library, Arizona State University.

24. George H. Haynes, *The Election of Senators* (New York: Henry Holt, 1906).

25. Jay S. Bybee, "Ulysses at the Mast: Democracy, Federalism, and the Sirens' Song of the Seventeenth Amendment," *Northwestern University Law Review* 91 (1997): 500–572; 538–544 (on corruption and deadlock). It is ironic that the very system that brought the American colonial citizens to appreciate the power of elections—they hated the governors, who were appointed by the king, but loved their legislatures, which they elected—brought US citizens not only to resent their appointed governors but eventually also to hold their legislatures in contempt.

26. Todd J. Zywicki, "Beyond the Shell and Husk of History: The History of the Seventeenth Amendment and Its Implications for Current Reform Proposals," *Cleveland State Law Review* 25 (1997): 165.

27. Frederic Austin Ogg, *National Progress, 1907–1918* (New York: Harper and Brothers, 1918), 150.

28. Erik J. Engstrom and Samuel Kernell, "The Effects of Presidential Elections on Party Control of the Senate under Indirect and Direct Elections" (paper presented at the History of Congress Conference, University of California, San Diego, December 5–6, 2003).

29. Leslie Wheeler, "Woman Suffrage's Gray-Bearded Champion Comes to Montana, 1889," *Montana Magazine* 31, no. 3 (1981): 2–13.

30. Many states enfranchised women to vote in school elections; Texas and Arkansas enfranchised women to vote in primary elections, the only elections that mattered in those one-party states. Alexander Keyssar, *The Right to Vote: The Contested History of Democracy in the United States* (New York: Basic Books, 2000), tables A17, A19; table A20 (full enfranchisement). See also Ogg, *National Progress*, 152.

31. Keyssar, *Right to Vote*, table 20.

32. Dewey W. Grantham, *Southern Progressivism: The Reconciliation of Progress and Tradition* (Knoxville: University of Tennessee Press, 1983), xvii.

Index

Activism, 67
   anti-Chinese, 96
   farmer, 99
   labor, 14, 29, 186n114
Address to the People, viii–ix, 2, 81
African Americans, 7, 10, 70
   citizenship and, 155
   migration of, 43, 44, 165n60
   suffrage and, 44
   support for, 165n65
   See also People of color
Agriculture, 49, 89, 163n36, 168n115
   fostering, 61
   investment in, 37
   production of, 36
Albuquerque Morning Journal, 108, 109, 111, 125
   on direct democracy, 117
   progressives and, 183n57
   on Republicans/constitution, 117
Amendments, 8, 25, 89, 109, 116, 119, 130, 134
American Association for Labor Legislation, 184n83
Anaconda Silver Mining, 64
Antebellum generations, 19, 20, 26, 144, 145
   constitutions of, 22–23
   political thoughts of, 29–31
Aragon, J. J., 120
Arbitration of labor disputes, 97, 124
Arizona Constitution (1910), 105, 110
   corporations and, 111
   direct democracy and, 115
   fellow servant doctrine and, 151–152
   recall and, 116
   writing, 144

Arizona constitutional convention of 1910
   corporations and, 13, 29, 52, 103, 124–129
   delegates, 12 (table), 113, 115, 116, 118, 120–121, 149
   democratizing reform, 113
   direct democracy at, 114
   duration of, 12 (table), 113
   leaders, 114, 116
   key role of party, 103, 105, 112, 120, 130–131, 149, 180n7
   protections for labor, 120–122
Arizona Gazette, 108, 109, 111, 118
   corporate control and, 127
   recall and, 116
Arizona Republic, 182n48
   direct democracy and, 113
   recall and, 116
Arizona Republican, 108, 109, 111
Arizona Supreme Court, 106
Arkansas General Assembly, 179n153
Assumption of risk, 92, 93, 120, 123, 124, 148, 152
Astor, J. J., 32

Baker, A. C., 123
Bakken, Gordon Morris, 173n39
Banks, 45–55, 146, 148
   creation of, 30, 46
   hostility toward, 30, 31, 47
   limited liability corporations and, 145
   taxing, 55
Barela, Casimiro, 70
Baum, Marsha, on borrowing, 14
Baxter, George, 93, 177n124
Beard, Charles, 132
Bensel, Richard, 6, 21

192 Index

Biggs, Marion, 85
Bill of Rights, 23, 60, 124
Binder, Michael, 144
Blackfeet, violence by, 162n24
Blacklists, 88, 92, 105, 112, 148, 180n5
Blackwell, Henry, 154
Board of Control, 78, 79
Board of Health and Vital Statistics, 180n5
Bolan, John, 122, 141
Boosterism, 19, 169n1
Borrowing, 14–15, 19–20, 142
    Colorado, 71, 74, 76, 92, 93
    Oregon, 113, 114, 133–134
    from other western states, 142–143
    See also Colorado; Oregon
Botts, Charles, 41, 43, 161n10
    on banks, 47
    commercial republic and, 163–164n46
    currency and, 30–31
    suffrage and, 40
Breen, Peter, 14, 69, 98
Bromwell, Henry, 14, 68, 73, 74
    on Colorado constitutional convention, 10
    history of Republican leadership, 68
    and Irrigation Committee, 73, 74
    leader of Granger faction at Colorado convention, 14, 68
    prior convention experience, 14
    railroads and, 83
    water and, 79
    women's suffrage and, 159n29
Brosnan, Cornelius, 54, 55, 168n114
Brown, Joseph, 75, 174n59
Browne, J. Ross, on Virginia City, 36–37
Bryan, William Jennings, 107, 132
Bryce, Lord Charles, 11, 158n25
Buchanan, James, Young and, 161n12
Bureaus of labor, 101
Burritt, Charles, 69, 78, 187n3
Bursum, Holm Olaf, 107, 118, 124, 180n11, 187n3
Butte, 64, 98
    strikes in, 64

California Bill of Rights, 163n45, 164n60
California Constitution (1850), 110, 167n108, 187n1
    banks and, 28
    bill of rights, 60
    California territory, 27–28
    Californios and, 22, 33, 43
    corporations and, 28
    development of, 32
    limited liability and, 56
    railroads and, 83
    suffrage in, 42
    water rights and, 80
    writing, 59, 66, 147
California constitutional convention of 1849, 11, 17, 23–24, 27, 164n54, 167n110
    banks and, 45–46, 48, 146
    corporations and, 31, 46, 48, 50, 56, 76, 80, 84–85, 148
    delegates, 12 (table), 165n71
    duration of, 12 (table)
    key issues of, 4–5, 22, 56
    leaders, 30–31, 34, 39, 40
    legacy of, 31–32, 35, 144
    North-South antagonism at, 13, 41
    rules for, 144
    suffrage and, 29, 40, 42
    water and, 15, 74, 76
California constitutional convention of 1878
    California Supreme Court, Hale and, 173n48
    delegates, 12 (table), 68
    duration of, 12 (table)
    key issues of, 17, 79–80, 92, 110, 146, 147–148
    leaders, 68, 100
    railroads and, 83–85, 141–142
    "shall not" sections of, 16
    tenor of, 96
    water law, 66, 72–73, 75, 76–77
Campbell, Anthony, 93, 177n122
Capital, 47, 87, 167n103
Carey, Charles, 35–36, 68
Catron, Thomas, 107, 117

Cattlemen, dominance of, 65–66, 79
Central Pacific Railroad, 31, 50, 51, 142
Chamberlain, George, 153
Chausovsky, Jonathan, 179n155, 195n103
Cheyenne City Council, 177n123
Cheyenne Daily Leader, 79
Cheyenne Weekly Leader, 169n1
Child labor, 92, 95, 104, 121, 122
Child labor laws, 121, 132, 149
Chinese, 70
    citizenship and, 97, 155
    growth of, 96
    hostility toward (*see* California constitutional convention [1878])
    labor, 92, 96–97
    migration of, 43
    political attention to, 14
    population of, 66
Chollar mine, 55
Civil War, 20, 21, 29, 31, 41, 44, 124, 139, 177n125, 179n155
    railroads and, 82
Clagett, William, 86, 94–95, 149, 176n106
Clark, William Andrews, 63–64
Clark, William M., viii–ix, 4
Cleveland, Grover, 177n122
Cline, Dorothy I., 111, 119, 180n10
Cobb, Lamar, on Republican Party/government control, 115–116
Coeur d'Alene, 64, 69, 98, 171n16
    gold at, 61, 62, 63
    mining war in, 64, 69
Collins, John A., 52, 54
Colorado
    Bureau of Labor Statistics, 170n11
    economic development of, 61, 63
Colorado Constitution (1876), viii, 74, 110
    bill of rights, 60
    commissioner of mines and, 94
    railroads and, 83–84
    water and, 74, 77
    writing, 6, 59
Colorado constitutional convention of 1876
    Address to the People, viii–ix, 2
    corporations and, 70, 73, 77, 92
    delegates, 67, 68
    duration of, vii, 12 (table)
    Granger faction at, 14
    labor, 88, 92, 97, 98
    leaders, 68
    mining and, 62, 63, 92, 105
    railroads and other corporations, 69, 81–83, 86, 129
    tenor of, 23, 141
    water, 66, 70–74, 76, 141
Colorado General Assembly, ix
Colorado Supreme Court, eight-hour law and, 159n32
Common carriers, 86, 126
Common Carriers Liability Law, 123
Common law, 72, 122, 124, 135, 140
    change of, 22, 77
    defenses, 110
    rule of, 93
    tradition, 17–18
Common right of water, practice of, 77
Compensation, 92
    for an injury at work, 89, 110, 125, 130
    workmen's, 123, 125, 130, 131, 134
Comstock Lode, 27, 36, 37, 142, 145
    demise of, 57
    discovery of, 32, 38
Confederacy, 45, 155, 163n32
Confederate veterans, 29
    suffrage and, 41, 42, 44
Connelly, Patrick, 122, 141
Constitutional conventions, 4, 5, 12 (table), 22, 25, 26, 28 (table), 38–41, 45–46, 55–56, 66, 68, 79, 101, 138–144
    constitutions and, 8–11, 13–18, 155–156
    debates at, 10, 13, 18, 104, 129, 138, 139–140
    delegate character, 12 (table)
    deliberations at, 13, 19–20, 31, 36, 111, 120–121, 143–144
    demography/economy and, 104
    double liability, 48, 56, 146, 166n82
    election to, 28
    institutional characteristics of, 9, 156

Constitutional conventions *(continued)*
   labor and, 92, 150, 151
   leadership at, 11
   mission of, 1–2
   newspaper coverage of, 18–19, 29, 168n1
   politics and, 67, 104
   proceedings of, 59, 140, 157n1
   representation at, 144, 149
   state government and, 60
   statehood and, 59
   taxation and, 52
   territories and, 104–112
   voting provisions and, 41–42
Constitutionalism, 9, 16, 92
Constitutions (state)
   constitutional conventions and, 8–11, 13–18, 155–156
   corporations and, 146
   defeat of, 139
   democratizing reform, 25, 103, 104, 109–110, 113–118, 131, 133, 149, 151
   development of, 4, 6
   distinctive provisions protections for labor, 89, 150
   as enabling documents, 17
   as fundamental law, 1
   generative capacity of, 16
   institutional/legal settings and, 22
   legislation in, 8, 15, 16, 143
   politics and, 5
   region and, 20
   revision of law of master and servant, 24–25, 93, 104, 120–124, 129
   studying, 18–22
   time and, 3
   understanding, 18
   voting on, 9, 10
   writing, 3, 11, 30, 39, 59, 61, 135, 138, 142, 156, 158n25
Contracts
   ironclad, 92, 94, 110, 120, 178n128
   making, 89
Contributory negligence, 110, 120, 123, 124, 149, 152
   employee, 123
   questions of, 123
Copper, 62, 63, 64
Copper Queen mine, 105, 106, 140
Corporate behavior, 125, 129, 143
Corporate law, writing, 24
Corporate regulation, 24, 25, 59, 70, 87, 103, 104, 111, 127, 129, 132, 137, 143
Corporate taxes, 13, 22, 52, 145
Corporation commissions, 1, 118, 129
   creation of, 125, 126
   debate about, 128
   scope/power of, 127, 128
Corporations, 10, 45–55, 81–88, 124–129
   accommodating, 146
   associations and, 56
   bankrupt, 149
   creating, 46, 48, 125, 142, 144
   economic stakes and, 82
   general laws and, 45
   hostility toward/wariness of, 31, 71, 76
   influence of, 126
   issues with, 30, 81
   material assistance to, 125
   monopolizing tendencies of, 81
   need for, 48–49
   obligations of, 146
   organization by, 46–47
   police power and, 88, 98, 147
   power/franchises of, 88
   railroad, 82, 86
   special laws and, 29–30
   support of, 111
   views on, 23, 128, 147
Corruption, 46, 133
   concerns about, 30, 154
   democracy and, 172–173n36
   legislative, 15, 16, 66
   political, 29–30
Costigan, Edward, 129
Criminal justice, 60, 157n10
Cross, C. W., 75, 174n58
Crutchfield, James E., 126
Cunniff, Michael, 105, 116, 141
   bio, 105–106

on corporate control and, 127
on law of master and servant, 123–124
Currency, 39, 46
   federal, 48, 166n79
   issues with, 30–31, 48
   paper, 45, 47, 48, 166nn79–80

Daugherty, Harry, 107, 141
Deady, Matthew, 3, 49, 50, 56–57, 140
Debt, 145, 160n44
   constitutional limits on government, 83
   imprisonment for personal, 161n9
   state, 16
De la Guerra y Noriega, Jose Antonio, 42, 164n57
Delegates to constitutional conventions, 1, 2, 3, 56
   concerns of, 19, 139
   corrective measures by, 4
   debates among, 5–6, 13, 38–39, 158n15
   deliberations by, 5–6, 8, 11–12, 19, 21–22, 23, 52
   democratic republican government and, 156
   election of, 9, 67–68
   federal legislation and, 143
   industrious/pragmatic, 138
   labor-management conflict and, 97
   partisan tendencies and, 9
   policies/institutions and, 26
   precedent and, 14
   state government and, 21, 60
   strategies/tactics/precedents and, 140
   superiority of, 10
   work of, 11, 25–26, 72, 126–127, 137, 138
DeLong, Charles, 50–51, 55, 140
Democracy, 40, 137
   corruption and, 172–173n36
   defined, 114–115
   embracing, 133, 155
   Herrenvolk, 155
   labor and, 150
   less, 134–135
   more, 117, 129, 131, 134, 142, 150, 152–155

Democratic Party, 85, 103, 105, 107, 112, 140
   labor and, 124
   pro-slavery faction of, 36
Democratic republic, 2, 4, 8, 138
Democratizing reform, 25, 103, 104, 109, 113–120, 131, 149, 151, 153
Denver Daily Tribune, 169n1, 174n50
Departments of agriculture, 1
Departments of labor, 1, 60
Dimmick, Kimball Edward, 44, 165n64
Dinan, John, 2, 3
Direct democracy, 103, 107, 117, 119, 129, 135, 149
   adoption of, 118, 131, 133, 144, 150, 153, 186n114
   constitutional provisions for, 24
   creating, 134
   criticism of, 114–115
   deliberations about, 5
   malapportionment and, 153
   opposition to, 113, 114, 115, 117
   peculiar geography of, 113
   support for, 113, 114, 115, 118, 133, 134, 144, 153, 183n48
Disfranchisement, 45, 155, 185n107
Double liability provisions, 48, 56, 146, 166n82
Dudley, William, 85, 176n102

École des Mines, 170n7
Economic change, 19, 132
Economic depressions, 7, 66
Economic growth, 61, 127, 147
Education, 1, 5, 17, 70, 150, 174n55
Eight-hour laws, 88, 89, 95, 100, 105, 132, 134, 149, 159n32
Einhorn, Robin, 167n105
Electoral College, 14, 41, 157n4
Ellinwood, E. E., 105, 106, 123, 126, 127, 128, 184n83
   on corporation commissions, 128
   on recall, 116
Eminent domain, 72, 76, 78, 87, 147, 176n114
Emma Mine, 64, 171n15
Emmons, Samuel, 170n7

Employer liability, 67, 110, 122, 123, 134, 135
Enabling acts, ix, 13
Estee, Morris, 84, 85, 175n95
Express companies, charges by, 126

Fall, Albert, 118, 126
Family law, 7
  migration to, 33, 162n17
Farmers, 82, 144
  capital of, 49
  delegates/bullying of, 10
  irrigation and, 79
  labor and, 131
  mobilization of, 13
Farmers' Alliance, 66, 71–72, 131, 146
  appearance of, 23
  direct democracy and, 134
Farmers' Union, 131, 132
Farming, 62, 141
Far West, 27, 41, 56, 57
Federal Deposit Insurance Corporation, 166n82
Feeney, Thomas, 105, 121, 122, 140–141
Fellow servant doctrine, 5, 92, 110, 120, 123, 125, 149, 177n126
  abrogation of, 88, 129–130, 131, 142, 151
  labor and, 151–152
  railroads and, 131, 151
Ferguson, Judson, 178n131
Fergusson, Harvey, 141, 187n6
Fergusson, Henry, 107, 118
Field, William T., 97, 107, 118, 178n147
Fitch, Thomas, Jr., 44–45, 50, 53, 167n93, 167n106
Founders, 1–2, 3, 116
Fourteenth Amendment, Oregon and, 163n32
Frank, Andre Gunder, on underdevelopment, 160n47
Fremont, John Charles, 14, 68
Fritz, Christian, on borrowing, 14

Garcia, Jesus Maria, 70
Gates, Charles, on delegates/corrective measures, 4

George, Henry, 35
Gilded Age, 16, 19, 72, 101, 104, 110, 111, 132, 148
  agendas of, 137
  bills of rights and, 60
  constitutions of, 23, 25, 31, 71, 104, 135, 150
  dilemmas of, 99–100
  labor protection and, 88
  politics of, 21
  positive rights and, 18, 60
  Progressive Era and, 24
Gold, 61, 62, 63
Gold rush, 22, 37, 56, 66
  impact of, 32, 34
  Oregon Territory and, 35–36
Gold standard, dominance of, 146
Gould & Curry, 54
Grand juries, 1
Grange faction, 14, 68, 82, 99, 134
Grantham, Dewey, democracy/South and, 155
Gwin, William, 40, 47–48, 146

Hacendados, 33
Hale, James, 73, 84, 148, 173–174n48
  water conflicts and, 77
Hall, Kermit, on state constitutions, 16
Hampton, on eight-hour law, 95
Hawley, Albert, 51, 53
Hayes, Rutherford B., 68
Haynes, George, 153
Headless ballot, 70
Health care, 17, 89
Helena Daily Herald, 81, 169n1
Hensel, Donald, 82, 175n87
Herrenvolk democracy, 155
Herrington, Dennis, 75–76, 174n55
Herron, Paul, 160n46
Hicks, John, 10–11, 16
Hill, Nathan, 62, 170n7
Homestead Act, 27
Homestead exemption, 132
Howard, Volney, 68, 75, 84
Hoyt, John W., 68, 87

Hudson's Bay Co., 32
Hunt, George W. P., 11, 105, 106, 180n6
 railroads and, 125
 territorial legislator proposal, 180n5

Idaho Bill of Rights, 60
Idaho Constitution (1889), 64, 110
 bill of rights and, 60
 railroads and, 86
Idaho constitutional convention of 1889, 11, 92
 corporations and, 77, 149
 delegates, 10–11, 12 (table), 13, 67
 duration of, 12 (table)
 and key issues, 5, 14, 61, 66, 88, 172n28
 leaders, 86, 149
 and mining, 63, 92, 94, 105
 tenor of, 23
 and water, 72, 76, 78
Idaho Weekly Statesman, 10, 11, 169n1
Illinois Constitution, 14, 82
Immigration to the West, 7, 33, 34, 36, 61, 89, 98
 African Americans and, 165n60
 large-scale, 146
Indiana Bill of Rights, 2, 40, 157n4
Industrial commissions, 128, 129
Industrial economy, 36, 144, 145
Industrial relations, 14, 17
Industry, 38
 growth of, 146
 issues with, 28–29
Initiative, 105, 113, 115, 117, 119, 129, 153, 163n36
 adoption of, 133
 opposition to, 114
 support for, 114, 116, 118
 using, 134
Injuries
 compensation for, 89, 110, 125, 130
 fatal, 135
 liability for, 92, 93
 personal, 92
Institutions, 1, 26, 60, 156
 management, 100
 political, 57
 social, 39
Interstate Commerce Commission (ICC), 20, 86, 143
Ironclad contracts, 110, 120
 banning, 92, 94, 178n128
Iron foundries, growth of, 163n40
Irrigation, 59, 65, 66, 72, 80–81, 148
 cattlemen and, 79
 ditches for, 76
 farmers and, 79
 preventing, 77
 settlement and, 71
 systems of, 74, 78, 81
Irrigation committee, 73, 78

Jackson, Andrew, 29, 30, 32, 53
Jacksonian evenhandedness, 16, 46, 55, 56, 57, 89, 144
Jacksonian principles, 46, 52–53, 56, 57, 99
Johnson, David Alan, 22, 161n10, 163n27, 165n71, 165n114, 167–168nn110–111
 Botts and, 164n46
 California boundary debates and, 164n50
 Gilbert and, 164n56
 on political inheritance, 28
 on state constitution, 167n108
 vote tracking by, 140
Johnson, Grove Lawrence, 163n44
Johnson, Hiram, 163n44
Johnson, J. Neely, 39, 160n44
Johnson, Paul, 46, 49, 53, 55, 165n71
Jones, James McHall, on associations, 46
Judicial federalism, 60
Juries, size of, 157n10

Kammen, Michael, 2
Kanazawa, Mark T., 175n87
Kaye, Judith, on common law tradition, 17–18
Kearny, Denis, protest from, 76
King, J. F., on time/constitutions, 3
Kingan, Samuel, 106, 114, 115
Kleppner, Paul, 108

Knights of Labor, 69, 134
Kogan, Vladimir, 144
Kousser, Thad, initiative and, 133

Labor, 34, 47, 89, 105, 144, 145
    agenda of, 104, 120–121, 122, 129–130, 131
    competition and, 96
    contracts and, 94
    controlling, 124
    conversations about, 138–139
    democracy and, 150
    Democratic Party and, 124
    farmers and, 131
    fellow servant doctrine and, 151–152
    hours of, 92, 99
    management and, 13, 24, 59, 88, 97, 100, 110, 111, 128, 146, 148, 171n6
    prison, 92, 96
    protection for, 23, 25, 70, 88–89, 90–91 (table), 92–101, 110, 121, 124, 129, 132, 135, 137, 140, 141, 148, 149, 151, 159–160n43
    safety of, 143, 151
Labor law, 101, 104, 150
Labor Party, 105, 113, 153, 180n6
Land grants, 33, 83
Lane, Joseph, popularity of, 36
Law of master and servant, 24, 93, 103, 104, 120–124, 148, 151–152
    issues about, 25, 110
    modification of, 129
    See also Assumption of risk; Contributory negligence; Fellow servant doctrine
Lead, 62, 63
Leadville, 63, 69
Legislation in constitutions, 7, 15, 16, 143
    class, 89, 98
    federal, 143
    special, 46, 119, 120
Legislatures (state and territorial), 68, 87
    apportionment of, 69
    contempt for, 154
    corruption of, 15, 16
    labor and, 125
    railroads and, 125
    regard for, 11, 154
    territorial, 9, 11, 16, 74, 77
Leshy, John, 118, 144
Lewis and Clark, 33, 162n17
Liability, 93
    employer, 67, 110, 122, 123, 134, 135
    limited, 30, 49, 135
    stockholder, 87, 106, 126, 128, 166n82
Limited liability corporations, 5, 22, 28
    abolition of, 87
    banks and, 145
    concerns about, 29–30, 48, 50, 56, 57
    hostility toward, 111
    mining and, 37
Lincoln, Abraham, 14, 36, 41, 115–116, 139
Literacy tests, 129, 134, 135, 155
    abolition of, 105, 150
    proposals for, 118–119
Lockwood, A. J., 168n116
    on capital/patriotism, 167n103
    mine taxation and, 52
Locomotive engineers, direct democracy and, 113
Los Angeles, 74
    railroads and, 84
Ludlow, 63
Lynch, A. R., 127, 128, 184n97

Madison, James, 139
Malapportionment, 133, 153
Management
    institutions/creation of, 100
    labor and, 13, 24, 59, 88, 97, 100, 110, 111, 128, 146, 148, 171n6
    water, 72, 73, 79, 80
Manufacturing, 79, 148
McGinnis, Tru Anthony, Labor Party and, 180n6
Mead, Elwood, 78
Mexican Americans, 7, 10, 70
    New Mexico Constitution and, 107, 118, 119–120

political attention to, 14
Republican Party and, 24, 103, 107, 120, 150
rights of, 104, 107
settlement by, 73, 106
voting and, 42
Mexican War, impact of, 34
Meyer, Elbert, on Colorado Constitution, 6
Migration, 35
banning, 43, 44
Militias, outlawing private, 98, 100
Miller, George, 141, 175n87
Mine commissioners, 101
Mine inspectors, 1, 60, 124, 149
Mine owners, 38, 54
Miners, 9
mine owners and, 38
protection of, 124, 149
wages for, 37
Miners' Protective Association, founding of, 37
Miners' Union, work of, 37–38
Minimum wages, setting, 99
Mining, 4, 6, 36, 64, 79, 106, 148, 170n7
beginning of, 63
conflict in, 5
dominance by, 14
farming and, 141
growth of, 31–32, 35, 55, 86, 170n11
investment in, 38
labor-management conflict in, 88
limited liability corporations and, 37
placer, 22, 34
practices of, 62
railroads and, 51, 83, 86
regulation for, 94, 101
successful, 61
taxation of, 52, 53–54, 55, 57
tax exemptions for, 53
underground, 94
unions, 37–38, 113, 170n11
wages in, 37
water and, 73, 74, 76
wealth from, 53–54

women and, 95–96
Mining industry, 23, 53, 55, 61, 63, 82, 105, 146, 168n115
characteristics of, 64
growth of, 62, 66–67
health of, 55
influence of, 32, 52, 65
taxes and, 52, 54
water rights and, 72–73, 141
Missionaries, 35, 161n13, 162n24
Mississippi Constitution, 177n126, 179n153, 184n91
fellow servant doctrine and, 142
Mississippi legislature, 68
Modern World-System, The (Wallerstein), 21
Moeur, B. B., 121
Moffett, S. E., on railroad corporations, 86
Montana Constitution (1889), 86, 110, 187n1
writing, 11, 59, 110
Montana constitutional convention of 1889, 13, 64
corporations and, 52, 65, 71, 80
delegates, 12 (table), 71, 80, 92, 97
duration of, 12 (table)
election to, 67
key issues of, 5, 13, 65–66, 71, 76, 86
leaders, 11, 14, 67, 69
mining and, 52, 61, 63–64, 92
tenor of, 23
women's suffrage and, 154, 155
Montana Stockgrowers' Association, 65
Montejano, David, 32
Moore, Ely, on government systems, 29
Moral choices, 29, 70
Morgan, John, 86
Mormons, 32, 164n50
Morriss, Andrew, 79, 169n2
Mortgages, taxes on, 66
"Mostly Anchor and Little Sail" (Hall), 16
Munn v. Illinois (1877), 20, 84, 86, 143
Murdock, Nelson, 54, 55

Native Americans, 7, 10, 27, 43
citizenship and, 155

Native Americans *(continued)*
  political attention to, 14
  population, 34
  relations with, 161n13
  Spanish settlement and, 33
  suffrage and, 44, 164n58
Nativists, 29
Neuborne, Burt, 17, 18
Nevada Constitution (1864), 55
Nevada constitutional convention of 1864, 27, 38, 40
  banks and, 45–46
  Confederate soldiers and, 42, 44
  corporations and, 31, 37, 45–46, 50, 52, 55
  delegates, 12 (table), 31, 39, 40, 44, 50, 52, 55, 142
  duration of, 12 (table)
  and fellow servant doctrine, 152
  key issues of, 22, 28–29, 37, 41
  leaders, 40
  and mining, 55, 61, 63, 96, 105, 140
  North-South antagonism at, 13
  special charters and, 30
  Stanford and, 50
  and suffrage, 29, 41, 43–44, 45, 155
New Deal, 19
New Hampshire constitutional convention, 185n107
New Mexico Constitution (1910), 13, 104, 109, 110, 112
  amendment and, 25
  corporations and, 111
  direct democracy and, 119
  labor and, 124
  Mexican Americans and, 107, 118, 119–120, 130
  Taft and, 25, 103, 130
  writing, 144
New Mexico constitutional convention of 1910, 103, 130–131, 149
  corporations and, 103, 124–129
  delegates of, 12 (table), 24–25, 107, 108, 120
  deliberations and, 111
  direct democracy and, 113, 117
  duration of, 1, 12 (table)
  key role of party, 24, 103–104, 108
  labor and, 120–121
  leaders, 107
  Mexican Americans and, 14, 19, 103, 120
  protections for labor, 110
  Republicans at, 103, 107, 111, 112
  roll call votes at, 111–112
  secrecy and, 111, 112
Newspaper coverage, 18–19, 29, 168–169n1
New York constitutional convention of 1894, 185n107
Nineteenth Amendment (women's suffrage), 134, 173n39
Noll, Roger G., 175n87
Nonpartisans, at California Convention of 1878, 68, 74, 144, 176n102
North-South antagonism, impact of, 13, 36, 41, 145
Nourse, George, 51, 53, 54

O'Donnell, Charles, on regulating freights/fares, 84
Ogg, Frederic Austin, 154
Oklahoma Constitution, 22, 124
  corporations and, 132, 184n92
Oklahoma constitutional convention of 1907, 131
Olney, Cyrus, 49
Oregon Constitution (1857), 113
  corporations and, 48, 50, 126
  writing, 57
Oregon constitutional convention of 1857, 27
  banks and, 30, 45–46
  corporations and, 30–31, 45–46, 48–50, 87, 126, 140, 146
  delegates, 12 (table), 22, 48, 50, 55, 56
  duration of, 12 (table)
  and farming, 14, 22, 27, 35, 36, 49
  Indiana Bill of Rights and, 2
  key issues of,
  leaders, 30

and migrants, 34, 35
North-South antagonism at, 13
suffrage and, 29, 43–44,
Oregon Territory, gold rush and, 35–36
Ores, refractory/rebellious, 61–62
Organizations, labor, 46, 49, 105
  popular sentiment about, 128
Ostrander, Gilman, on California/Nevada, 38

Palmer, Louis, 92, 93, 177n127
Parker, Dorothy, 31
Parsons, Andrew, 105–106, 115, 116
Partisanship, 15, 39, 103, 108, 137
Pasteur, Louis, germ theory and, 162n24
Paul, Rodman, 31, 61, 63
Pearce, Richard, Hill and, 170n7
Peculiar geography, 113, 133, 153
Pennsylvania Constitution, "shall not" sections of, 16
People of color, 29
  suffrage and, 22, 42, 43, 44, 181n22
People's Party, 23, 147
  Direct Democracy and, 113
  railroads and, 125
Periphery, 21
  managing, 23, 59, 70, 81–82, 99, 101
Persily, Nathan, 133, 153
Petitions, 9, 94, 117–118
Phelps-Dodge interests, 106
Pinkerton detectives, 98, 139
Pisani, Donald J., 173n47
Plumb, S. J., limited liability corporations and, 87
Police power, corporations and, 88, 98, 147
Political economy, 7, 100
Political rights, 60
Politics, 8, 14, 19, 21, 26, 29, 70, 146, 195n105
  antebellum, 28
  competitive, 99
  constitutions and, 5
  national, 7
  normal, 151
  party, 15, 103, 108

populist, 71
progressive, 104, 150
shaping, 67
study of, 6
"Politics without Parties: The Western States from 1890–1984" (Kleppner), 108
Poll taxes, 134, 135, 150, 155, 180n5
Pomeroy, Earl, 34, 162n17, 171–172n21
Population growth, 32, 62, 162n17
Populist Party, 23, 67, 140, 172n28
Populists, 10, 17, 69, 71, 105, 108, 144, 171n21, 176n106, 186n114
  agenda of, 24
  mobilization of, 13, 66
  workers and, 88
Portland Federated Trades, 134
Positive rights, 17, 18, 60
Poverty, 121, 158n12
Price, Rodman, 34, 146, 162n20
Primary elections, 119, 129, 134, 149
  women's suffrage and, 186n117, 189n30
Prison labor, 92, 96
Private ownership, right of, 76
Privileges, 60, 79
Progressive Era, 13, 19, 26, 104, 132, 155
  Gilded Age and, 24
  politics of, 21, 137
Progressives, 24, 103, 183n57
Prohibition, 134
Property
  assignment of, 7
  securing, 77, 99
Property law, writing, 24
Public employment, 94
Public good, 46, 87, 88
Public lands, distribution of, 70
Public policy, 8, 144
Public schools, viii
  bilingual, 104
  segregation in, 24, 104, 107, 120, 150
Public service corporations, 106, 125–126, 127
  rates of, 128
  restrictions on, 128

202 Index

Racism, 96
Radical Republicans, 20, 41
Railroad commission, 82, 84–85, 86
Railroads, 7, 10, 14, 22, 45–55, 62, 66, 81–88, 83, 93, 138, 147, 148, 181n19
  assisting, 51–52, 142
  charges by, 126
  consolidation of, 86
  debates about, 23, 82
  decisions about, 141–142
  fellow servant doctrine and, 131, 151
  growth of, 82
  hostility toward, 23
  issues with, 28–29, 124–125
  land grants and, 83
  legislatures and, 125
  managing, 124
  mining and, 51, 83, 86
  monopolizing tendencies of, 81
  public interest and, 87
  regulation of, 82, 85, 88, 100, 125
  state governments and, 51
  subsidizing, 51, 84
  taxing, 84
Ranching, 6, 14, 64–65
  growth of, 61, 62
  initiatives, 163n36
  investment in, 37
Recall, 113, 117, 119, 129, 134, 153
Reconstruction, 20, 21
Reed, Thomas, 93, 177n123
Referendum, 25, 105, 113, 115, 117, 129, 130, 134, 153
  opposition to, 114
  support for, 114, 116, 118
Reform, 8
  democratizing, 25, 103, 104, 109, 113–120, 131, 149, 151, 153
  progressive, 25, 69, 103, 149
Region
  and economic development, as collective identity, 1, 26
  and geography, relation to other regions, 33, 145
Regulation, 86, 126–127
  corporate, 24, 25, 59, 70, 87, 103, 104, 111, 127, 129, 132, 137, 143, 184n92
  mining, 94, 101
  railroad, 82, 85, 88, 100, 125
Religion, freedom of, 60
Republic, definition debated, 114
Republicanism, 40, 157n4
Republican National Committee, 107
Republican Party, 41, 85, 103, 112, 140, 167n93, 174n48, 181n21
  government control and, 115–116
  Mexican Americans and, 24, 107, 150, 181n19
Rickards, Governor John E., progressive measures and, 67
Riparian rights, 10, 72, 73, 74, 77, 141
Roberts, C. M., corporate control and, 127
Rocky Mountain Husbandman, on range husbandry, 171n17
Rocky Mountain News, 169n1
Roll call votes, 111–112, 148
Roosevelt, Franklin Delano, 103
Roosevelt, Theodore, 103, 134, 143
  Common Carriers Liability Law and, 123
  on democracy, 152–153
Royal School of Mines, 170n7

Safety, 89, 92
  worker, 124, 143, 151
San Francisco, 38, 76
  population of, 35
San Francisco Alta, 42
Santa Fe New Mexican, 108, 111, 112, 119, 181n22
  direct democracy and, 113, 117, 118
  statehood and, 109
Santa Fe Ring, New Mexican society and, 107
Scheiber, Harry, 96
School elections, women's suffrage and, 189n30
Scrip, 67, 88, 92, 180n5
Secondary sources, 18, 168n1
Segregation
  forbidding, 24, 104, 150
  school, 24, 104, 107, 120, 150

Segura, Nepulmuncio, 120
Seligman, E. R. A., 13
Seminoles, extermination of, 32–33
Semple, Robert, 39
Senators, popular election of, 119, 149, 153, 154
Settlement, 7, 61, 82, 137
Shafter, James M., on railroads, 83–84
Silver, 61, 62, 63
Silver Bow, 69
Silver-lead mining, 63
Simms, Mit, 121
Slave owners, 27, 43, 165n60, 167n105
Slavery, 27, 43, 44, 98, 163n32, 165n60
Smelting industry, 72
Smith, Daniel A., 186n114
Smith, Delazon, 2, 39, 40, 157n4
Smith, George, 93, 177n125
Smith-Flood legislation, 119
Socialists, 105, 112
South Carolina Constitution, 184n91
Spanish-American War, 105
Spring Valley Water Company, 76
Standard Oil, 177n122
Stanford, Leland, 31, 50, 51, 52, 142
State governments, 24, 51
  empowering, 100–101
  prerogatives of, 60
Statehood, 28 (table), 88, 109, 116, 139
  advantages of, ix
  constitutional conventions and, 59
  granting, 13, 103
  resistance to, 10
Stewart, Senator William M., 173n47
Stockgrowers Organization, 171n19
Stockholders, 48, 110, 145
  liability of, 87, 106, 126, 128, 146, 166n82, 188n13
Stock raising, 64–65, 66, 79
Strikes, 64, 124
Suffrage, 7, 40, 41–45
  African Americans and, 44
  Confederate veterans and, 41, 42, 44, 45
  denying, 22, 42, 43
  educational qualification for, 70

Mexican Americans and, 24, 42
Native Americans and, 44
people of color and, 22, 42, 43, 44, 181n22
questions of, 29
race and, 5, 41, 42, 43
See also Women's suffrage
Sutherland, Alexander, 98, 139, 178n149
Swisher, Carl, 17, 68

Taft, William Howard, 24, 103, 109, 114, 116, 181n21, 182n47
  amendment and, 119
  New Mexico Constitution and, 25, 130
Tammany Hall, 36
Tarr, G. Alan, 20, 60, 169n2
Taxes, 66
  bullion, 168n113
  collecting, 53, 74
  imposing, 53, 74, 146
  property, 167n108
  resisting, 145
  slave owners and, 167n105
Territories, 28 (table), 61–66
  concerns of, 145
  constitutional conventions and, 104–112
  foreign investors and, 59
  settlement of, 31–38
Thatcher, Henry, 69, 83
Timber industry, settlement/growth and, 14
Time to statehood, 28 (table)
Tinnin, Wiley, 4, 74, 100, 158n12
Toole, Joseph K., 11, 69, 97, 172n36
Transportation, 59
  rates/controlling, 87
Treaty of Guadalupe Hidalgo, 40, 42, 56, 70
Trounstine, Jessica, 108
Turner, Frederick Jackson, 31

Union Pacific Railroad, 86, 177n123
Unions, denial of, 124
US Constitution, 1, 2, 16, 42, 114

US Exploring Expedition, 33
US Geological Survey (USGS), 170n7
US House of Representatives, 41, 68
US Supreme Court, 44, 99
Utah Constitution (1895), 16, 17, 97, 110
    bill of rights, 60
Utah constitutional convention of 1895,
        13, 97, 98, 92
    corporations and, 88
    delegates, 12 (table), 59, 92
    duration of, 12 (table)
    key issues of, 5
    leaders, 161n12
    and mining, 14, 61, 64, 105, 171n15
    and suffrage, 154, 173n39
Utah–Northern Pacific, 62

Vigil, Agipeto, 70, 159n29
Virginia City Enterprise, 38
Virginia Constitution, 184n91
Voting provisions, 41–42, 95, 104, 150
Voting Rights Act, 119

Wallerstein, Immanuel, 21, 59–60, 160n47
Wallis, John, 29–30, 165n70
Washington constitutional convention,
        13, 98
Water, 70–81
    appropriation of, 71, 75–76, 78, 79, 148
    corporate monopolization of, 81
    issues, 72, 81, 141
    mining and, 73, 74, 76, 141
    private sector provision of, 80
    as property, 77, 78
    settlement and, 71
Water companies, 71, 80, 138, 148
Water law, 24, 76, 100
    Pueblo rights, 73
Water management, 72, 73, 79
    hostility for, 80
Water masters, 101
Water rates, 74, 77, 78
Water rights, 10, 71, 79, 80, 148
    appropriation and, 75–76
    debates about, 23, 70, 73, 74, 75

designing, 72, 73, 76
systems of, 70
Watkins, William, 44, 165n65
Webb, Wilfred, 106
Webster, Daniel, 30–31, 47
Weinberger, Jacob, corporate control and,
        127
Wells, Edmund, 106, 114
West
    compared to the South, 6–7, 21
    early development and settlement,
        7–8, 13, 14, 23, 27, 31, 32
    geography, 6, 144
    major industries, 6, 35
    as periphery, 6, 21, 23, 59, 70, 99
West, Oliver, 134, 186n116
Western Federation of Miners, 69
Western state constitutions. *See* Constitutions (state)
White, George, 82–83
White supremacy, 21, 43
Wickersham, George, 182n48
Willamette Woolen Mill, 166n91
Williams, George, 30, 49, 50, 56, 140
Williams, Robert F., on judicial federalism, 60
Wilson, Edgar, 77
Wilson, Woodrow, 24, 103, 129
Winsor, Mulford, 114
    on child labor, 122
Women's suffrage, 15, 42, 95, 149, 154–155,
        159n29, 159n32, 186n117, 189n30
    passing, 134, 173n39
    support for, 23
    Wyoming and, 164n54, 173n39
    See also Suffrage
Working conditions, monitoring, 94, 100
Workingmen's Party, 20, 66, 68, 76, 84, 85,
        92, 174n55, 174n58
    agitation of, 161n9
    anti-Chinese sentiment of, 96
Workmen's compensation law, 123, 125,
        130, 131, 134
Wozencraft, Oliver, 43, 164n58
Wyoming Constitution (1889), 110

bill of rights, 17, 60, 98
  corporations and, 88, 147
  eminent domain and, 176n114
  railroads and, 86
  water management and, 23, 79–80,
  writing, 11, 59, 110
Wyoming constitutional convention of
    1889, 13, 78, 93
  corporations and, 88, 147
  delegates, 12 (table), 92
  duration of, 12 (table)
  key issues, 5, 13, 64, 69, 95
  leaders, 68, 79, 87
  mining and, 79, 92, 94
  tenor of, 23
Wyoming Council, 65
Wyoming Stock Growers Association,
    65, 79

Young, Brigham, removal of, 161n12

Zackin, Emily, 18, 89, 159–160n43
Zinc, 62, 63
Zywicki, Todd, 154

www.ingramcontent.com/pod-product-compliance
Lightning Source LLC
Chambersburg PA
CBHW060952230426
43665CB00015B/2169